IMAGES
of America

BEACON FALLS

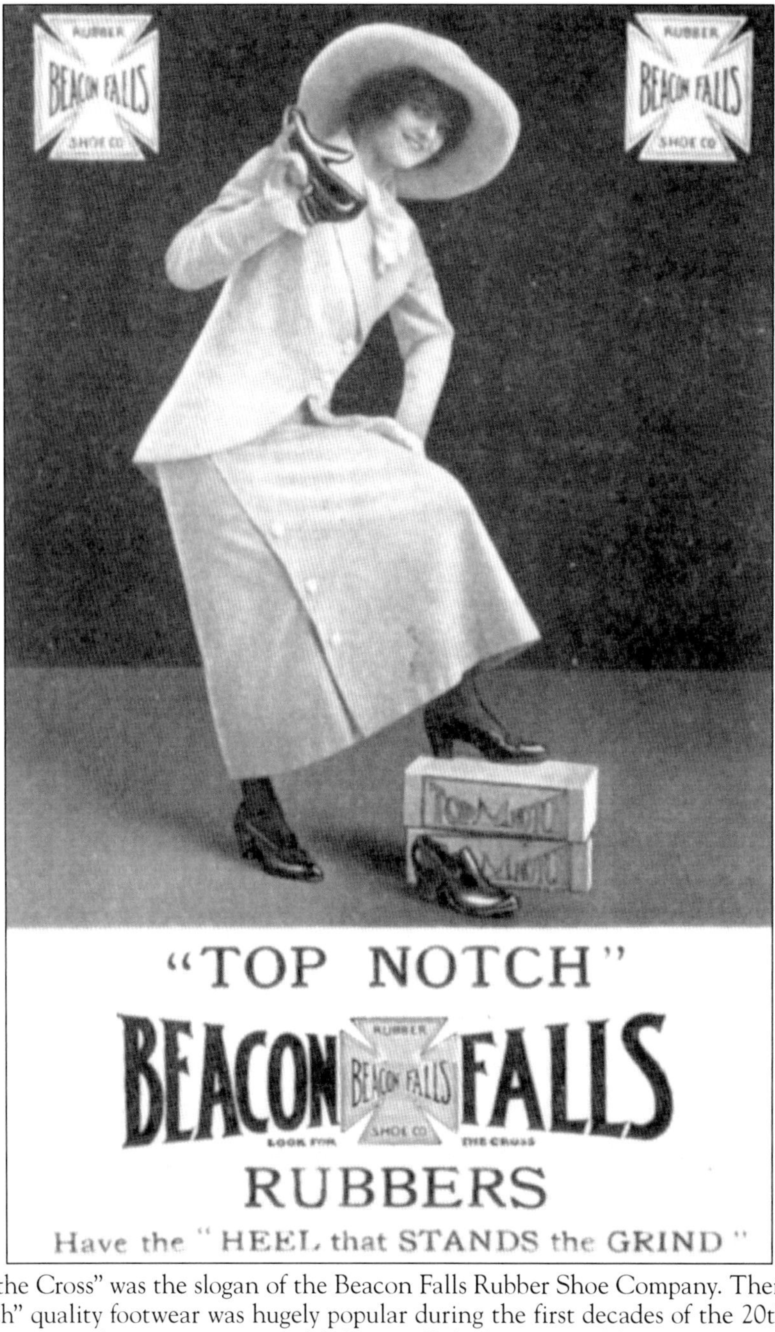

"Look for the Cross" was the slogan of the Beacon Falls Rubber Shoe Company. Their brand of "Top Notch" quality footwear was hugely popular during the first decades of the 20th century. Here in a c. 1915 advertisement, a model shows off the latest in rubber overshoes, known for generations simply as "rubbers." (Michael A. Krenesky.)

ON THE COVER: Beacon Falls residents young and old show their patriotism and civic pride as they celebrate the end of World War I in November 1918. The Beacon Falls Rubber Shoe Company, whose truck is being used to carry the American National Red Cross banner, can be seen in the background. (Mark Heiss.)

IMAGES
of America

BEACON FALLS

Mark Heiss
with the Beacon Falls Historical Society

ARCADIA
PUBLISHING

ISBN 978-0-7385-9143-8

Published by Arcadia Publishing
Charleston, South Carolina

Printed in the United States of America

Library of Congress Control Number: 2011939419

For all general information, please contact Arcadia Publishing:
Telephone 843-853-2070
Fax 843-853-0044
E-mail sales@arcadiapublishing.com
For customer service and orders:
Toll-Free 1-888-313-2665

Visit us on the Internet at www.arcadiapublishing.com

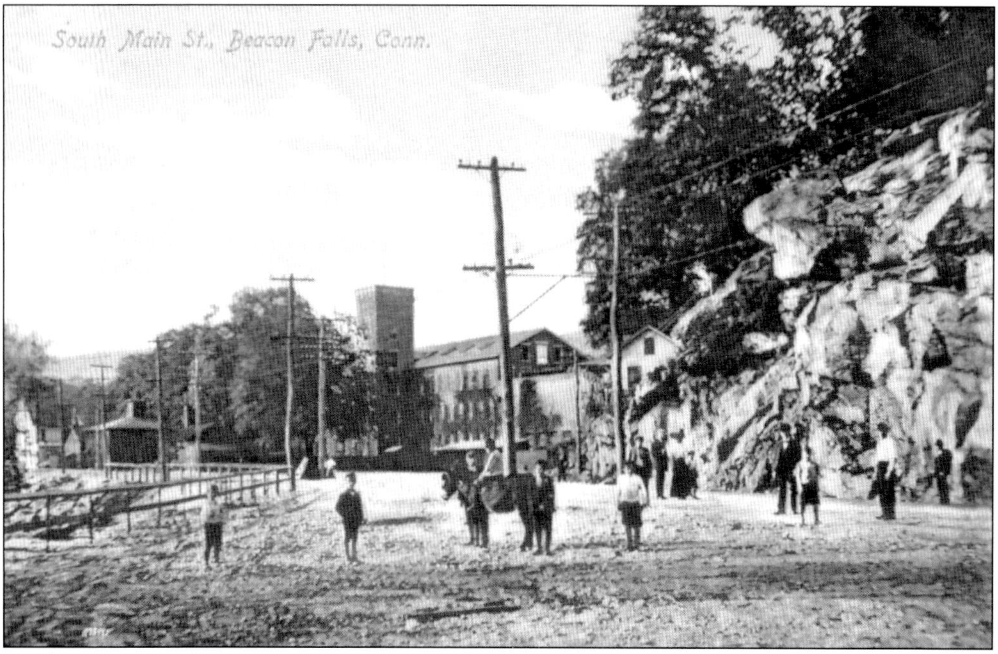

Mother always said not to play in the street, but there is little danger in allowing children to play right in the middle of Main Street in Beacon Falls. At least that was true in 1900, when this postcard photograph was taken. Then, residents were much more likely to see a horse here than an automobile. (Michael A. Krenesky.)

Contents

ACKNOWLEDGMENTS

Unless otherwise noted, all images are courtesy of the Beacon Falls Historical Society. Other images are credited as follows: Mark Heiss (MH), Beverly Wilcox Krenesky (BK), Michael A. Krenesky (MK), Marion Lennon Zollo (MZ), Edward Betkoski (EB), Robert Vernon and Donna Vernon Price (RDV), Leonard and Harriet D'Amico (LHD), Joan and Bill Weed (JBW), James Woodward (JW), Alice Gelmini Baldwin (AGB), Arthur Tucker (AT), and the Holloway family (HF).

A book such as this is a collaborative effort. The author is grateful for the help and encouragement from numerous individuals, including Beth Heiss, Matthew Heiss, Lissie Cain, former municipal historian Michael A. Krenesky, Nancy Betkoski, James Woodward, Harriet and Leonard D'Amico, Ben Catanzaro, Gloria McGeever, Mary Jane Winne, Gerry and Charlie Vesterman, Sue Gerchy, Edward J. Chicoski Jr., Joan and Bill Weed, Sandra Swan, John Holloway, Edward Betkoski, Marion Lennon Zollo, and Raymond Lennon.

A special thank-you to president of the Beacon Falls Historical Society Beverly Wilcox Krenesky, whose knowledge of Beacon Falls history is unsurpassed.

The author would like to make a special acknowledgement to the late Michael Krenesky, who as the town's first municipal historian recognized the need to remember Beacon Falls's past and who with his wife, Beverly Wilcox Krenesky, was a founding member of the Beacon Falls Historical Society, which was chartered in 1990. Michael's self-published book *My Beacon Falls* was a key resource for organizing this book.

Finally, the author would like to thank Barbara and Gordon Heiss, who throughout their lives always provided encouragement and the confidence to try new things.

INTRODUCTION

Situated in the heart of the Naugatuck River Valley, Beacon Falls is one of the smallest and youngest towns in the state of Connecticut. Though the area that later became Beacon Falls was originally inhabited by the Paugasuck Indians, European settlers slowly expanded into the area in the mid-1600s. They congregated into villages within the New Haven and Connecticut colonies, and towns were born. The town of Derby—and later Bethany—contained the village of Beacon Falls for a time.

By 1700, settlers found that the fertile soil alongside the Naugatuck River, made so because of the frequent floods that occurred here, was ideal for planting. One such settler, Capt. Ebenezer Johnson, of Derby, purchased much of the land on which present-day Beacon Falls sits. He settled in the Pines Bridge area of town. In 1676, he took ownership of a young Indian boy named Toby, who remained with him for 12 years until Johnson decided to set him free. Early history texts indicate that Toby was sold much of the land along the river north of Pines Bridge for 10 pounds and a barrel of cider.

Toby's land included the wild, rocky valley north of the Beacon Falls village. With its steep cliffs and dense forests, this area led to many legends, including one legend that tells of an Indian princess who leaped from the top of a high rock upon learning of the death of her lover. The spirit of the maiden is said to appear in a narrow crevice about halfway up the hillside. At midnight on March 20 and September 20 of each year, the spirit appears in the form of a snake. On the head of the snake is a large carbuncle, which if anyone can secure it, will make him fabulously wealthy. It is for this reason that High Rock is also known as Squaw Rock. This area later became a popular vacation retreat.

During the 1700s and 1800s, the many streams that feed the Naugatuck River Valley were recognized as a source of power, and factories were established. In Beacon Falls, manufacturing of hard-rubber products and brass novelties led to manufacturing of woolen shawls, which led to manufacturing of rubber shoes. The factories provided employment that drew people to the area and often financed construction of nearby shops and homes. Eventually, the surrounding towns each surrendered land that was situated around this population center, and the town of Beacon Falls was created.

As the Roman orator Cicero once said, "To be ignorant of what occurred before you were born is to remain always a child. For what is the worth of human life, unless it be woven into the life of our ancestors by the records of history." His words capture the purpose of all historical societies: not to live in the past, but to recognize that everything we see today is built upon the work of those that came before us. Please join us for a look back at the history of Beacon Falls and celebrate the accomplishments of those who brought us to where we are today.

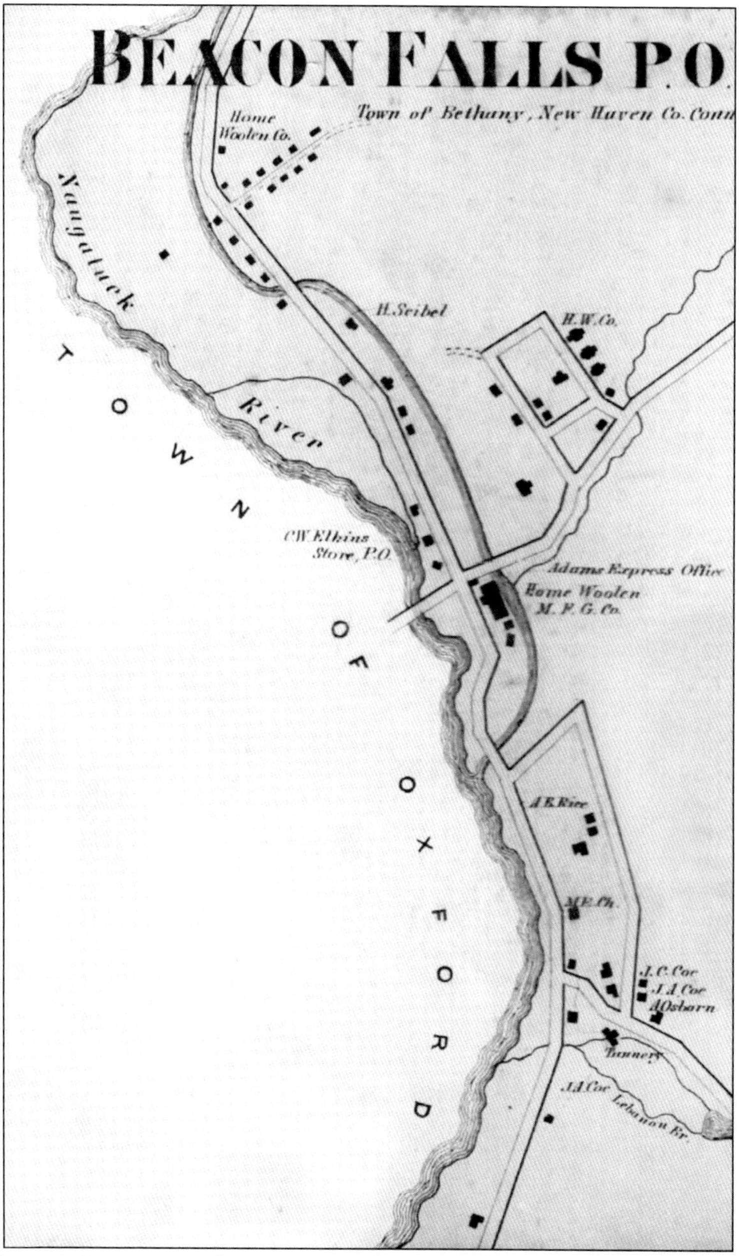

When this Beers Atlas map was drawn in 1868, Beacon Falls was still just a part of the town of Bethany and was separated from Oxford by the Naugatuck River. The Home Woolen Mill was the predominant factory in town. Notable is the canal that crosses under North Main Street and Burton Road. As with many factory towns of the period, the factory-owned homes shown behind the woolen mill and at the end of North Main Street and marked with "HW&Co." were rented to their employees. The 10 square miles of land that became Beacon Falls was separated from Bethany, Naugatuck, Oxford, and Seymour in 1871. So dominant was the woolen mill that consideration was given to naming the new town Home in its honor. But the name *Beacon Falls* eventually won out. The tannery on Lebanon Brook would later become the Homer D. Bronson Company. (MH.)

One

The Valley

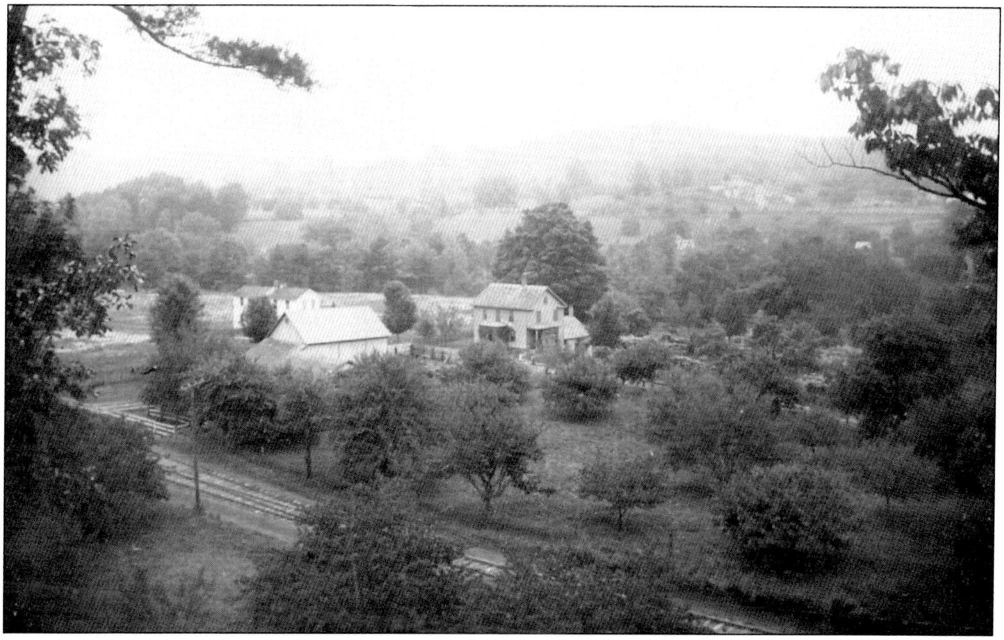

In May 1849, the railroad arrived at the Beacon Falls village. The railroad would change the Naugatuck Valley forever by making it easy to deliver goods manufactured here. In this photograph from the turn of the last century, the modern railroad runs alongside a traditional farm at the southern end of Railroad Avenue. This image looks east near where Lopus Road runs today. (MH.)

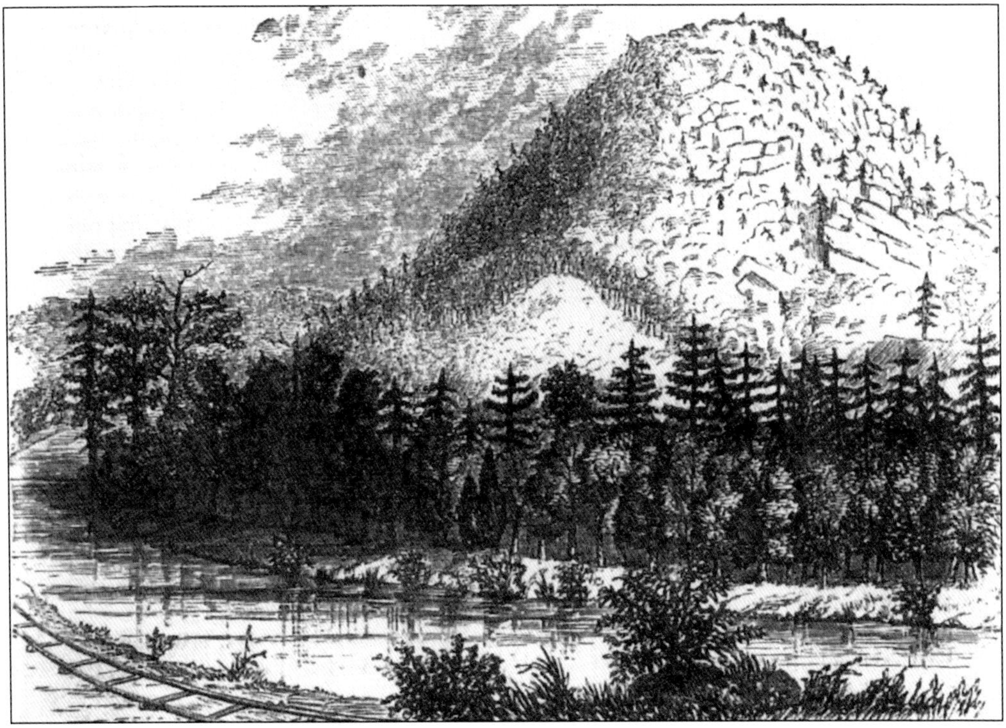

At 400 feet tall, the southern border of Beacon Falls is dominated by Rock Rimmon with its distinctive dome shape. This etching from 1858 looking east from the western bank of the Naugatuck River also shows the track of the Naugatuck Railroad in the foreground. The track was only nine years old at the time. A similar view from 60 years later appears below. (MK.)

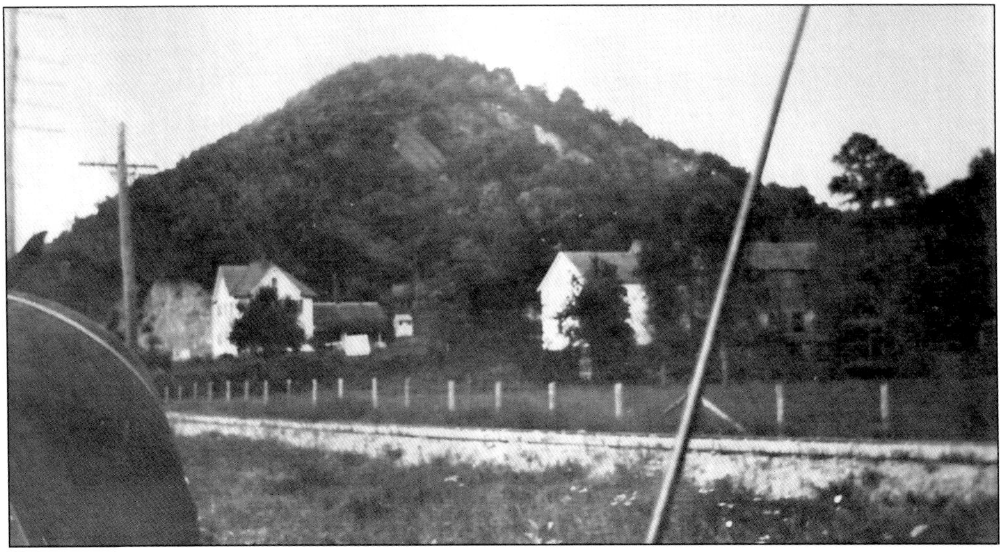

In the mid-1840s, Alfred Bishop, who had recently completed construction of the Housatonic Railroad line in western Connecticut, proposed construction of a railroad along the Naugatuck River Valley. The valley was already home to a staggering assortment of factories making everything from brass products in Waterbury to rubber products in Naugatuck. Bishop felt that these factories would financially support construction and operation of the new line. (MH.)

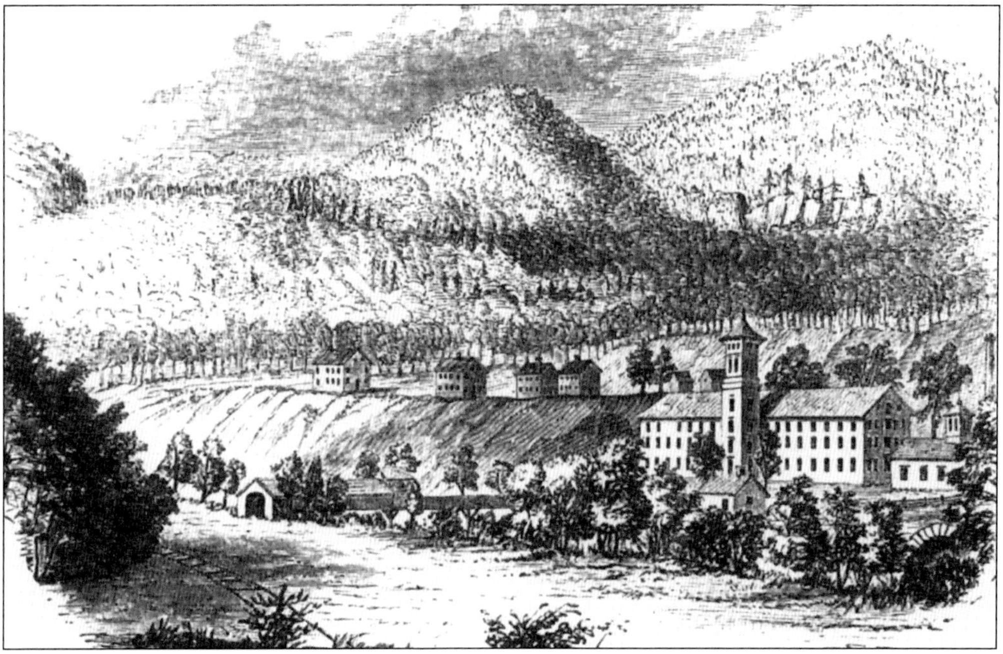

Here, an etching from 1858 shows the village of Beacon Falls with the American Hard Rubber Company factory building. The factory used a technique of molding rubber under high heat and pressure to make hard-rubber items that were previously made of ivory, wood, or glass, such as handles, whip sockets, and insulators. These hard-rubber items could then be carved by craftsmen. A canal provided waterpower to the mill. (MK.)

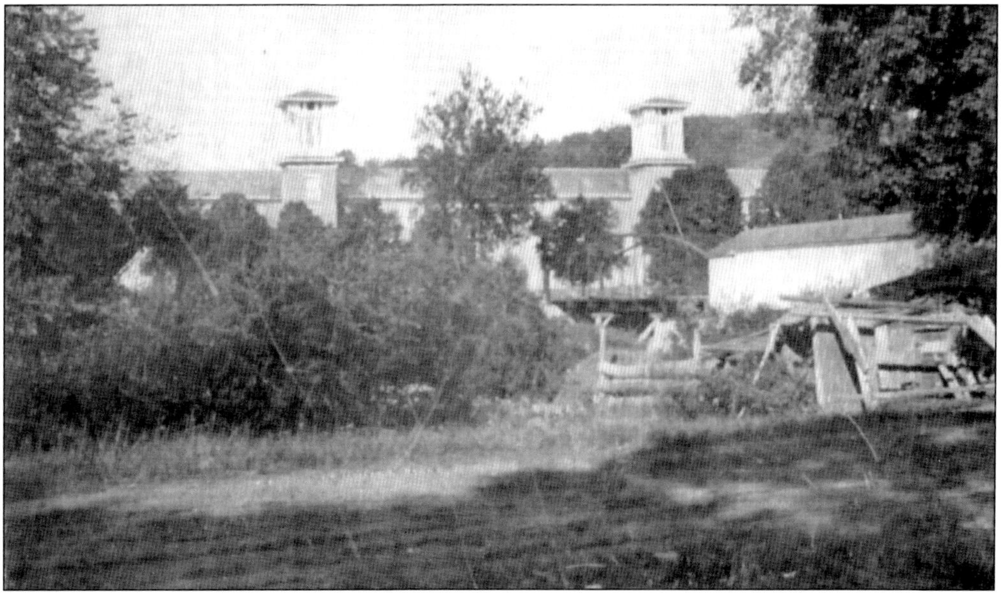

In 1862, the factory was taken over by the Home Woolen Mill, makers of woolen shawls, when the rubber factory divided and moved to Seymour and Long Island. The woolen mill expanded the one building into two in 1870. In one of the oldest known photographs of Beacon Falls, the factory is seen with its two towers still topped with wooden cupolas, also seen in the previous etching. (MK.)

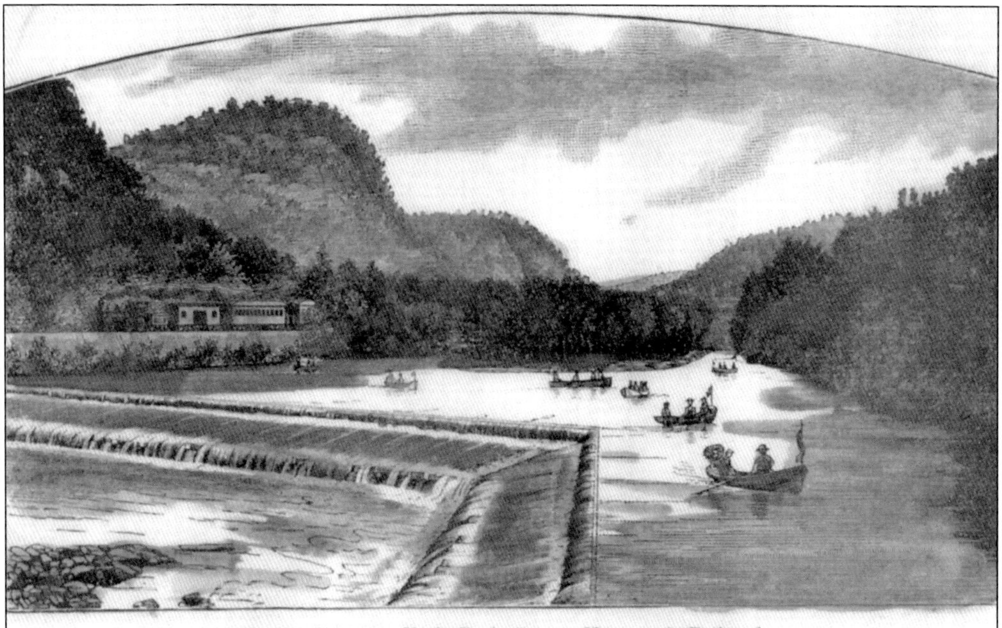

On the River at High Rock Grove, Naugatuck Railroad.

The Home Woolen Mill constructed a dam on the Naugatuck River two years after completion of the railroad. This dam would supply water via a three-quarter-mile canal to the factory on Main Street. This view shows a locomotive steaming south. Knowing the value of having a resort on its track, the railroad established High Rock Grove.

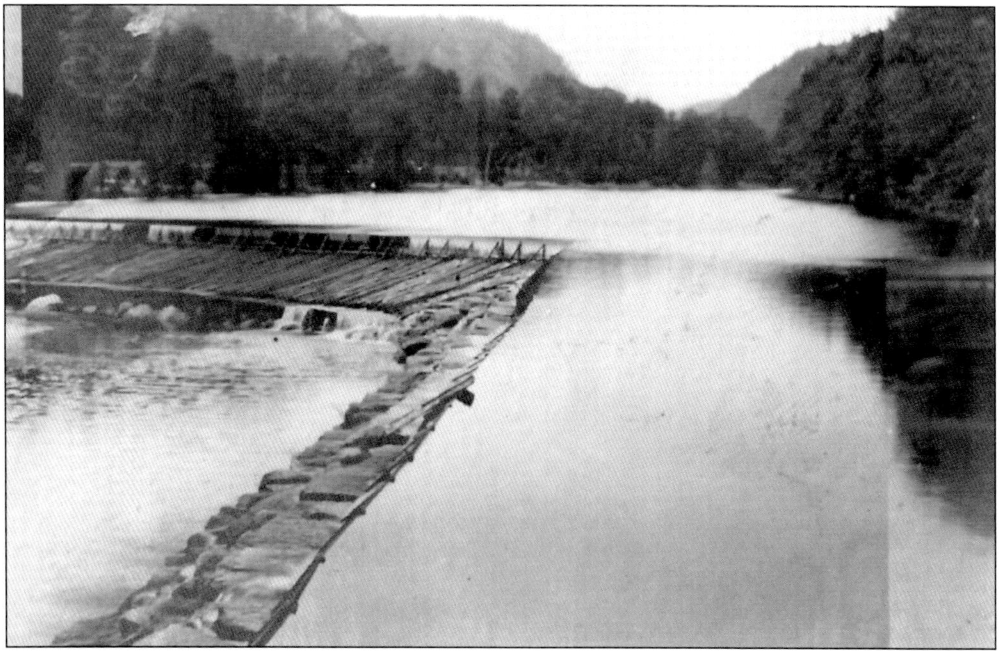

The Naugatuck Railroad established a seasonal stop called High Rock Grove at a small clearing at the most dramatic part of the valley. This would provide the railroad additional revenue on the normally slow weekends as day-trippers travelled to the park. As seen in the etching above, boating on the Naugatuck was a popular activity.

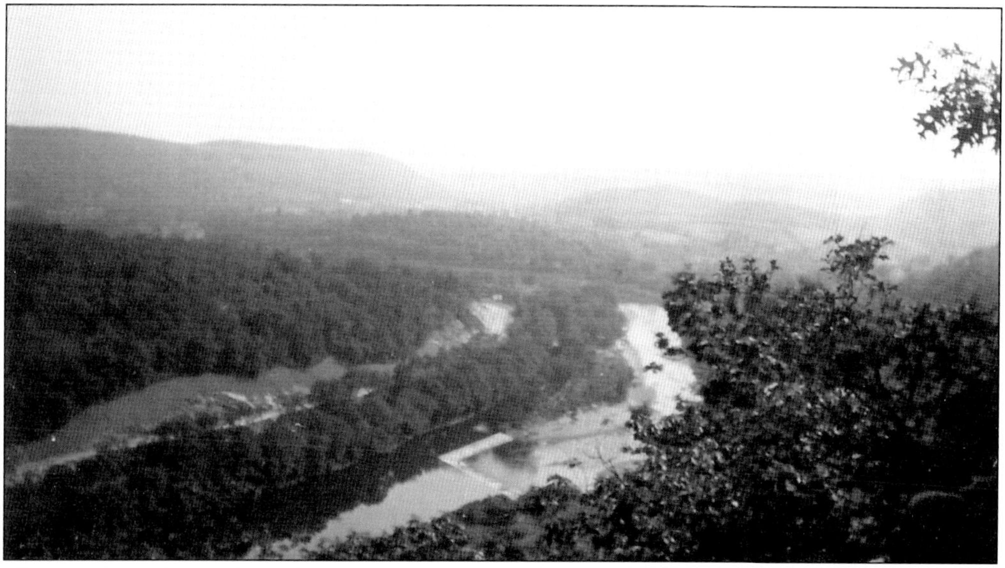

This southward view from the appropriately named peak called High Rock shows the *L*-shaped dam. The canal parallels the river before crossing under Main Street on its way to the factory in the center of town. The dam provided an unusually still, deep portion in an otherwise swift, shallow river. High Rock Grove offered swimming, hiking, boating, and more. (MH.)

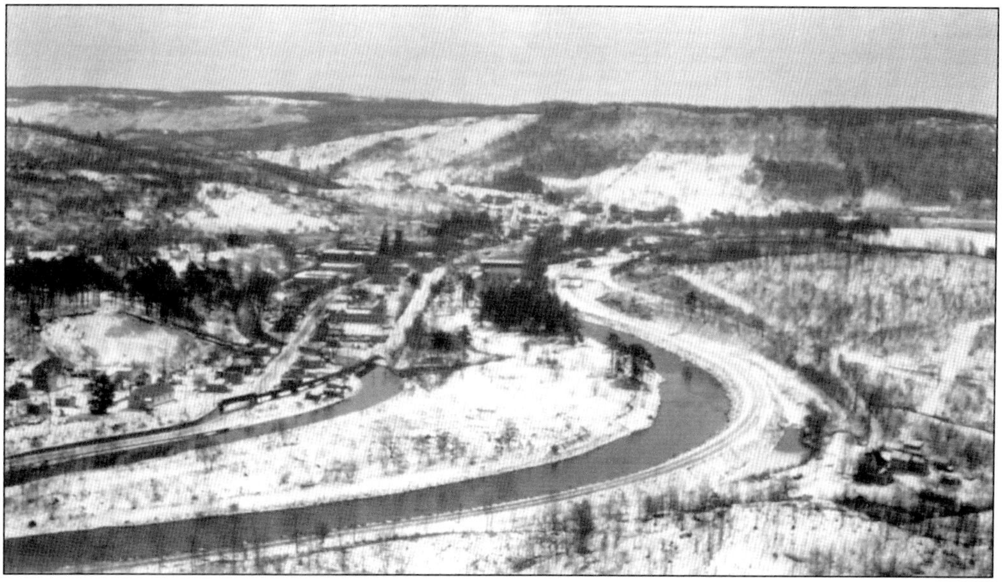

Slightly south of the previous photograph, both the canal (left) and the Naugatuck River are clearly visible. The canal followed a serpentine path as it traveled parallel to the river for a time, crossed under the trolley line, under Main Street, behind the homes on the eastern side of Main Street, and then under Burton Road before reaching the factory. (MK.)

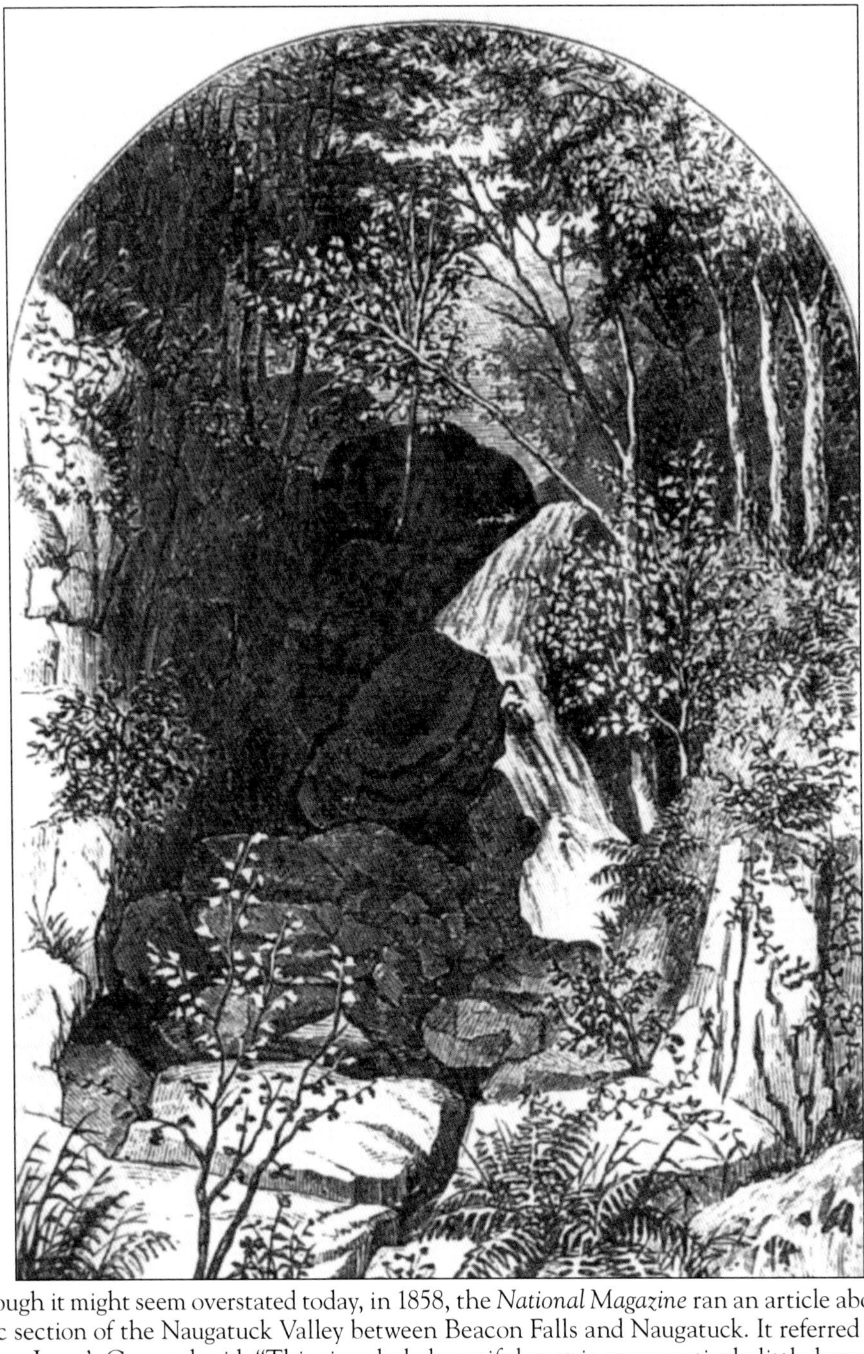

Although it might seem overstated today, in 1858, the *National Magazine* ran an article about the scenic section of the Naugatuck Valley between Beacon Falls and Naugatuck. It referred to this place as Jones's Gap and said, "This singularly beautiful spot is comparatively little known, but to the lovers of the picturesque it is well worth a visit. From Seymour to Naugatuck, a distance of about seven miles, every step of the way develops some charming point of view. The traveler by the train is so hurried through this singularly wild and picturesque scenery that he can form but an imperfect impression of its characteristic features." The adventurous can find this spot today by taking Lopus Road to Cold Springs Road, then continuing carefully on the dirt road to the parking area. (MK.)

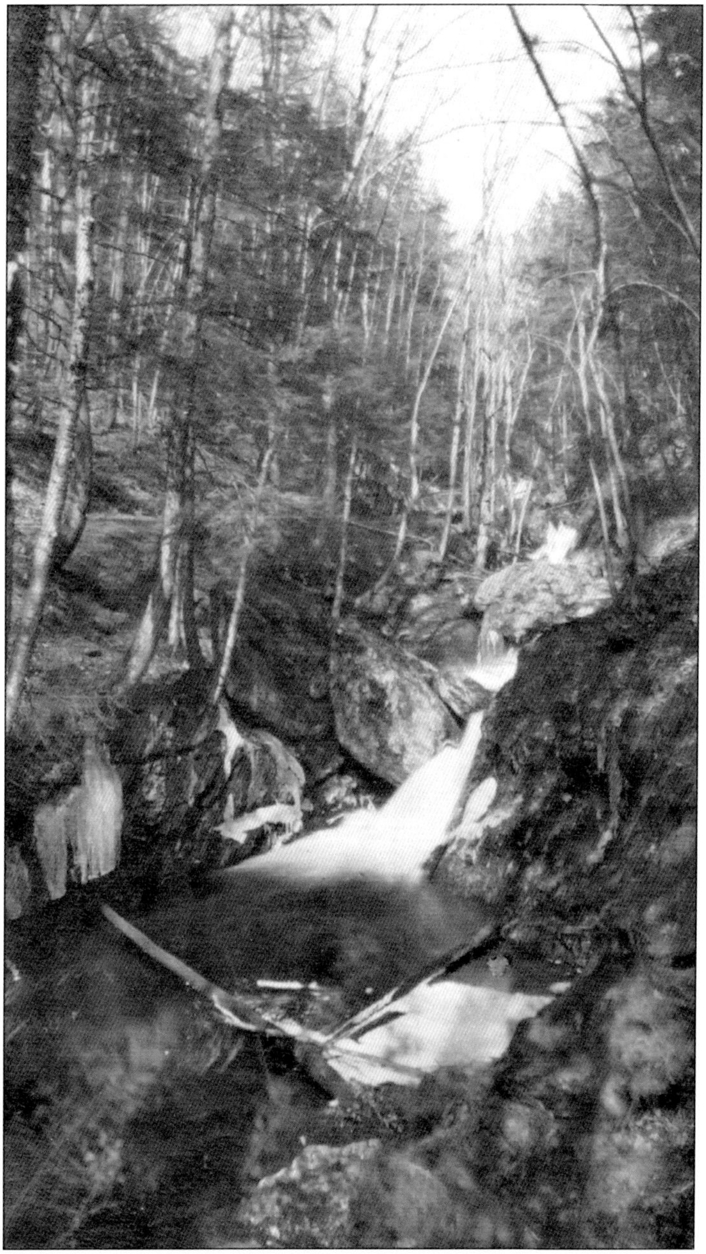

Taking in nature, a couple sits upon the rocks at the glen in High Rock Grove, still lovely in 1910. John Rockey in his *History of New Haven County* wrote in 1892, "In High Rock Glen, formerly called Sherman's Gorge are cool secluded walks cozy nooks and many turns abounding with picturesque effects which may be enjoyed to the music of gurgling waters leaping over moss covered rocks which vainly strive to confine them in their precipitous course. On High Rock is Lookout Point where is disclosed a view of sublime beauty, deep forests, stern rock covered hillsides and tilled fields with every shape and form of verdure may there be seen. The railway has provided a station at High Rock Grove and the place is much patronized by those seeking rest and enjoyment of sylvan retreats. It is also a favorite resort of picnic parties from all points in the valley." (MH.)

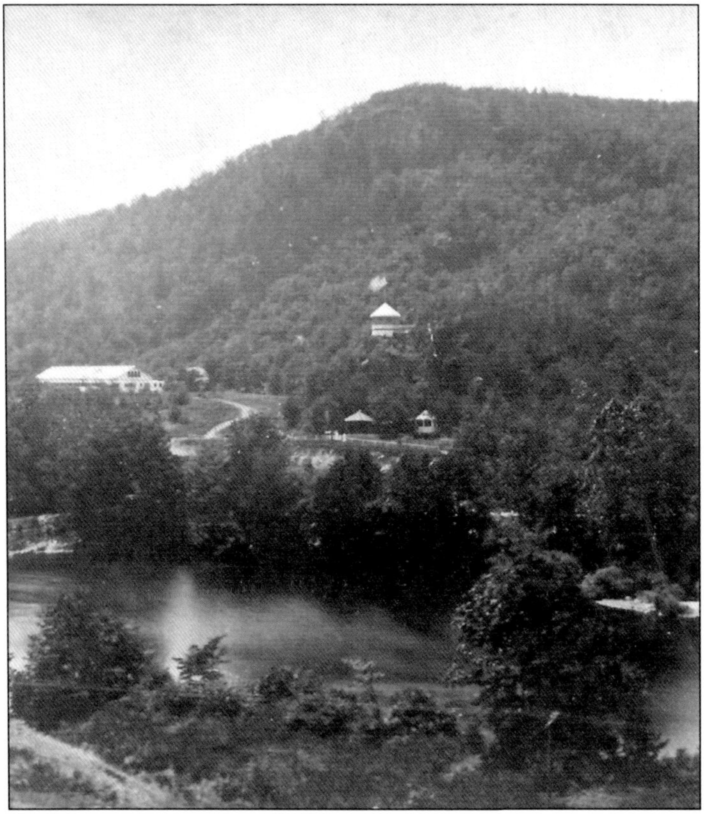

This rare stereopticon slide of High Rock Grove shows the park fully developed. The large building on the left is a skating rink. The gazebo with the flag was built on a rock outcropping. A contemporary account indicated that the park had two spacious pavilions and other houses, a croquet field, merry-go-round, skating rink, and boats for rowing on the river. The glen waterfall is to the right of this photograph. (MK.)

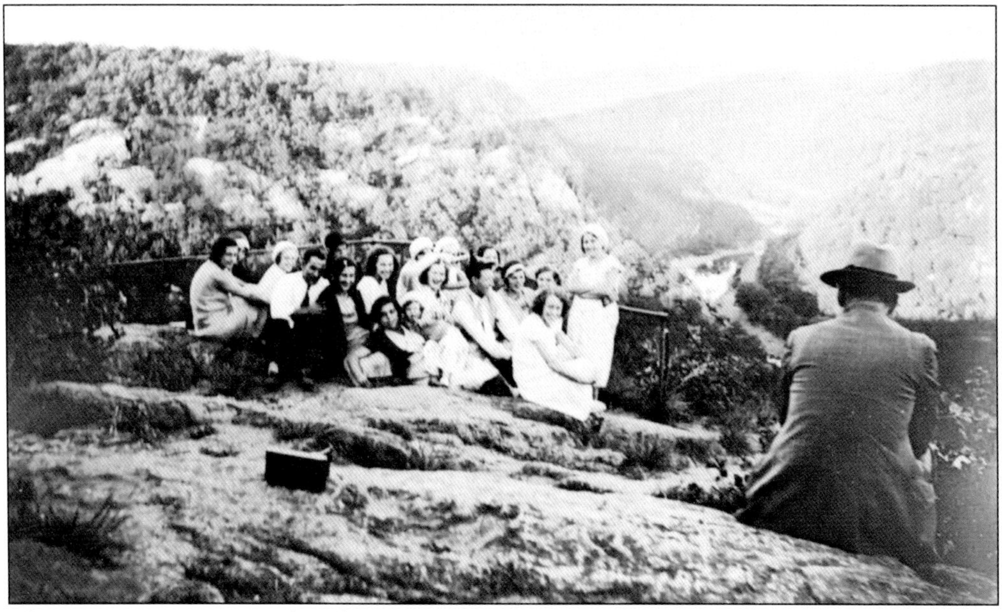

The signature attraction of High Rock Grove was a hike to Lookout Point for a commanding view of the Naugatuck Valley. On a clear day, Long Island Sound is visible. Toby's Rock at an elevation of 730 feet is seen behind these hikers. Scarcely a commuter on Route 8 today would imagine the presence of a popular resort in this isolated and now densely wooded spot.

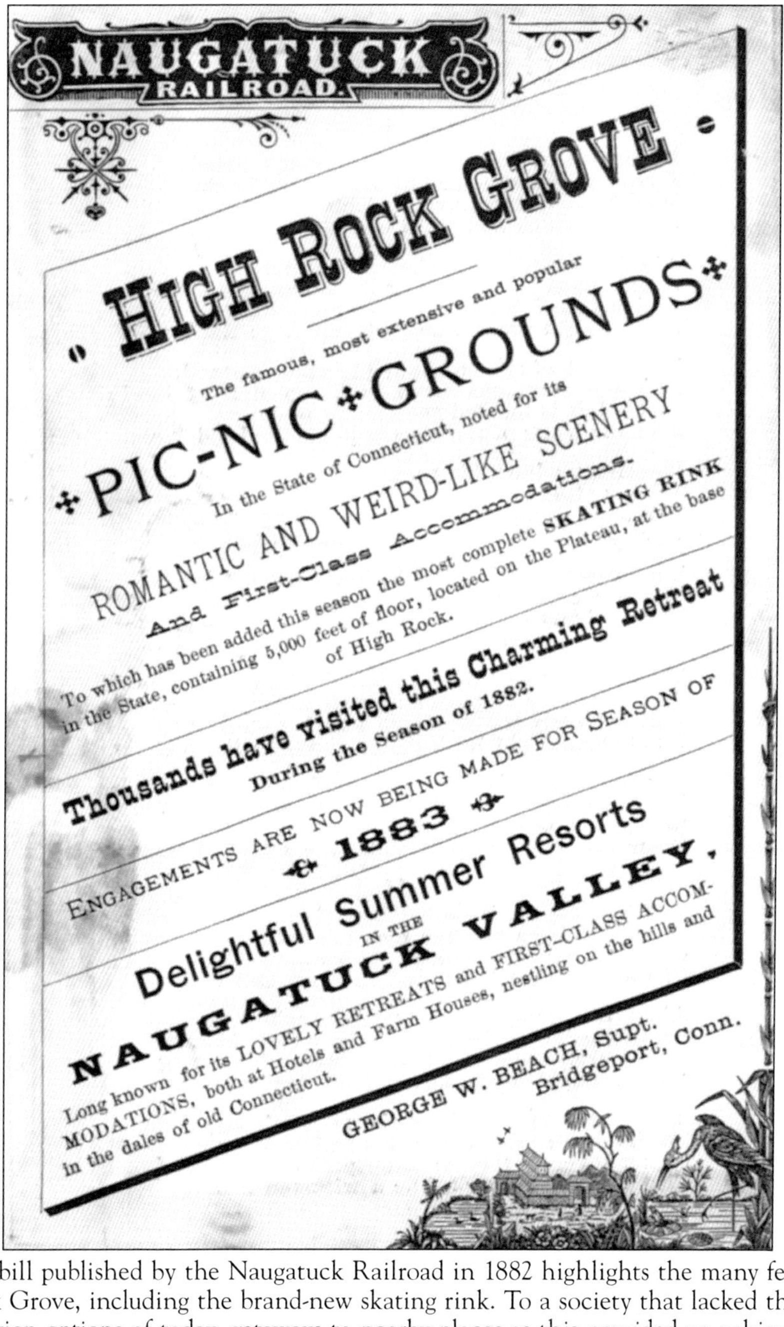

This handbill published by the Naugatuck Railroad in 1882 highlights the many features of High Rock Grove, including the brand-new skating rink. To a society that lacked the speedy transportation options of today, getaways to nearby places as this provided an achievable and affordable vacation and were just a train ride away. The same year, Samuel Orcutt wrote in his book *Indians of the Housatonic and Naugatuck Valleys*, "It was not until the summer of 1876, that the establishment of a picnic ground at this place, with all the modern conveniences, was attempted by the Railroad Company. Early in July, the new Grove was ready for use, and on the 12th of that month the first pic-nic was held there, and from that time to the present, it has been a resort for tens of thousands of visitors almost yearly, there having been as high as 80,000 visitors in a single season."

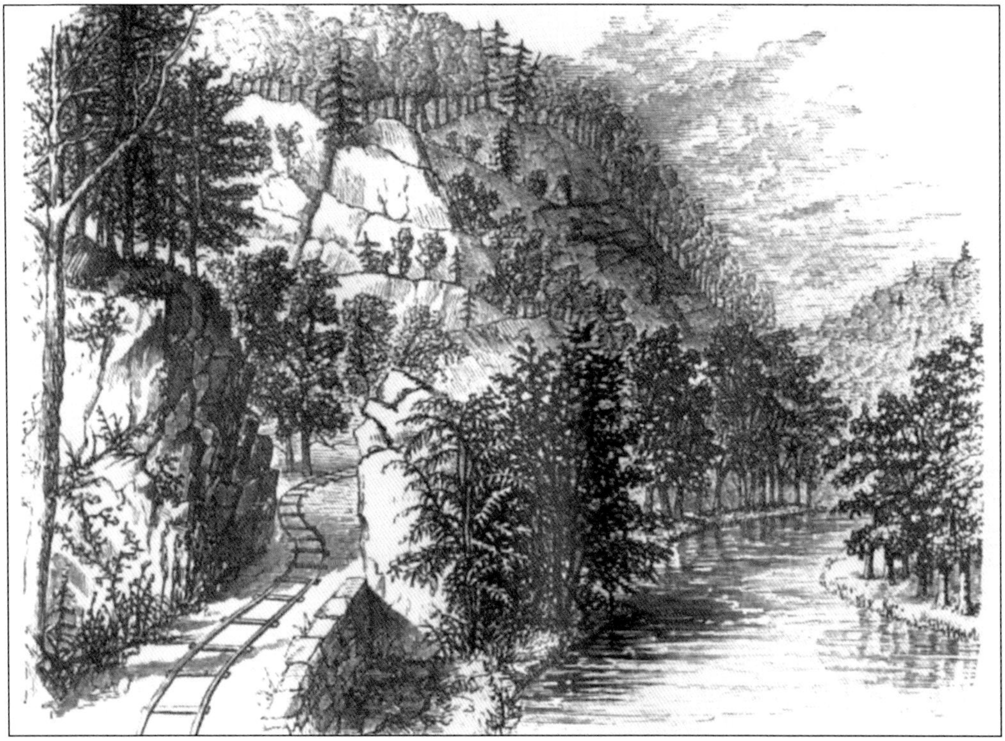

The *National Magazine* article continues, "Indeed, there are few portions of Switzerland or Norway where the pedestrian is better repaid for a ramble through them. Like our American scenery in general, this lacks the Alpine features so peculiar to those countries, but in the picturesque and wild it is scarcely excelled in either." (MK.)

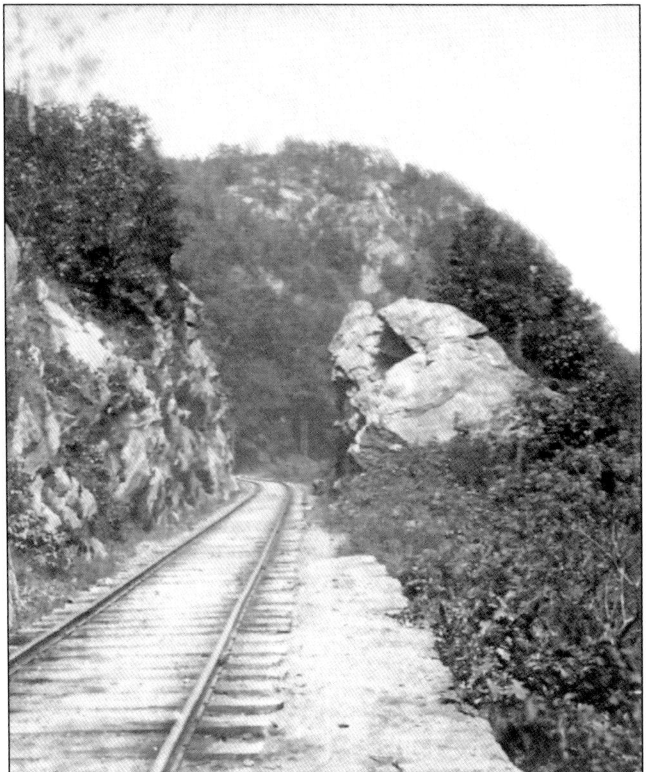

In this northward view, the railroad track passes through Sherman's Cut, much as it did in the etching from 1858 above. The builders of the Naugatuck Railroad understood the risks of a railroad line alongside this river with its frequent floods and the risk of rock slides in this steep-walled valley. (MK.)

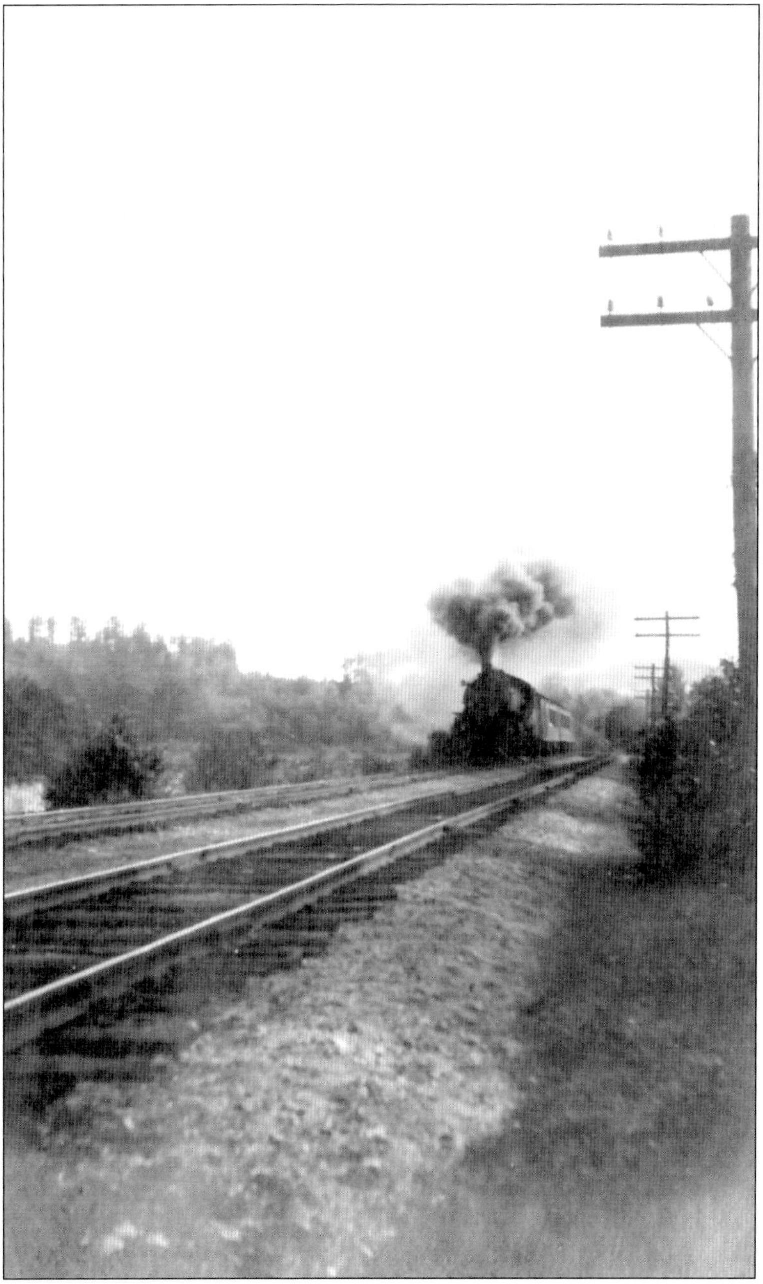

It is full-steam ahead in this 1911 view of a passenger train heading north during the era of steam power. At a total cost of $1.5 million for construction from Bridgeport to Winsted and for engines and cars, the Naugatuck Railroad proved itself well worth the investment. Alfred Bishop, who was the driving force behind the railroad, never saw it completed. He passed away just days before the first train arrived in Waterbury on June 11, 1849. It was George W. Beach, superintendent of the Naugatuck Railroad, who was responsible for developing High Rock Grove into a so-called pleasure resort. Improvements to the grove began in 1876. On April 1, 1887, the Naugatuck Railroad was leased to the great New York, New Haven & Hartford system, who then took financial control of the line in 1906. (MH.)

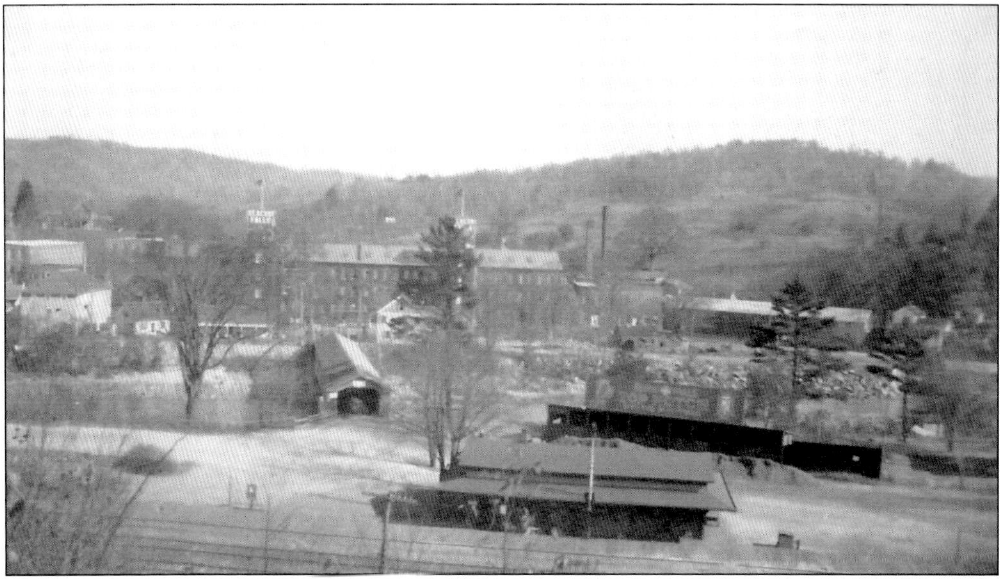

In 1868, the Naugatuck Railroad constructed a station in Beacon Falls seen in the foreground of this photograph. By the time this image was taken, several sidings had been added in Beacon Falls, one of which allowed railroad cars to cross Railroad Avenue to dump coal into sheds. These sheds are seen behind the station next to the covered bridge. (MH.)

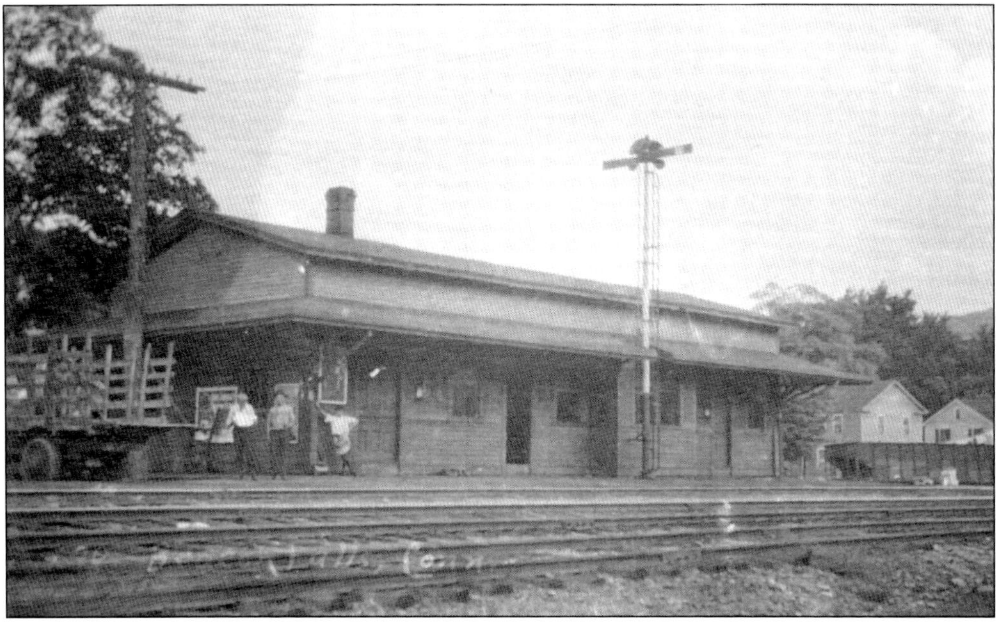

Julius Hart was assigned as the first agent of the Beacon Falls railroad station. Hart was previously a clerk in Cordon W. Elkins store on Main Street. A report to the State of Connecticut Board of Railroad Commissioners in 1883 stated that the Naugatuck Railroad had recently completed remodeling and improvements to this station.

This view of the Beacon Falls railroad station looks north from the platform. The covered bridge would be to the photographer's right. In the distance, one can make out the embankment where the road crosses over the railroad tracks. Today, the Beacon Falls railroad station is but a small glass enclosure reminiscent of a bus stop shelter.

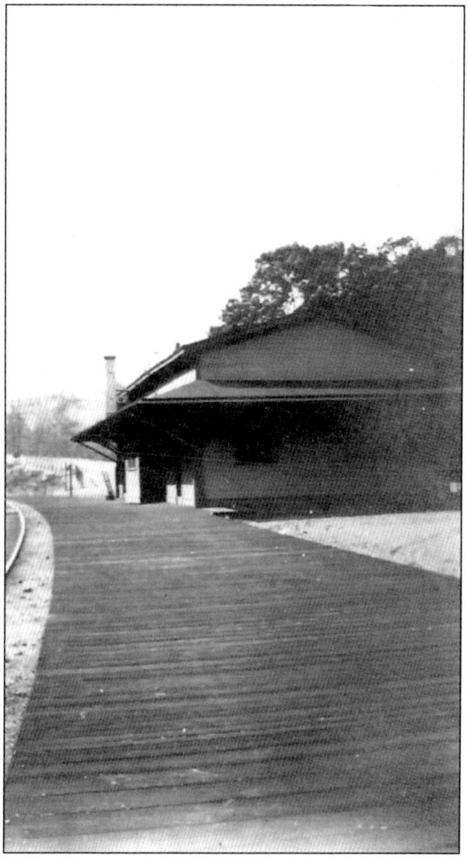

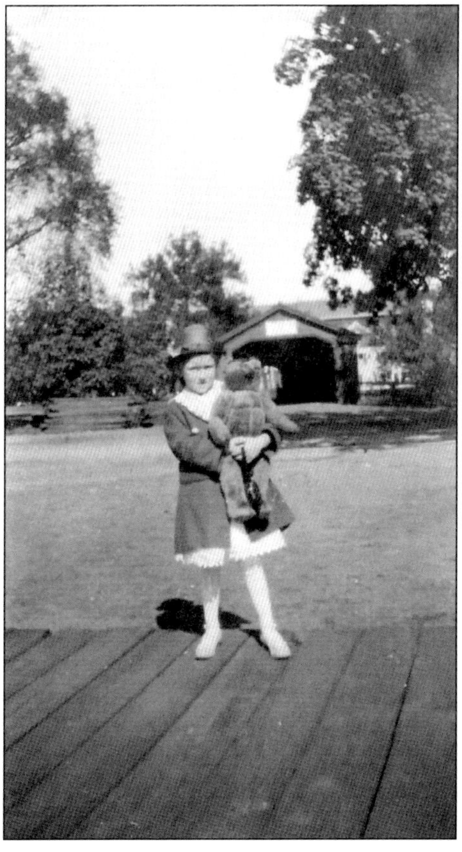

Little Dorothy DeBrichy waits for a train at the Beacon Falls station. Dorothy is accompanied by her teddy bear. These toys had only just come into popularity. Some years earlier, Pres. Teddy Roosevelt had an encounter with a bear while hunting, which led to the popularity of the stuffed bear as a toy. (LHD.)

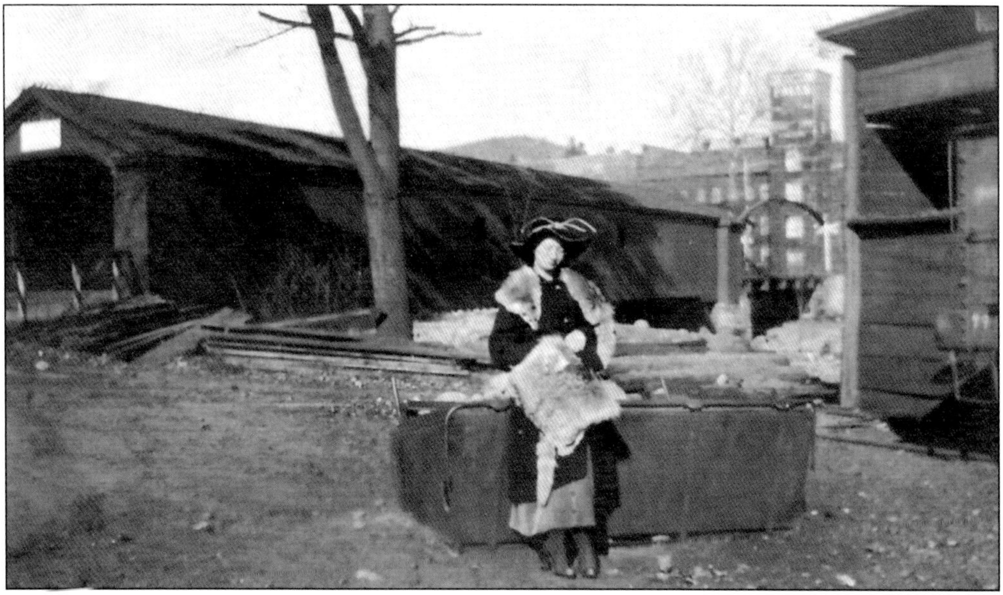

Estrid Morrits Campbell displays high fashion in a most unusual place—resting alongside the coal bins on Railroad Avenue. The fox stole complete with its head and tail, which is wrapped around her shoulders, was quite fashionable at the time. One can only guess where she was heading. (LHD.)

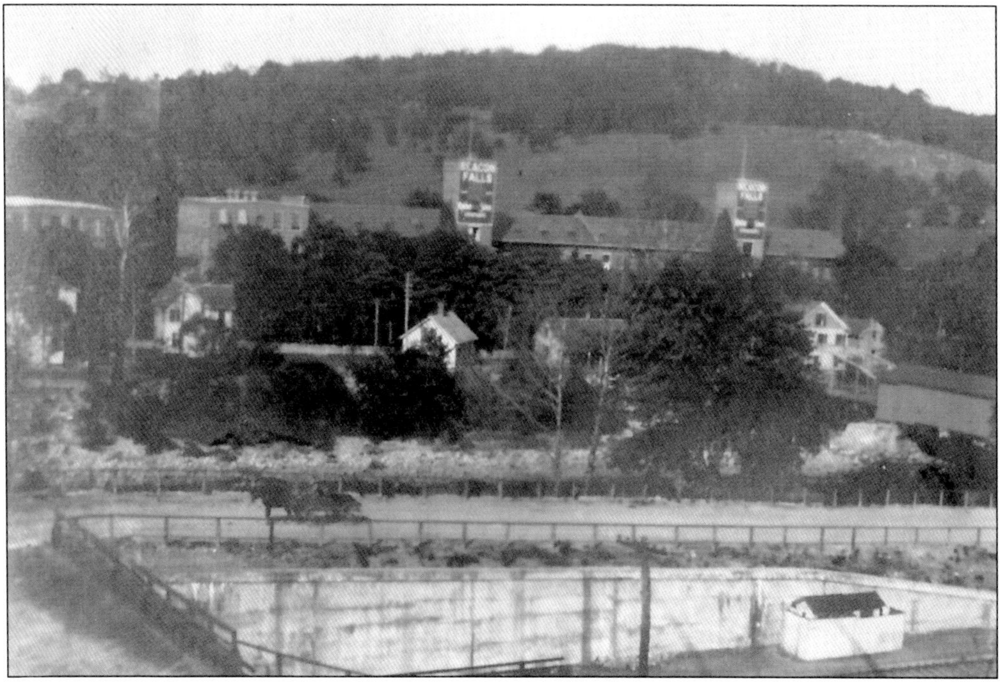

A horse-drawn wagon is approaching the bridge over the railroad tracks to Lopus Road. Other than the mode of transport, this very early view of Beacon Falls does not look too different from today. In the distance, there is a gap between the buildings of the Beacon Falls Rubber Shoe Company at Burton Road. In 1916, the Rubber Shoe Company built a trestle bridge-way over Burton Road, but this photograph predates that event.

These multi-tenant homes on Railroad Avenue were constructed to house factory workers. In these days before the development of the hill section of Beacon Falls behind the rubber shoe factory, most of the population of town lived here on Railroad Avenue or on Main Street. Multiple railroad sidings can be seen just across the street.

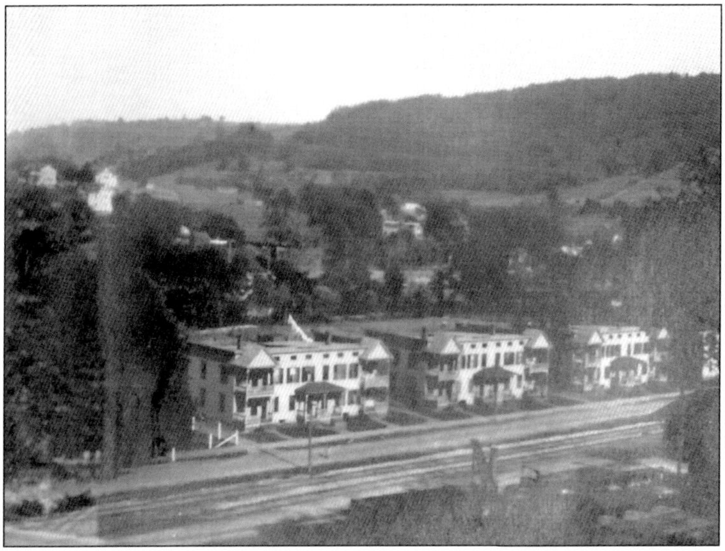

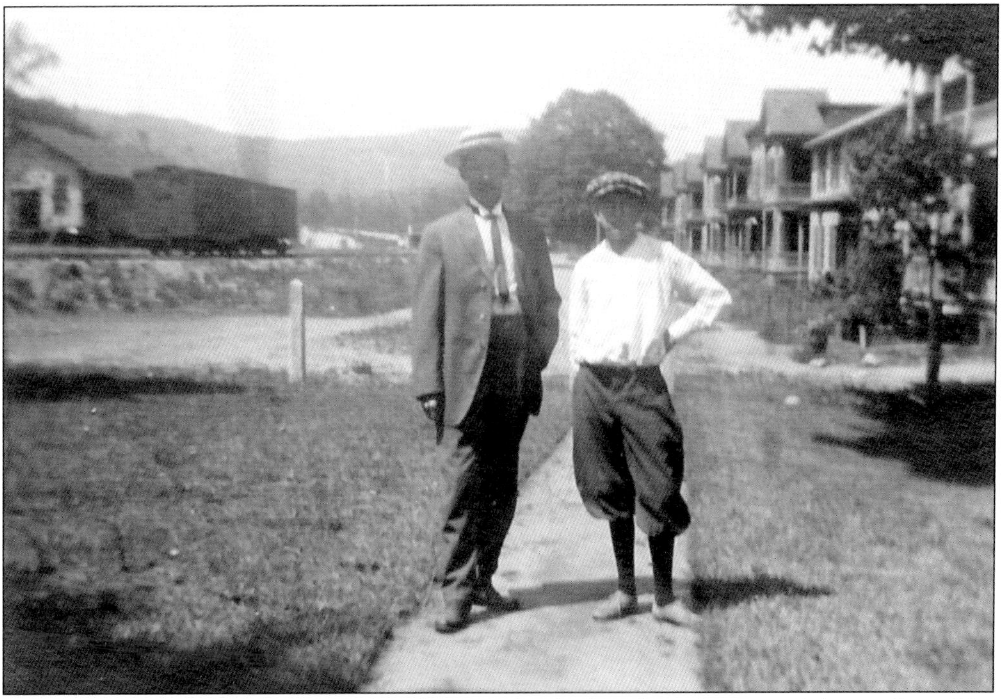

Life on Railroad Avenue is seen in this photograph, which perhaps features a father and son. The youngster is wearing knickers, which were commonly worn by prepubescent boys. Even though Railroad Avenue ends here, the sidewalk services additional homes beyond this point. Of note is the boxcar on the railroad siding. (MH.)

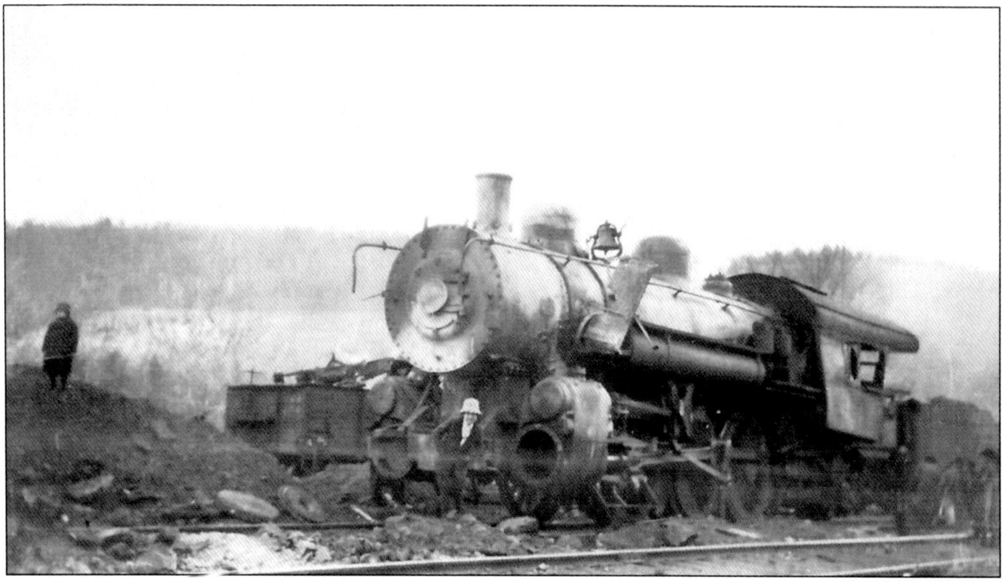

On December 1, 1916, a serious railroad accident occurred in Beacon Falls when a northbound passenger train rear-ended a freight train that was stationary on a siding off the main line. Here, the passenger train engine, a Pacific-type locomotive No. 1006, awaits removal. An investigation later revealed that the conductor on the freight train had failed to close the switch after the freight train was pulled onto the siding.

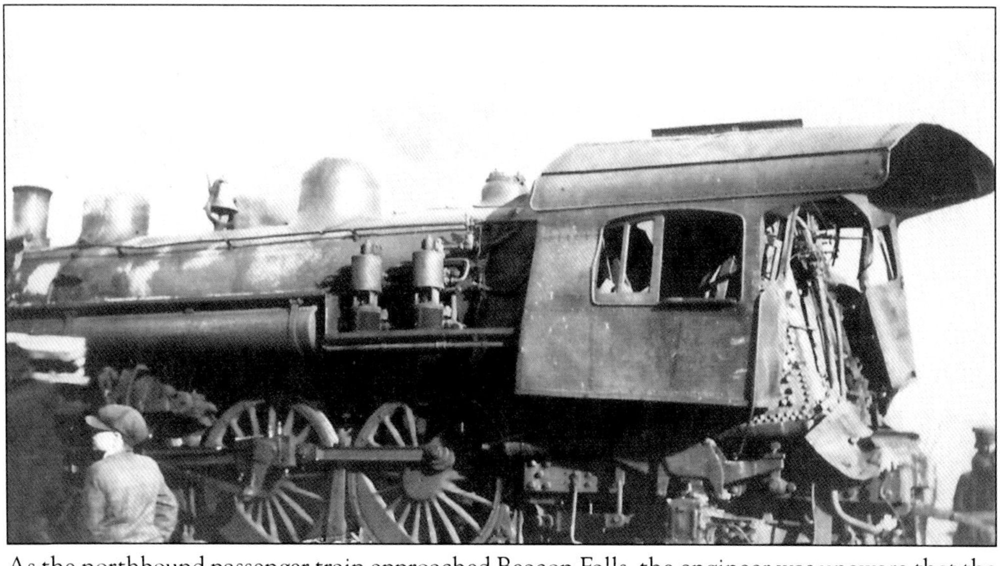

As the northbound passenger train approached Beacon Falls, the engineer was unaware that the switch ahead had been left in the wrong position. The crash instantly killed the engineer, Eugene Lake, and the fireman of the passenger train, Charles Slack, and injured nine passengers, two seriously. Here, the damage to the passenger train engine is evident, caused when the coal car was pushed into the cab of the engine.

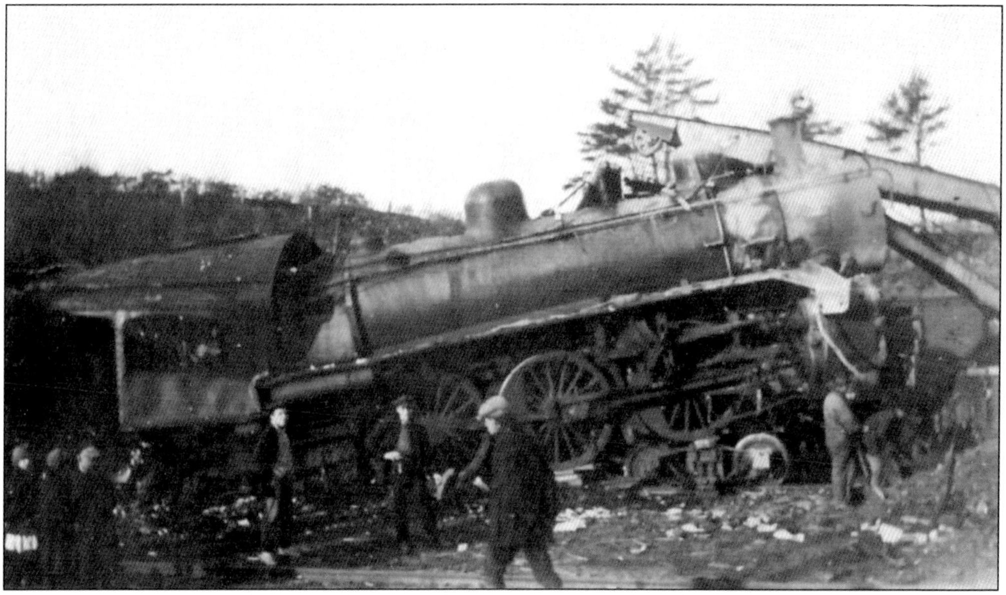

A crane lifts the engine back onto the tracks. In this view, debris from the demolished freight cars is scattered about. Railroad accidents were not uncommon during this time. Some of the more spectacular crashes were chronicled in songs that became hugely popular, including "Casey Jones" and "Wreck of the Southern Old 97." (MK.)

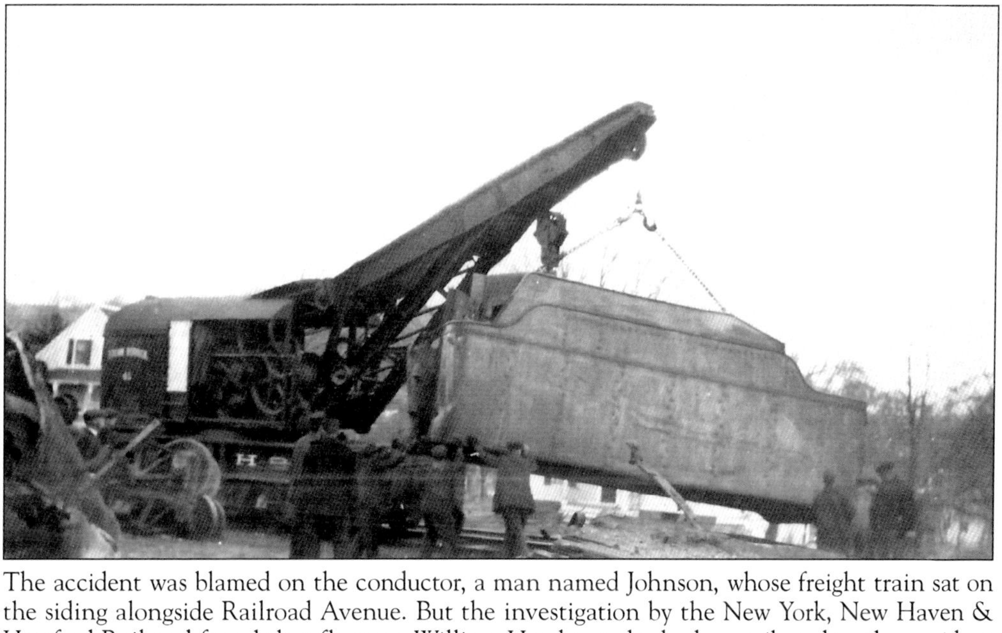

The accident was blamed on the conductor, a man named Johnson, whose freight train sat on the siding alongside Railroad Avenue. But the investigation by the New York, New Haven & Hartford Railroad found that flagman William Herchenroder had contributed to the accident by not noticing the position of the switch when he returned to the caboose. Here, the coal car, which is missing its undercarriage, is being lifted.

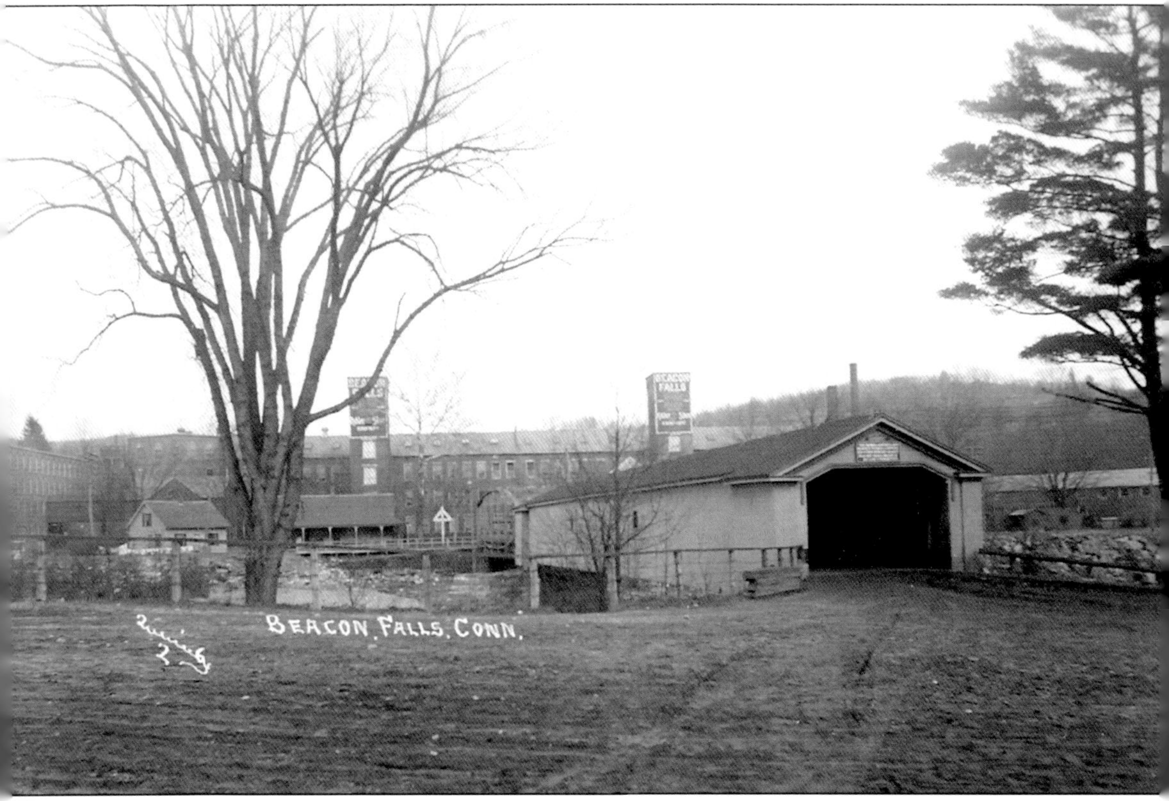

A passenger stepping off the platform at the Beacon Falls station would be faced with this view, captured by a postcard photographer around 1910. By this time, the Beacon Falls Rubber Shoe Company has taken over the factory once occupied by the Home Woolen Mill. In 1888, *The Blue Book: A Pocket Directory of Textile Manufacturers of the United States and Canada* indicated that the Home Woolen Mill in Beacon Falls contained 15 sets of cards to comb the wool, 74 looms for weaving, a dye house, 3 boilers, and 2 waterwheels. The primary product was "cassimeres" and worsteds. The mill employed approximately 300 hands. As late as 1892 when the Associated Mutual Insurance Company surveyed the site for the Beacon Mill and Power Company, the iconic towers were still topped with delicate wooden cupolas. But, less than 10 years later, the towers were topped with brick and sported the Beacon Falls Rubber Shoe Company's Top Notch cross pattée logo. (MH.)

Two

THE VILLAGE

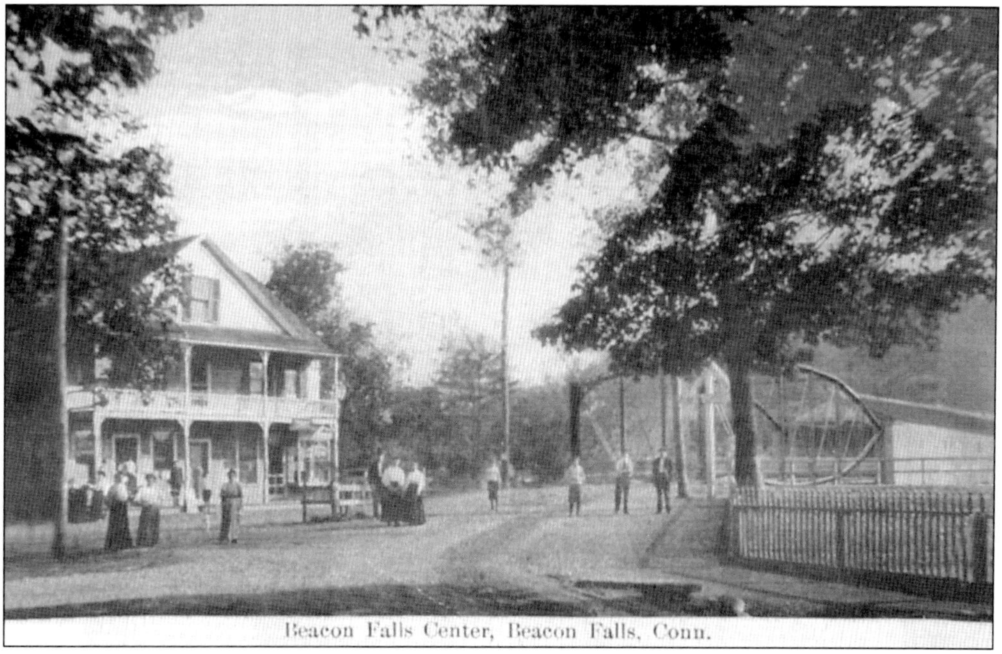

Standing in the middle of Main Street looking west, a postcard photographer captures downtown Beacon Falls. Until the late 1940s, there were buildings immediately across the street from the Beacon Falls Rubber Shoe factory buildings. At one time, the factory even ran a bowling alley located slightly south of here. (BK.)

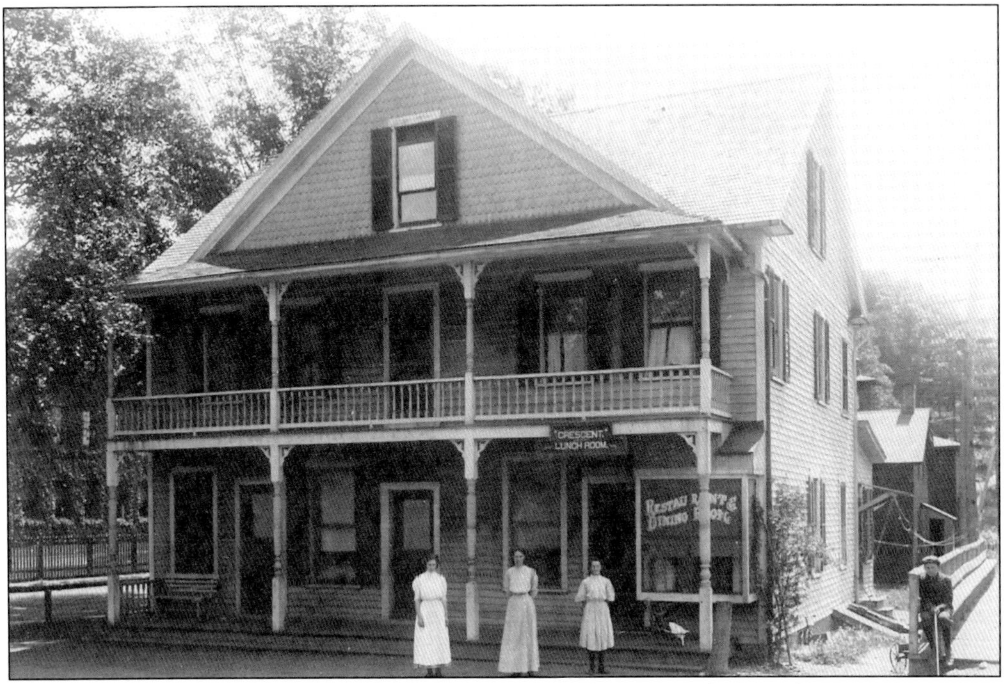

On the left approaching the bridge is the Crescent Lunch Room. This was the most convenient eatery to the railroad station across the river. Sarah Tucker operated the eatery and is seen standing between hostesses Sadie Malone on the left and Carrie Fahy on the right. Sadie and Carrie were sisters; their maiden name was Bronson. The second floor housed an apartment. (BK.)

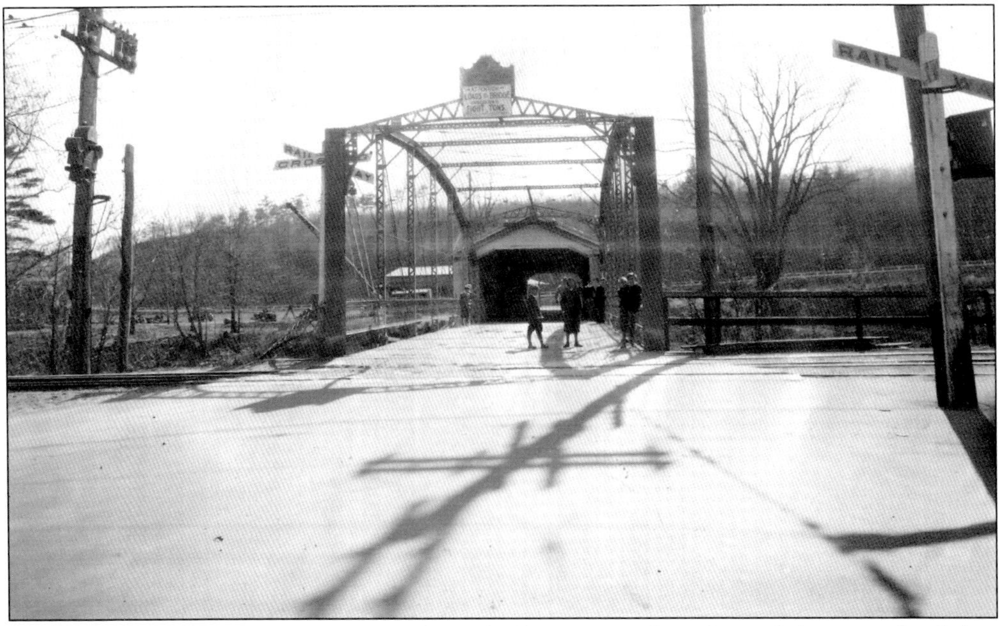

The first bridge in downtown Beacon Falls was built in 1835 and was located about 300 feet below the present location. That bridge, which at the time connected the towns of Bethany and Oxford, was deemed unsafe after the flood of 1855 and was replaced with a covered bridge just upstream. Part of the covered bridge was replaced in 1889, leaving a steel-and-wood bridge seen here. (BK.)

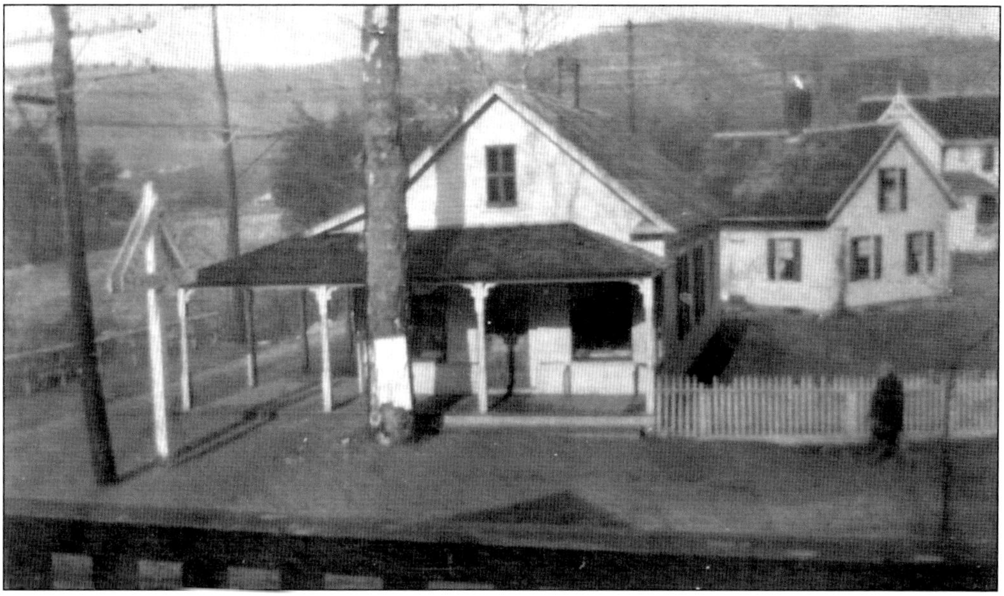

This picture, taken from the second-story porch above the Crescent Lunch Room, shows the drugstore across Depot Street. The drugstore had a broad wrap-around porch that doubled as the trolley stop. Visible is a triangular sign that reads, "Electric Railway Crossing." Behind the drugstore is a little house that was built at an unorthodox angle to catch the morning sun at the entrance to the house.

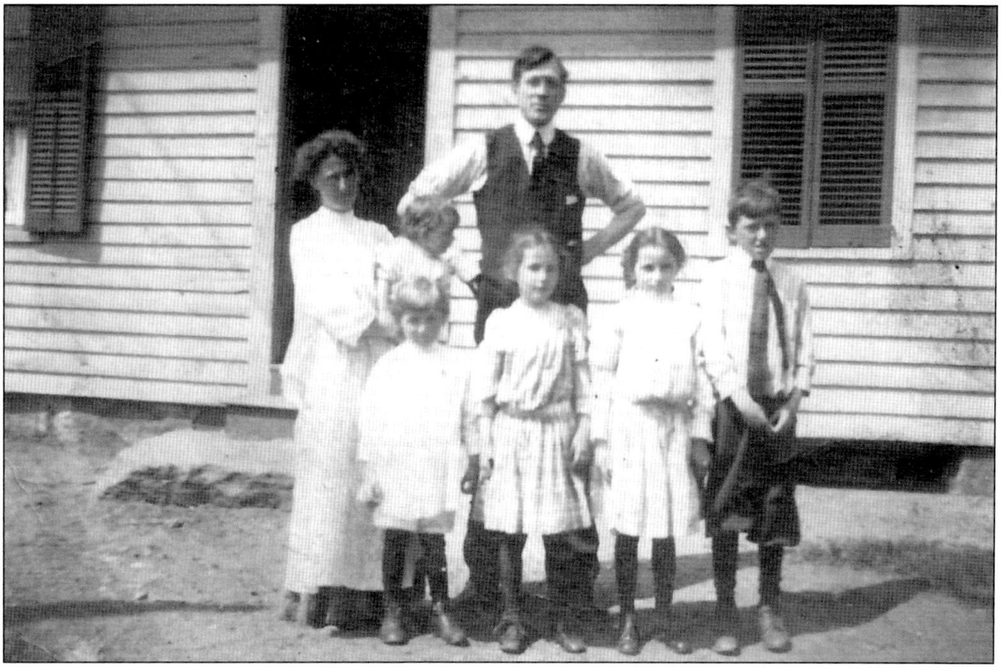

The little house beside the drugstore was home to parents Agnes and Cyrus Wilcox, seen here with their children. Young Leon is being held in his mother's arms, while (from left to right) Cyrus, Hazel, Mildred, and Harold stand in front. This house was later moved to a site on Skokorat Road. Harold Wilcox worked in the drugstore starting at age 15 and would remain there for 50 years. (BK.)

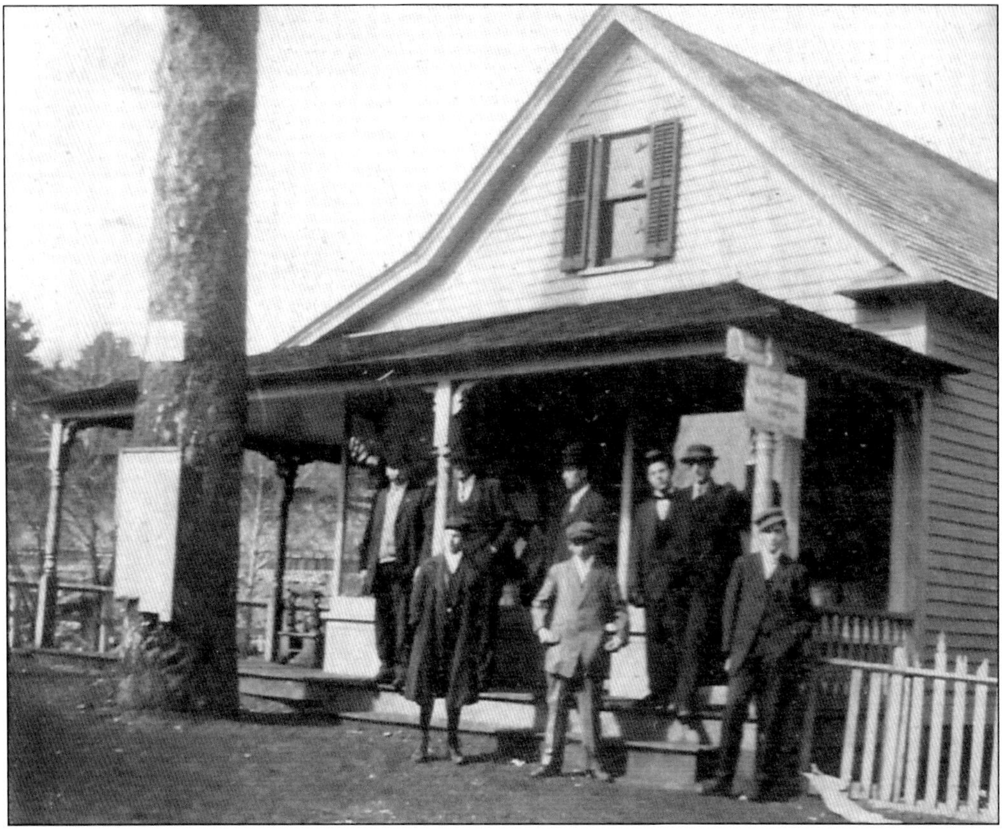

To catch up on town events, residents just had to stop at the drugstore. Always a gathering place, there would be someone at the drugstore with whom to share a story or two at any time of the day. The trunk of the tree was used for notices from the town about upcoming meetings. It was one of four places in town designated as signposts for displaying legal notices and announcing town assemblies.

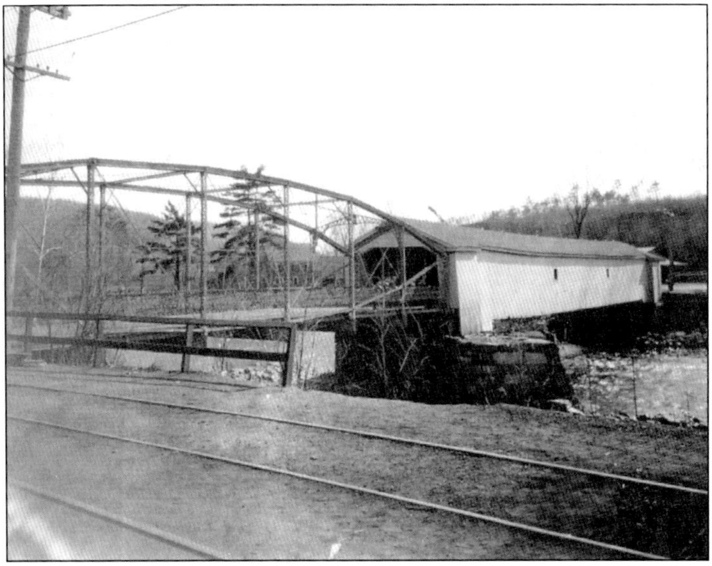

Looking south from the trolley stop at the drugstore, the Depot Street bridge is seen. In 1856, the American Hard Rubber Company offered to build a bridge in this new location. It was considered the peak of modernization. The three- and four-ton timbers came from local sawmills. To maintain the wood decking, riders would be fined $1 for trotting their horses too fast across the bridge. (BK.)

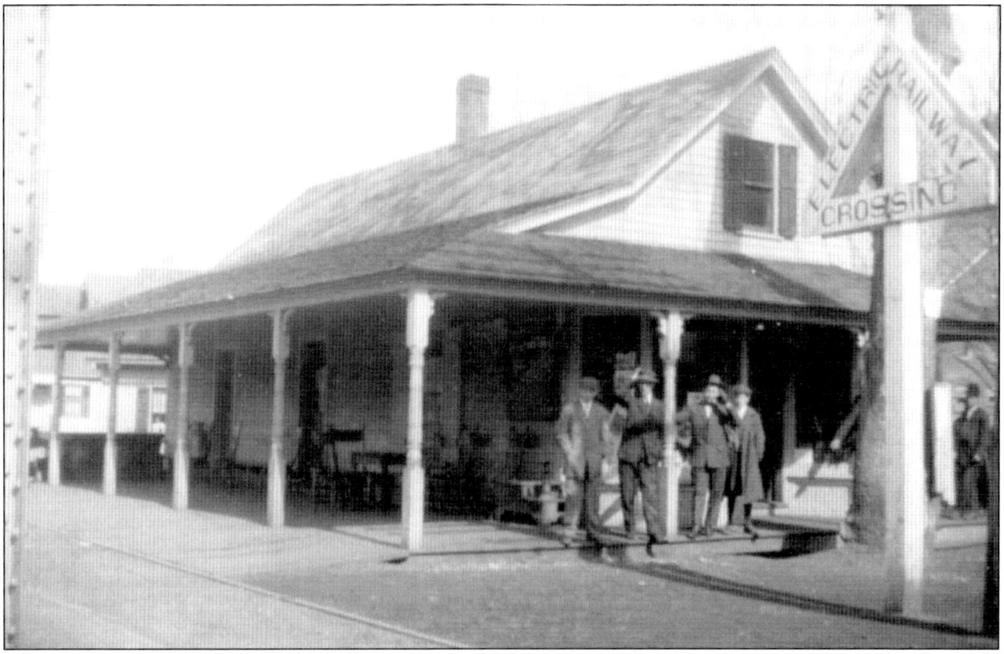

In 1906, the trolley opened from New Haven to Waterbury with half-hour service. Built two years later in 1908, the drugstore acted as the trolley stop. Druggist and chemist Leo F.J. Hoffstat was the first proprietor. The store became a drop-off for freight arriving by trolley. In the span of one day, the store recorded a staggering 276 cases arriving for customers.

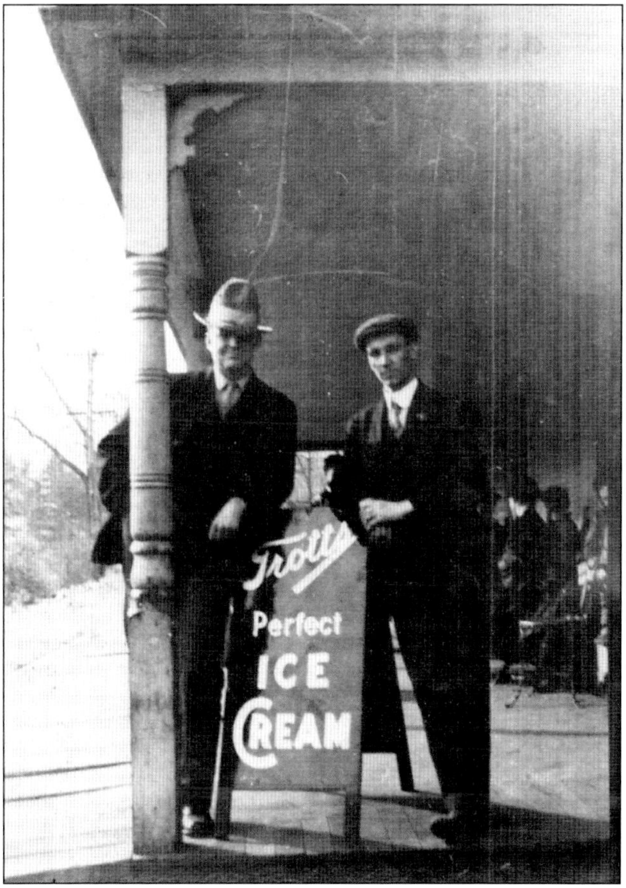

Bradford Wakefield (left) and Pat Malone pause for a photograph. Bradford Wakefield was first selectman from 1919 to 1925, serving seven one-year terms. Behind them, some residents are waiting for a trolley and perhaps enjoying a taste of Trott's Perfect Ice Cream. Trolley service in Connecticut was extensive. From Beacon Falls, a passenger could easily travel to Waterbury, New Haven, Bridgeport, or spend the day at Savin Rock Amusement Park. (BK.)

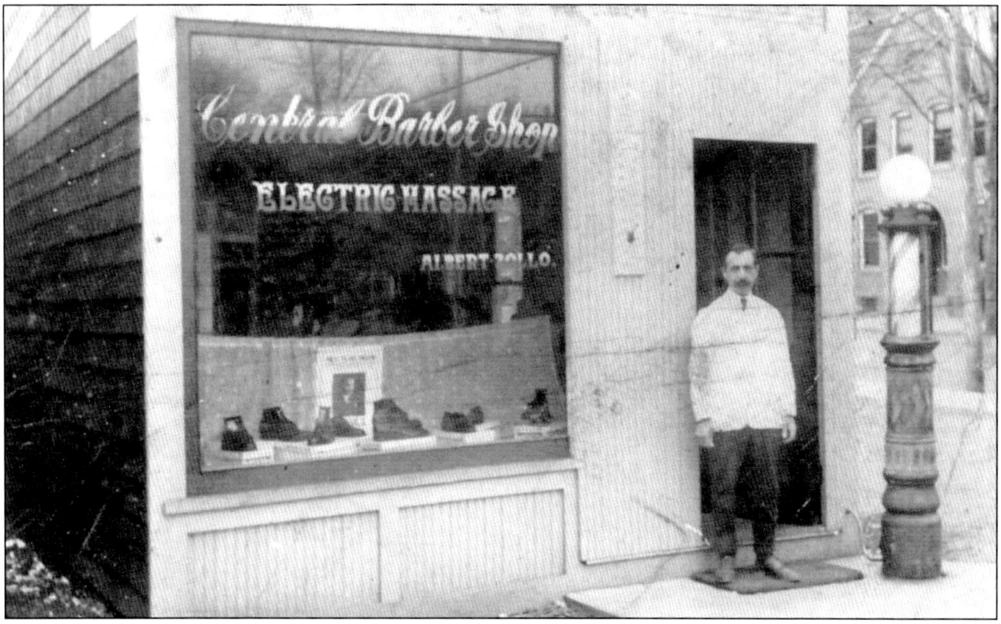

The Central Barbershop is what Al Zollo called his emporium. For a time, his shop was located next to the drugstore. When this building became a liquor store, Zollo converted the little house behind the drugstore into a barbershop. He and his family lived in the apartment above the Crescent Lunch Room. The Zollo family has been associated with numerous businesses in town over the years. (MZ.)

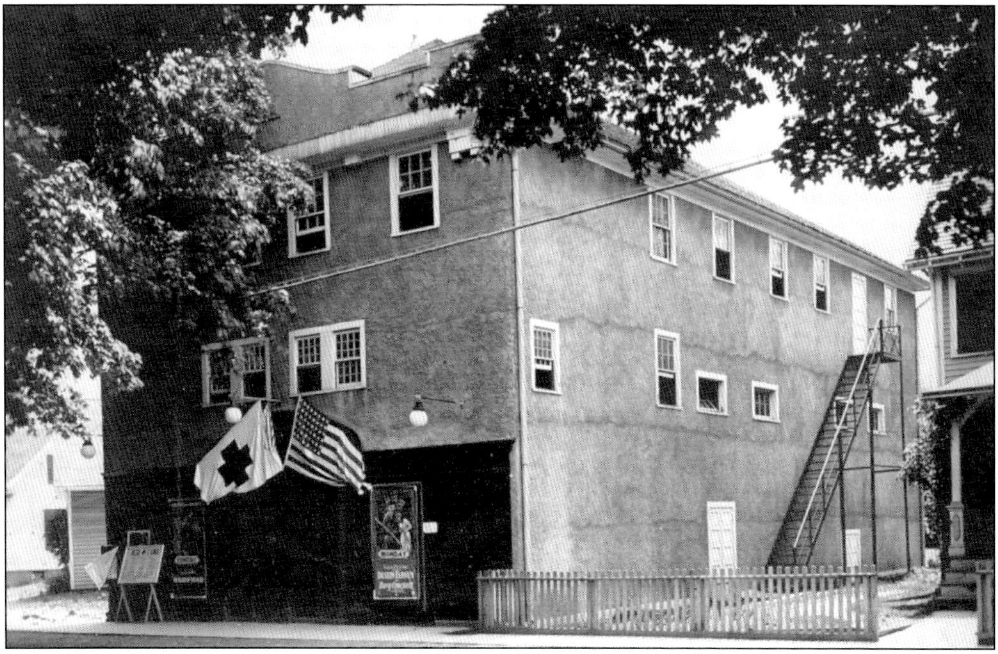

In 1915, the Beacon Falls Rubber Shoe Company built this moving-picture theater across from Burton Road. The building also included an assembly and dance hall. In this photograph, the one-sheet advertises the 1916 film *Davy Crockett*, a silent film starring Dustin Farnum in the title role. The building was also used by St. Michael's Roman Catholic Church while the new church on Maple Avenue was being constructed in 1941 and 1942. (BK.)

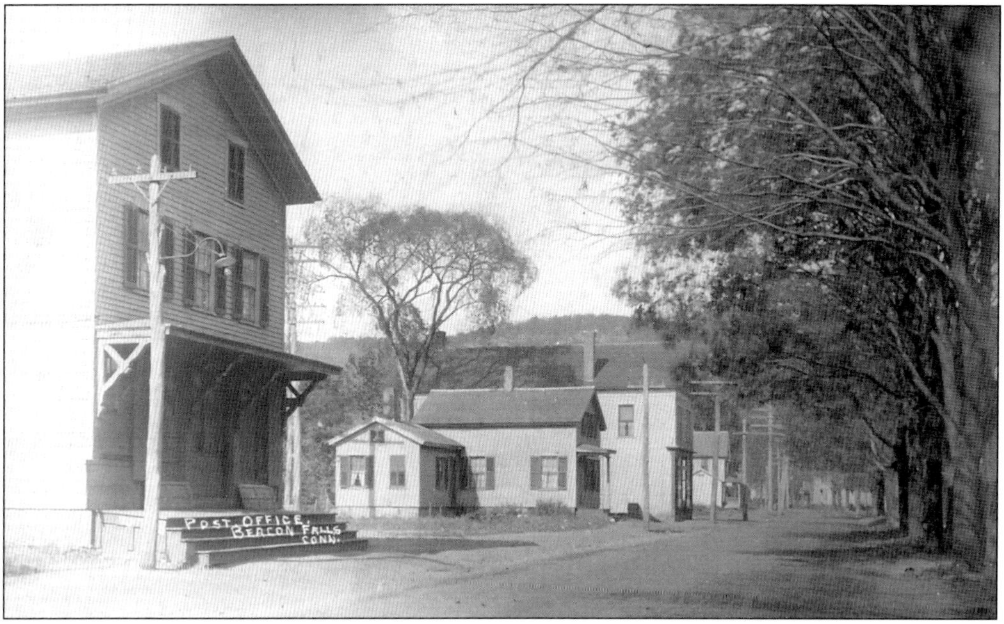

In the 1860s, the postmaster was Corydon W. Elkins, and the post office was in his store. Other stores in Beacon Falls in the late 1800s were operated by Virgil Buckingham, Beecher & Percy, and May & Isabel. In 1910, when this postcard photograph was taken, the post office was in Emerson Terrill's general store. It is not clear if this building was previously Elkins's store, as some have suggested. (MH.)

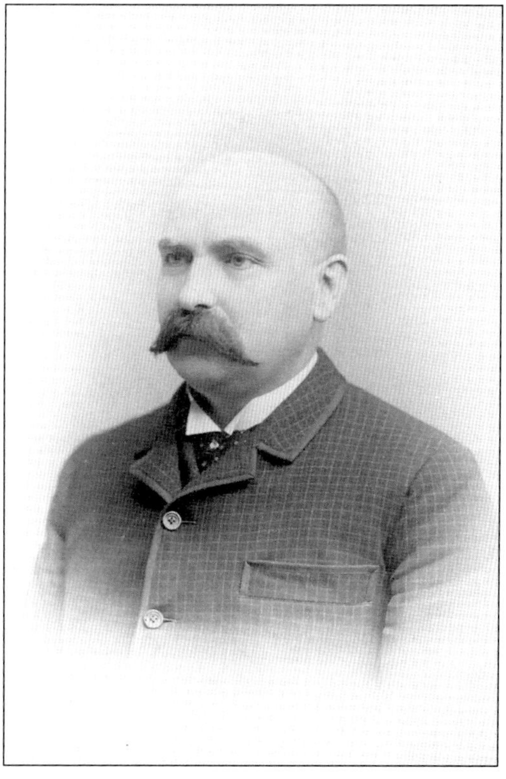

Emerson J. Terrill, seen here, established his general store in 1880. His cousin Emery L. Terrill later became Emerson's partner. Both were active participants in local government. Emery was town clerk and treasurer in 1889. Emerson was in the state legislature in 1888 when this photograph was taken, and he served as first selectman of Beacon Falls in 1889. Both Terrills were postmasters here in the late 1800s. (MH.)

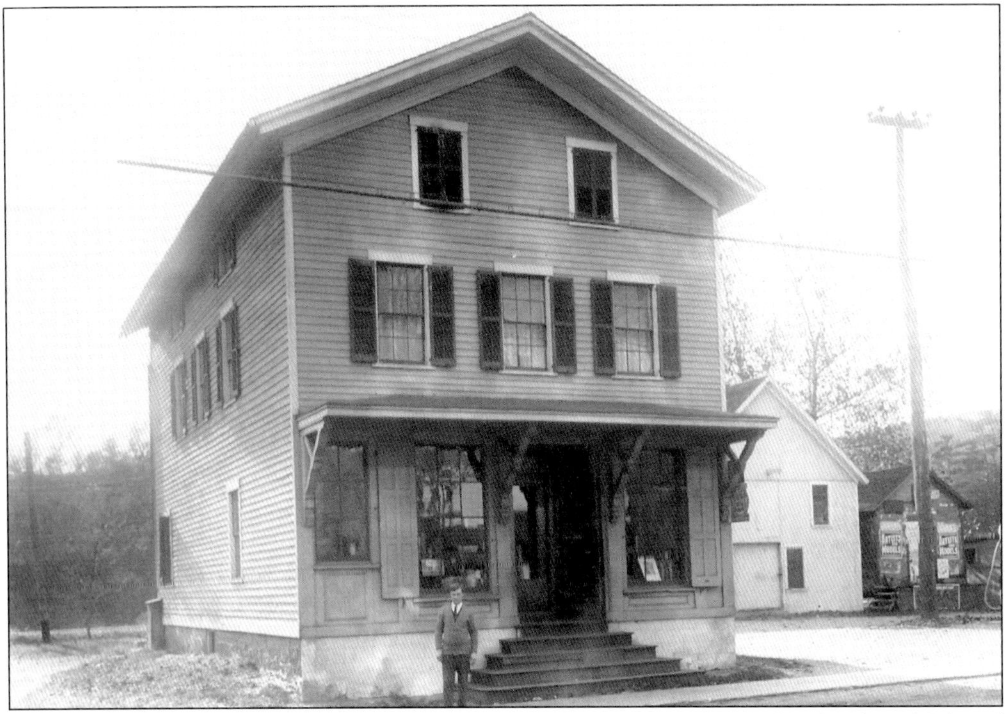

While the Terrill cousins were operating the general store in Beacon Falls, they hired Edward Gruber as a clerk. Edward took over the store in the first decade of the 20th century and ran the store until the early 1950s. This photograph taken in the 1910s features Edward's younger brother William "Willie" Gruber, who served as a clerk at the store and briefly took over operation of the store when Edward passed away in 1951. (MH.)

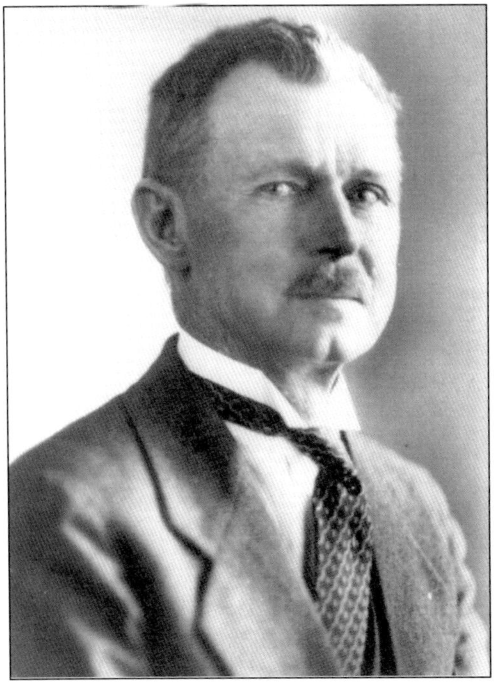

Edward Gruber appears in a formal portrait. He lived in the upper stories of the store with his wife, Amy Cook Gruber, and their daughter Charlotte Amy Gruber. John Cook, who lived on Burton Road, provided financial assistance to Edward when he acquired the store. Edward was married to John's sister Sarah, and John was married to Edward's sister Helen. (MH.)

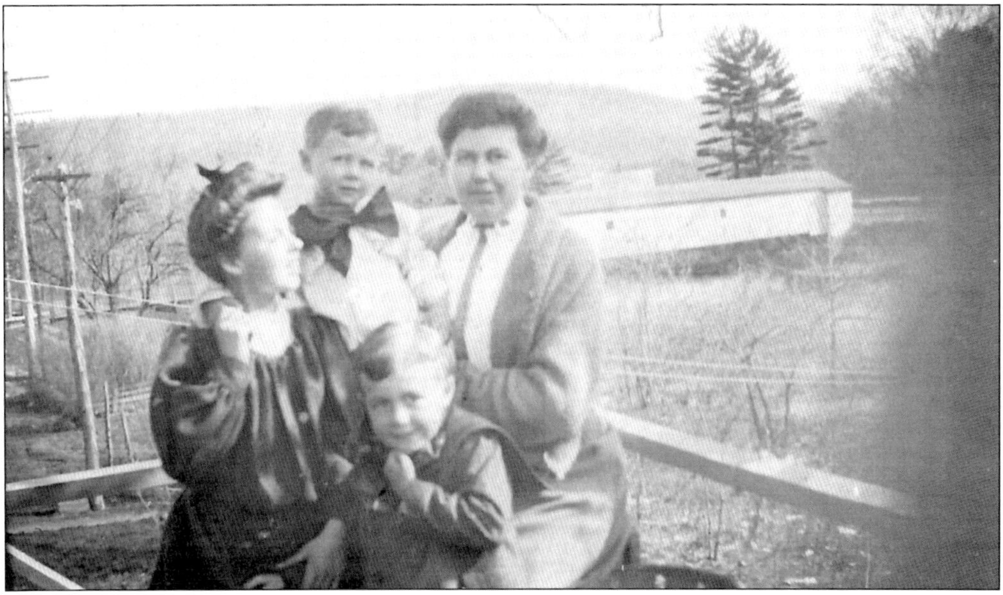

Gruber's Store was located essentially where the Irving Gas Station sits today on Main Street. The back of the store faced the river. Here, Edward's wife, Amy (right), poses with (clockwise) nephew Warren Cook, daughter Charlotte, and nephew Irving Cook. The covered bridge on Depot Street dominates the background. (MH.)

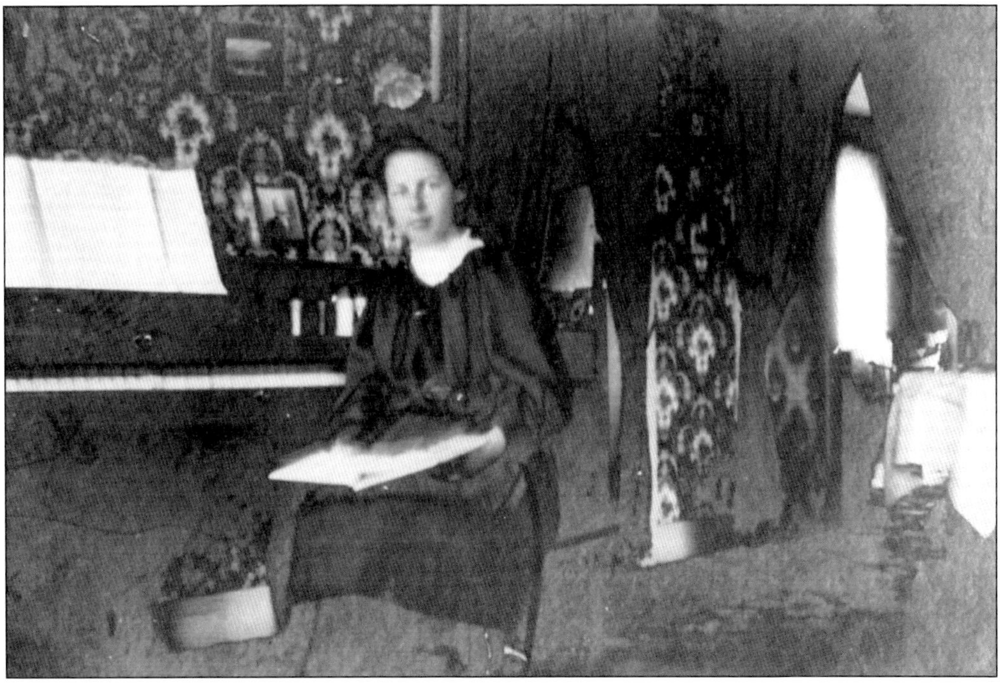

Edward Gruber's daughter Charlotte is shown practicing piano inside the living quarters of the store. The piano enjoyed much success during this period and was often the only way music was heard in most homes in these pre-radio, pre-television days. Edward Gruber was perhaps the first person in Beacon Falls to purchase a phonograph. His Edison Home Phonograph, a machine that played cylindrical rolls, survives today in a private collection. (MH.)

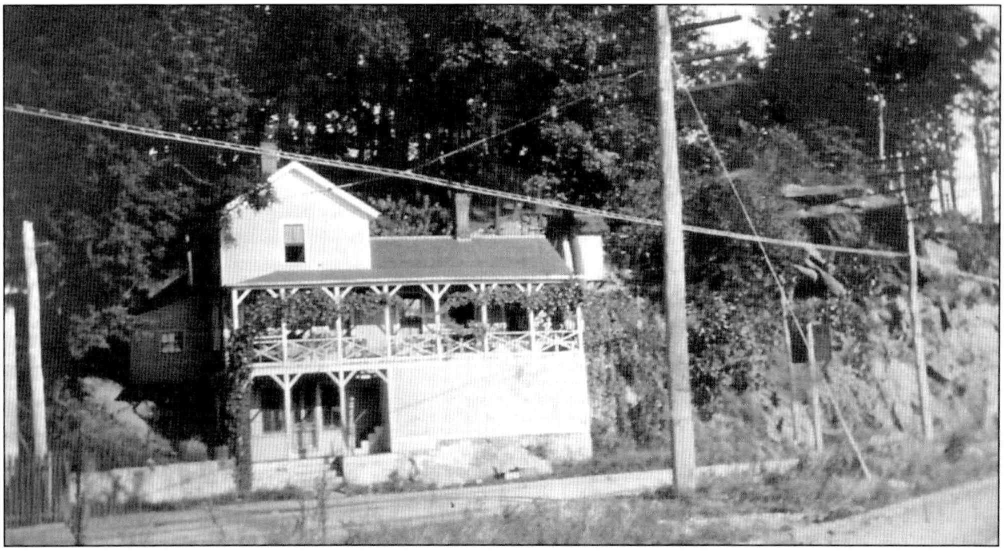

This structure was appropriately known as the Rock House. It literally was built into the rock formation before the corner was blasted away to make Main Street wider. In this perspective taken from the trolley tracks, the Rubber Shoe Company is just out of view to the left. A barbershop occupied the lower floor while the upper floors were living quarters. (BK.)

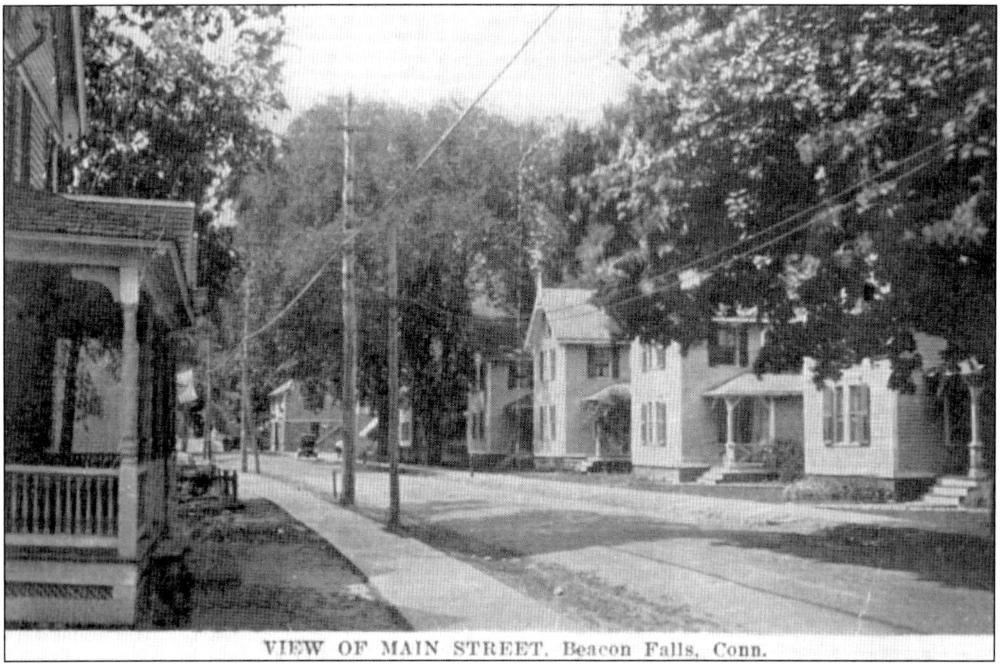

It is hard to imagine Main Street as a quaint residential street with a dirt road, but that is what it was when this postcard photograph was taken around 1910. This view looks north on North Main Street. Very little has survived on the left side of this image while several homes on the right remain. (BK.)

This 1910 photograph looks south from North Main Street. In 1905, Almon C. Judd, manager of the Elton Hotel in Waterbury, wrote *The Ideal Tour*, which guided travelers on "a trip of one thousand miles, so arranged that the motorist sees the best of New England scenery, travels over the best of New England . . . and stops at the best of New England hotels." It included a drive through Beacon Falls. (MH.)

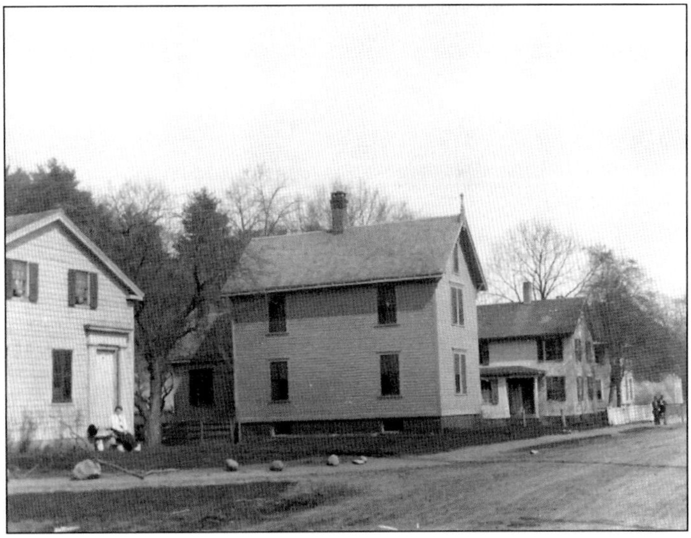

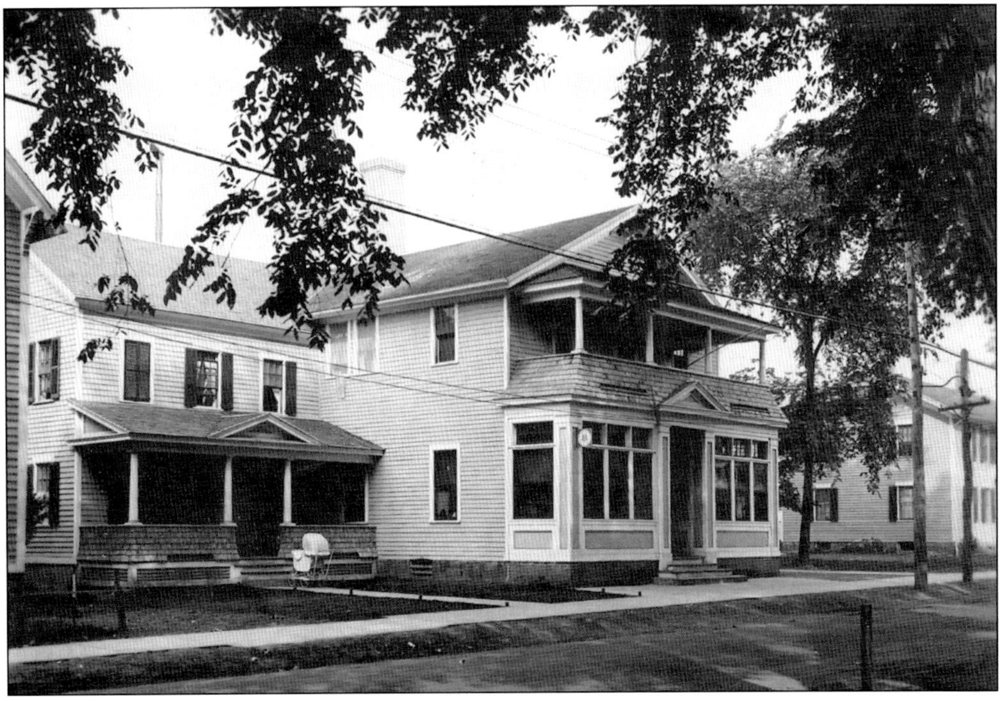

The Beacon Falls Rubber Shoe Company built numerous facilities in town, including a bowling alley and a movie theater. In 1915, they built the Top Notch Hotel on North Main Street, which is seen here. It contained 75 rooms and a restaurant and was often used to house employees. This building would eventually become home to the Connecticut State Police barracks before they were moved to Bethany.

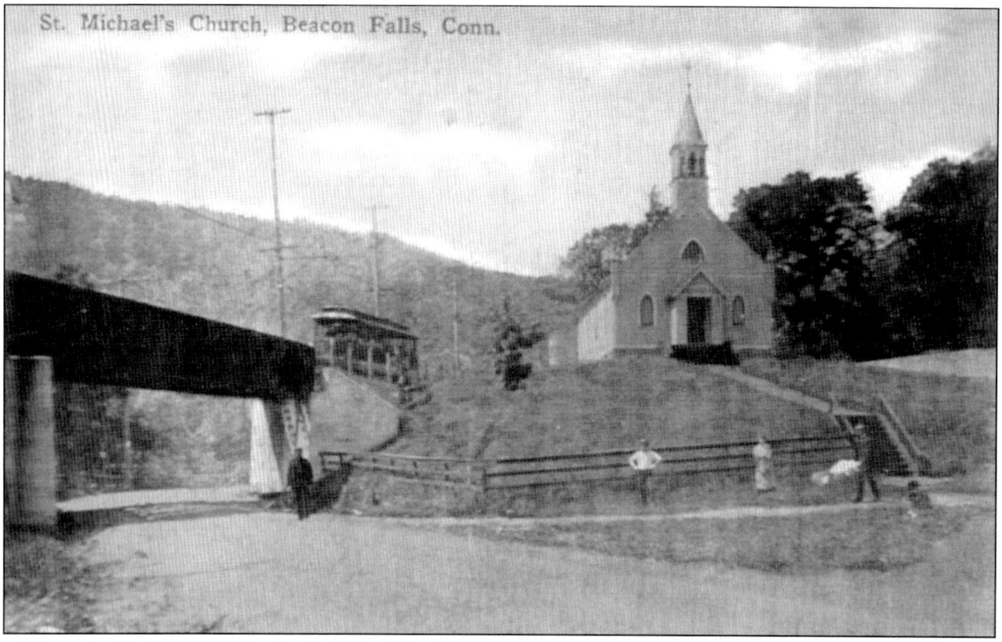

In 1885, St. Augustine's Catholic Church in Seymour established a mission in Beacon Falls. A church named in honor of St. Michael the Archangel was constructed on the corner of Church and Main Streets. This postcard shows the church as it looked around 1900. St Michael's was elevated to full parish status on November 15, 1924. Here, a trolley approaches Main Street. (MK.)

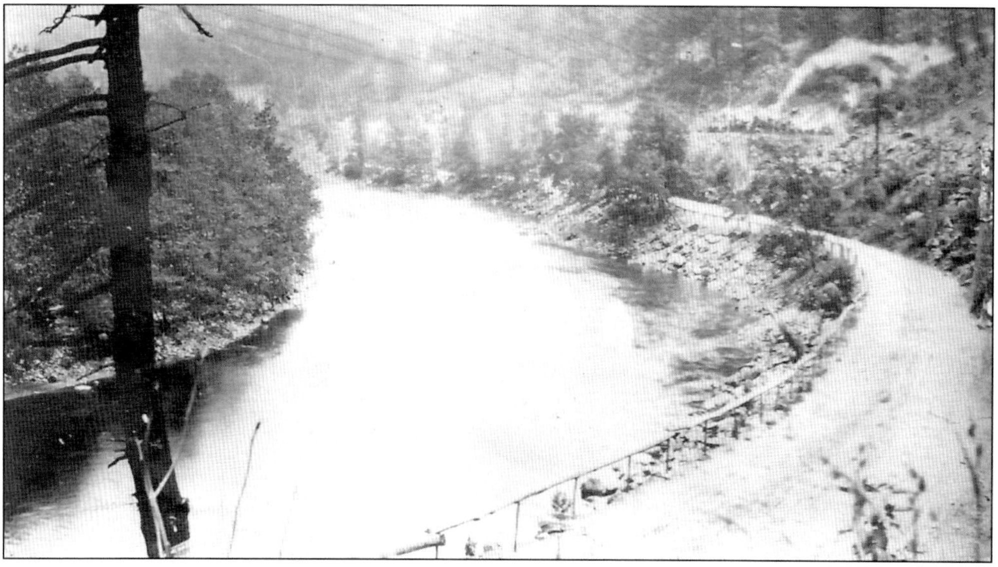

As Main Street heads north out of town, it enters the scenic High Rock area. On August 24, 1906, the Naugatuck Valley Electric Railway Company applied for approval to extend the trolley line from Naugatuck through Beacon Falls to Seymour. Near High Rock where there was precious little room, a trolley path was carved out of the hillside. This construction work can be seen progressing in the distance. (BK.)

Once the trolley track reached the outskirts of Beacon Falls from the north, it crossed over Main Street, then over the canal, and then ran behind the homes on the west side of Main Street. In this view, a cable is being strung along the track from an unusual scaffold on wheels. The pantograph on the trolley would ride on this electrified cable. (MH.)

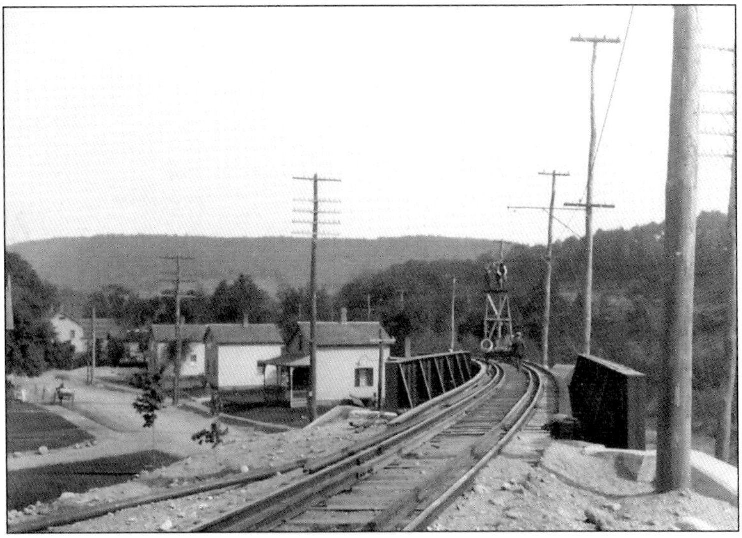

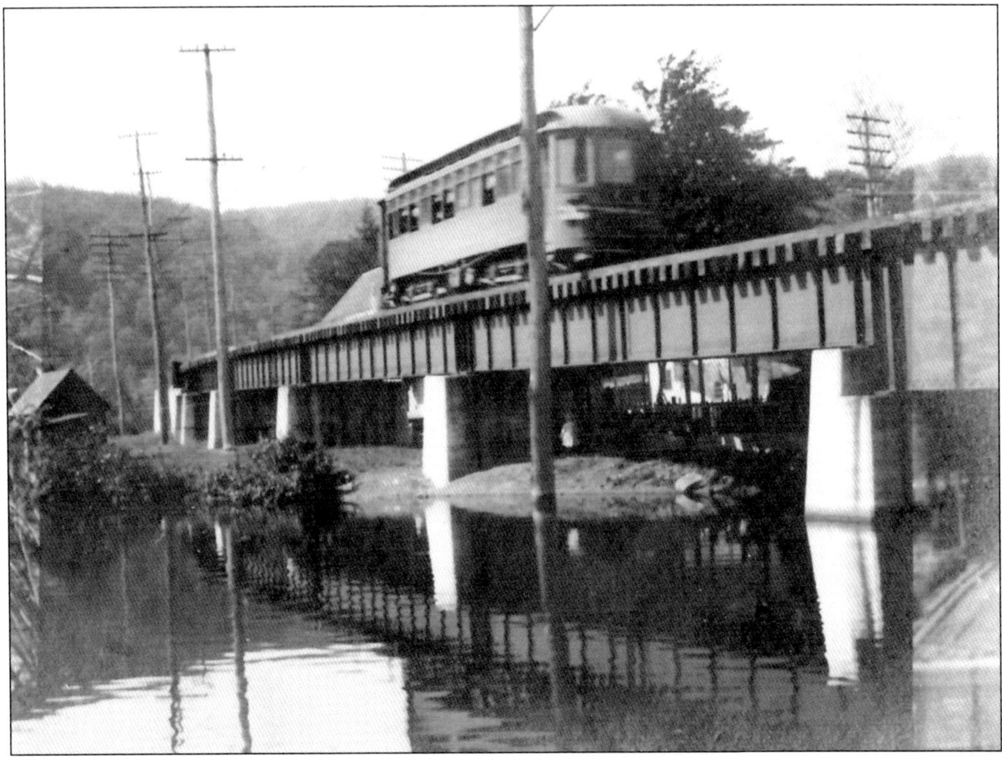

The trolley operated until 1935 when it was replaced with busses. In this view looking north, the roof of St. Michael's Roman Catholic Church is just barely visible behind the trolley. A new church was constructed on Maple Avenue when the land containing the old church was sold to the State of Connecticut in 1941 for highway construction. The new church opened its doors on June 21, 1942.

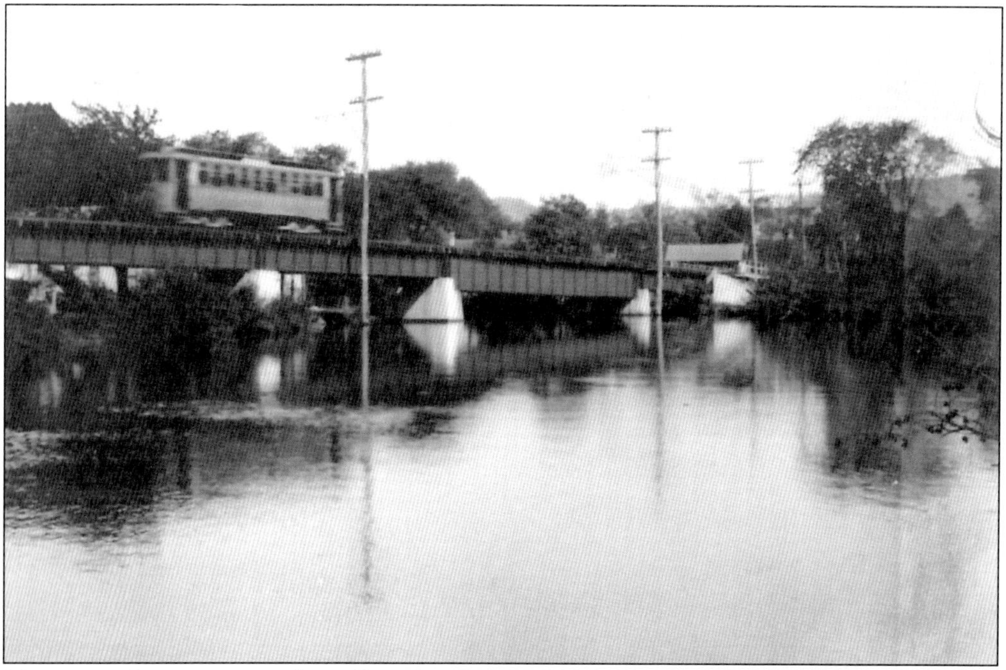

This is an alternate view of a trolley crossing the canal. When looking at nostalgic views of trolleys, it is often forgotten that trolleys had their share of mishaps. In 1917, when one trolley rear-ended another north of town, 30 people were injured. On December 26, 1909, a trolley jumped the track between Seymour and Beacon Falls and rolled down a 40-foot embankment into the frozen Naugatuck River.

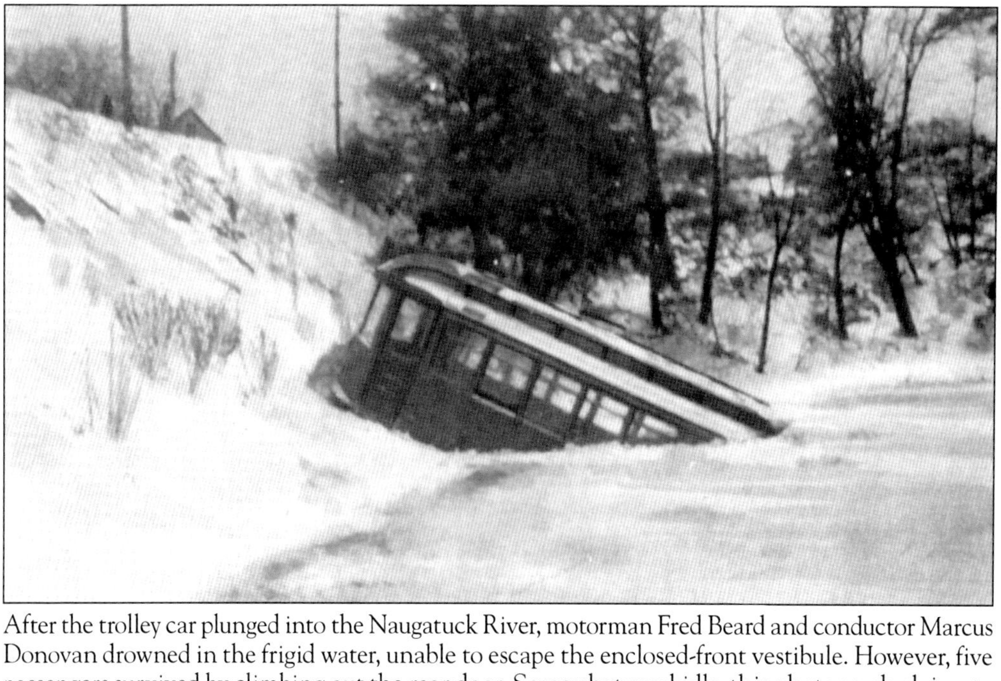

After the trolley car plunged into the Naugatuck River, motorman Fred Beard and conductor Marcus Donovan drowned in the frigid water, unable to escape the enclosed-front vestibule. However, five passengers survived by climbing out the rear door. Somewhat morbidly, this photograph claims to have been taken prior to the victims' bodies being removed from the vehicle. (MK.)

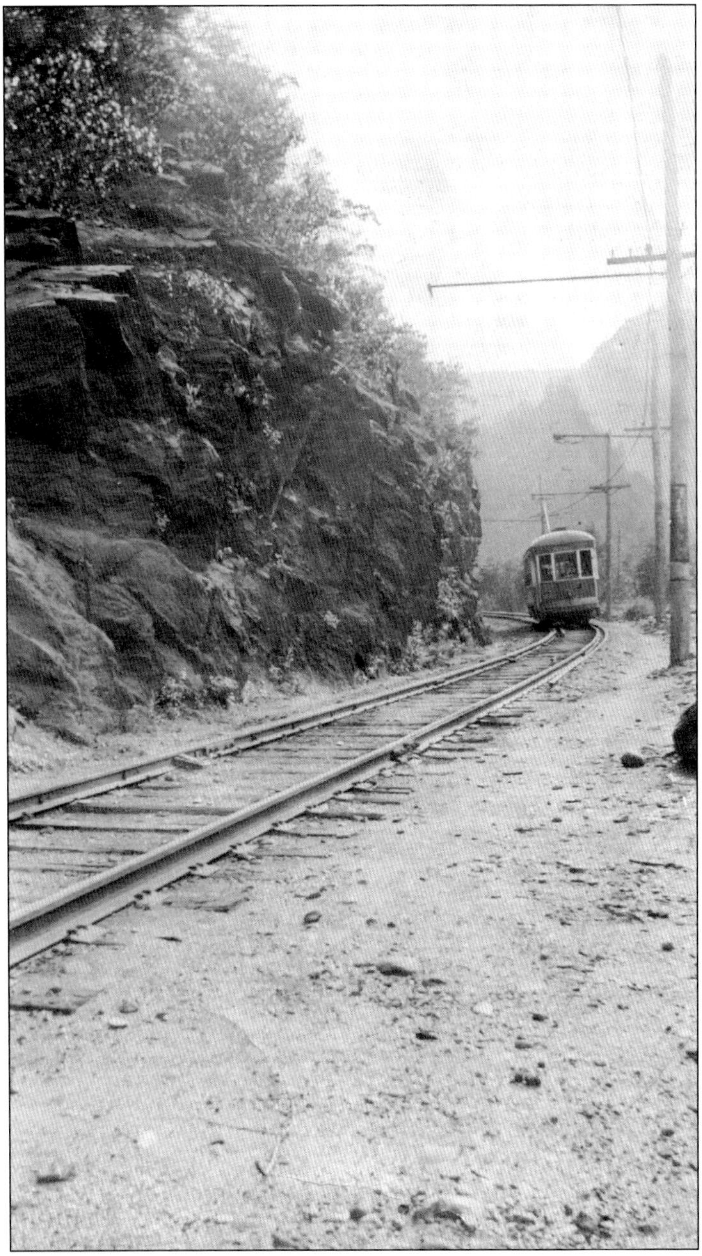

A trolley departs Beacon Falls en route to Naugatuck. The trolley track sat high on the hillside while the automobile road ran below alongside the river. In 1919, the State of Connecticut blasted and removed 15,000 cubic yards of rocks from the valley walls to eliminate the "extreme narrowness" that existed in several spots along the automobile road. When the trolley was discontinued in 1935, this track bed was converted into an automobile road for northbound traffic only, and the original automobile road was configured to carry only southbound traffic. For years, the "high road" and "low road," as they were called, provided drivers a curving, scenic, yet white-knuckle drive. Later, much of the hillside below the trolley track was blasted out to create the four-lane Route 8 as it exists today. But one can still make out brief segments of the high road carved into the hillside.

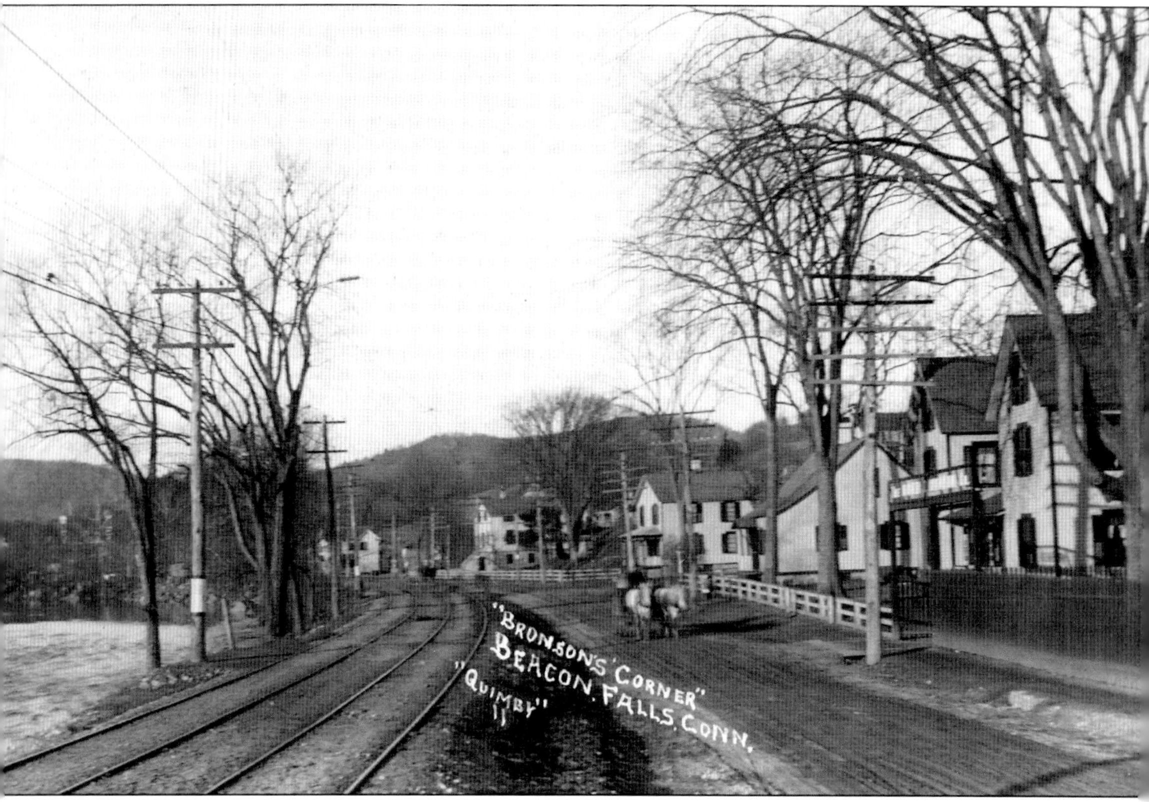

This postcard looks north at the intersection of Main Street and Bethany Road located just beyond the Homer D. Bronson Company headquarters on the right. The trolley line here has two tracks. These segments of double tracks allowed northbound and southbound trolleys to pass one another. This view has much of the feel of the divided Main Street of today. For a time, the trolley served another purpose in Beacon Falls, as school bus. In 1908, ten students in the Cotton Hollow section of town rode the trolley to downtown Beacon Falls so they could attend the Center School after the schoolhouse in Cotton Hollow closed. The expense of $100 for the year represented a significant savings over keeping the Cotton Hollow schoolhouse open, and the quality of education the students received was considered greatly superior. As reported by the Connecticut State Board of Education, the only negative for the students was "bad morals being learned from contact with rough people on the trolley and in the village." (BK.)

Three

Early Life

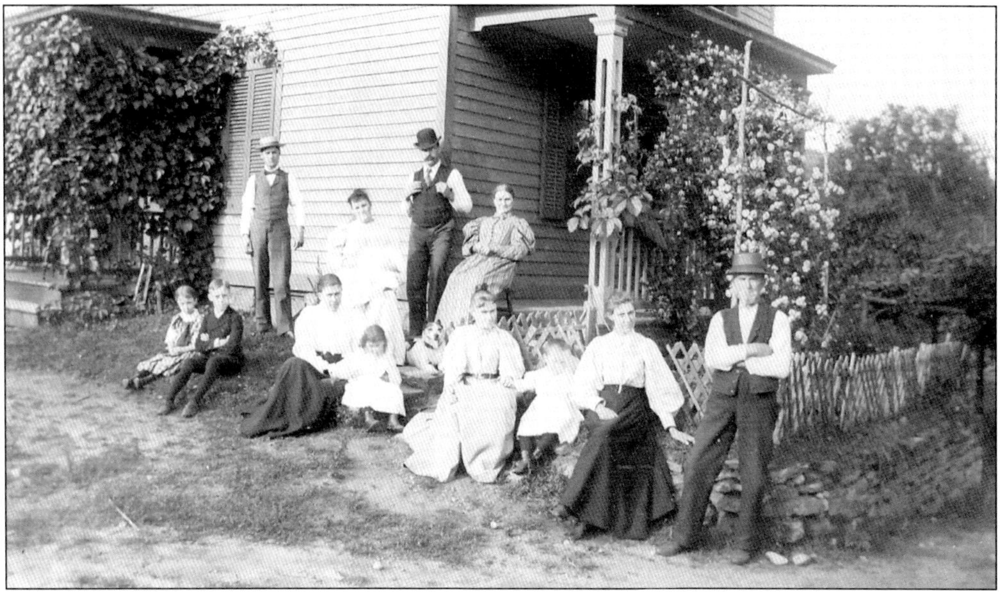

Life in a small town is a collection of individual family stories. One such story starts with this photograph from around 1895. It shows the Gruber family at home on the end of Railroad Avenue. Christian Gruber (right) moved to town from Windsor, Connecticut, when the Home Woolen Mill opened in Beacon Falls in 1864. His oldest children also worked at the mill. When the woolen mill closed, the elder Gruber took up farming. (MH.)

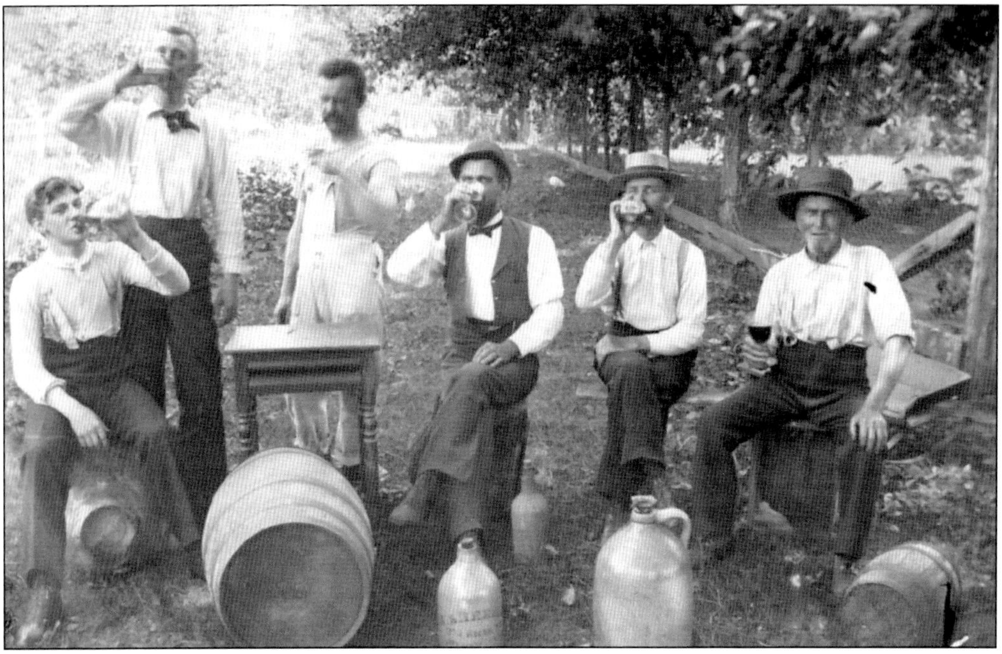

Christian Gruber (right) enjoys a little home brew with his sons. He was of German descent. When he arrived in Beacon Falls, there was already significant German population here, as many of the skilled carvers employed by the American Hard Rubber Company were originally from Germany. For a time, the north end of Main Street was referred to as "Germantown." (MH.)

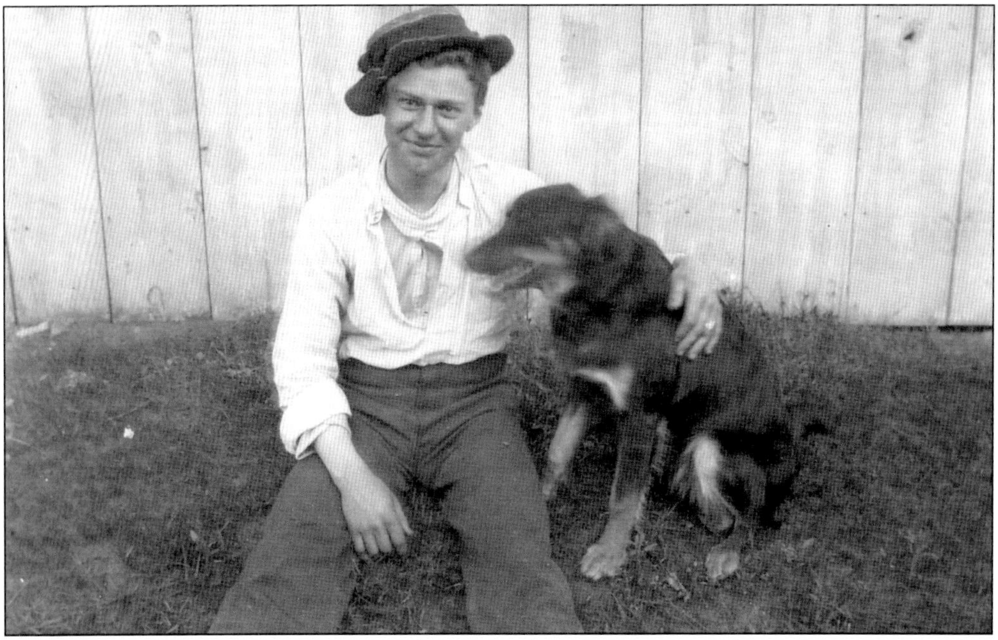

Here, one of the Gruber boys poses with his dog. When the Home Woolen Mill closed, the eldest members of the family left for Patterson, New Jersey, to follow the woolen trade. The younger members remained in Beacon Falls to work at the rubber shoe factory or were too young to work. (MH.)

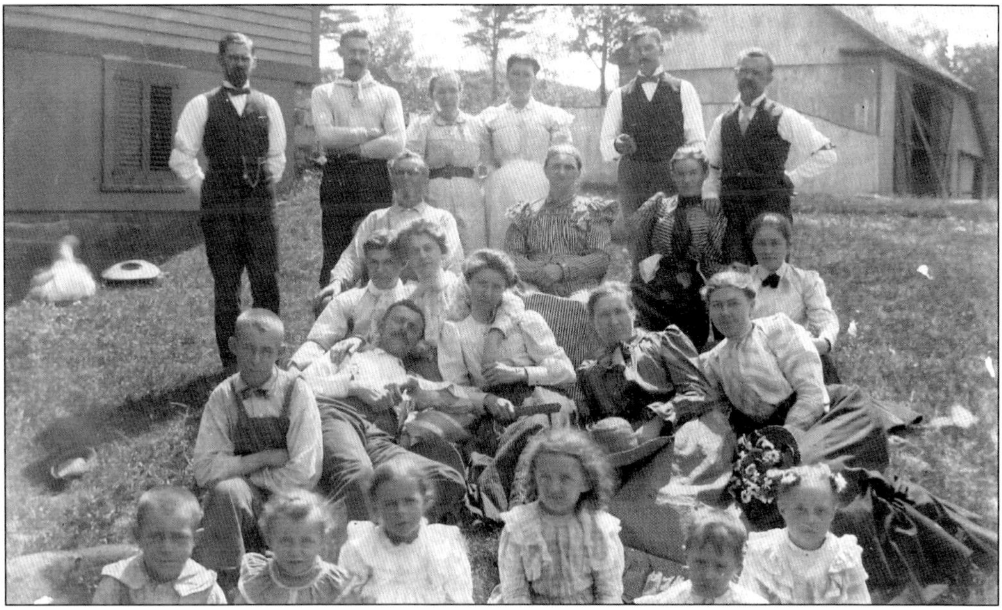

Christian and Susan Gruber are seated at the rear (left and center) during a family reunion around 1905. The eldest son, John (standing at the left rear), moved to New Jersey to pursue the woolen industry there. He eventually became the superintendent of the ill-fated Woodvale Woolen Mill outside of Johnstown, Pennsylvania. During the Johnstown flood, John Gruber is credited with rescuing victims of the flood as they floated past the partially collapsed woolen mill. (MH.)

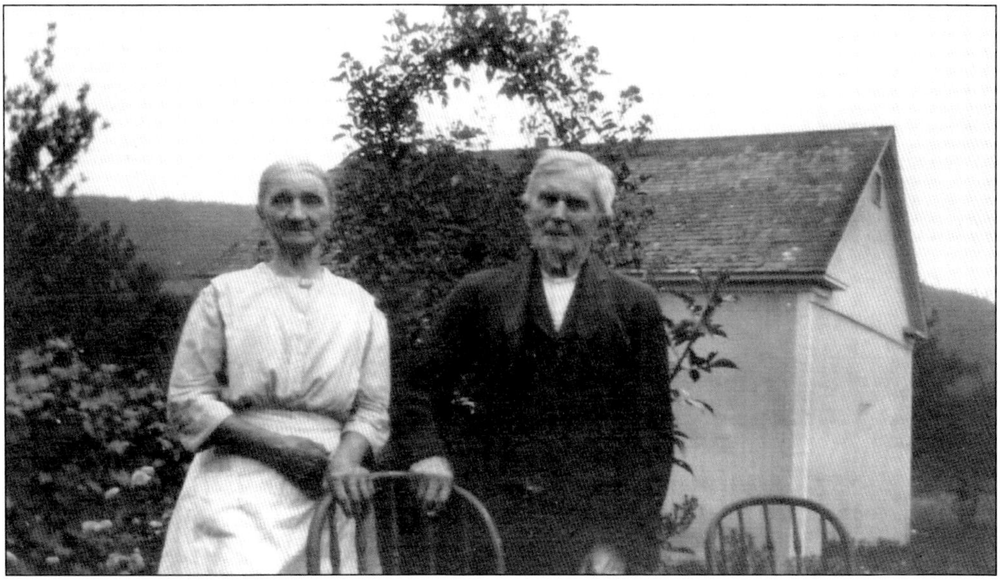

The elder Grubers pose for a photograph in July 1914; Christian is aged 90, and Susan is 84. The Gruber property stretched from the end of Railroad Avenue out toward Lopus Road. Today, a residential street is named for these former residents. The Grubers are interred at Pine's Bridge Cemetery nearby. Their oldest son, John Gruber, is interred in the lone mausoleum there. (MH.)

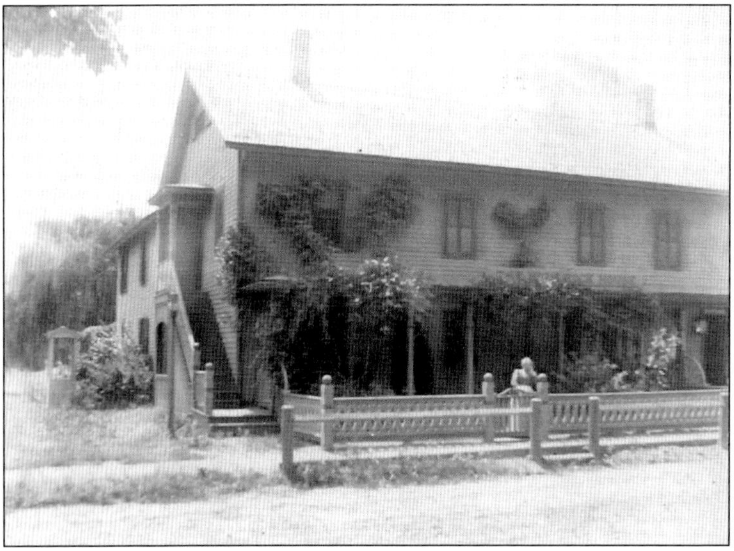

Another occupation in Beacon Falls was innkeeper. With High Rock Grove attracting thousands of visitors each year, both hotels and farmhouses were available to put up guests. A good place to stay on a trip to High Rock might have been here, High Rock House on North Main Street. (JW.)

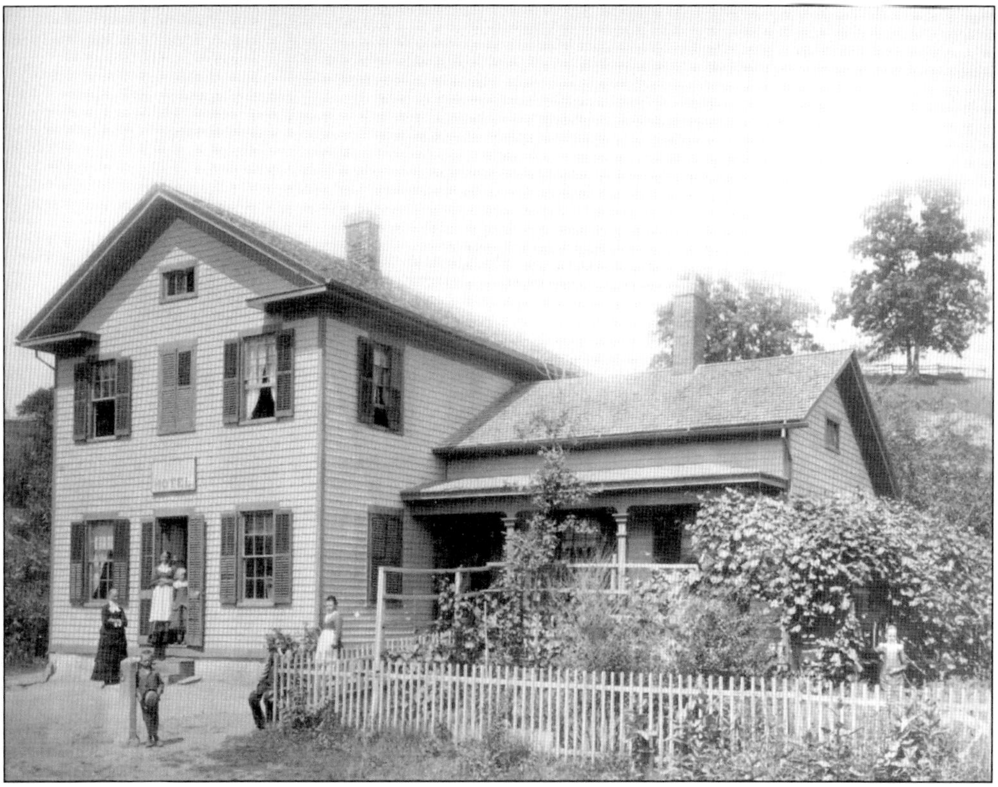

A little farther south down Main Street was the Beacon Falls Hotel, shown here. The hotel appears to be little more than an ordinary farmhouse of the period, but as an advertisement for High Rock Grove pointed out, Beacon Falls had "first class accommodations, both at hotels and farm-houses, nestling on the hills and in the dales of old Connecticut." This hotel sat near where the Beacon Falls Market sits today.

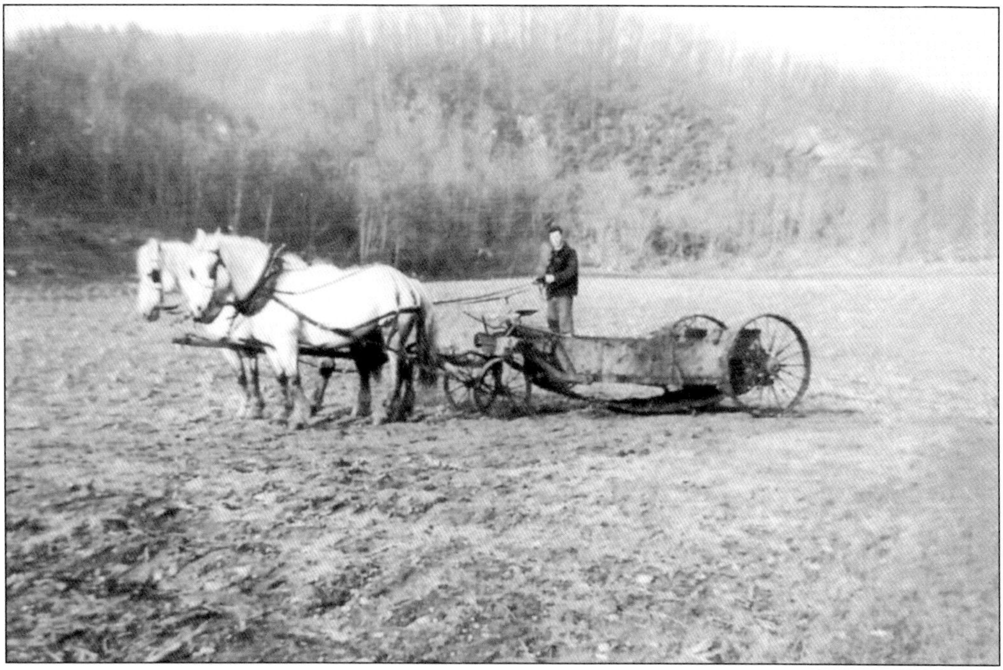

Many farms dotted Beacon Falls in the early 20th century. Here, Joseph S. Betkoski, of Spring Dairy Farm on Blackberry Hill, gets ready to fertilize the cornfield. In addition to the dairy, his family raised a variety of livestock and vegetables for local residents. Salted meat was stored in a barrel and kept in the cold cellar along with vegetables covered with sand or hay. (EB.)

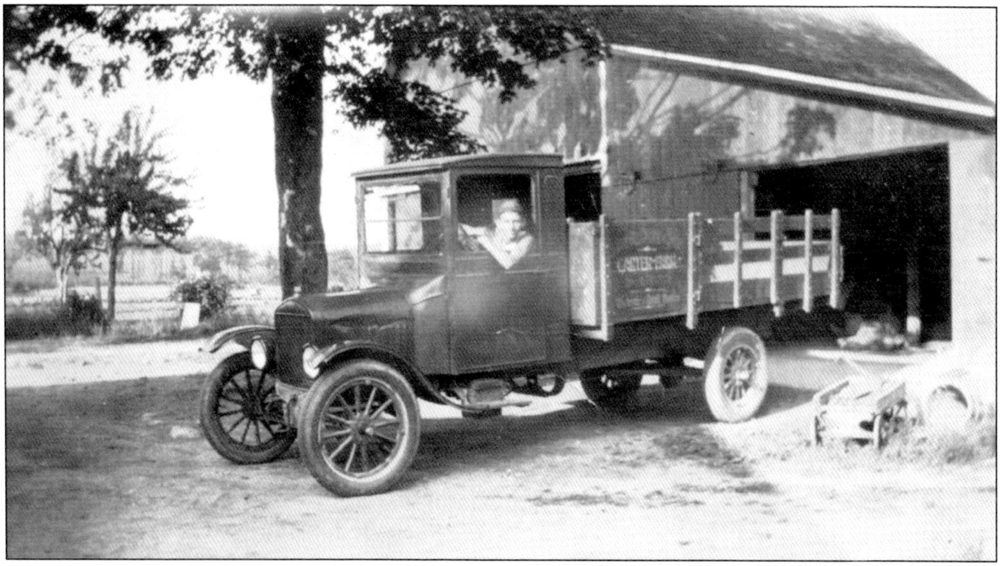

Edward Gelmini, who worked with his father, Luigi, and his brother Davio at their vegetable farm on Lopus Road, is seen sitting in the family Ford Model T pickup truck. They sold their vegetables at the Municipal Market on Meadow Street in Waterbury. Later, the produce was sold on the premises. All of Davio's children worked on the farm, and many Beacon Falls youths had their first jobs picking vegetables here. (AGB.)

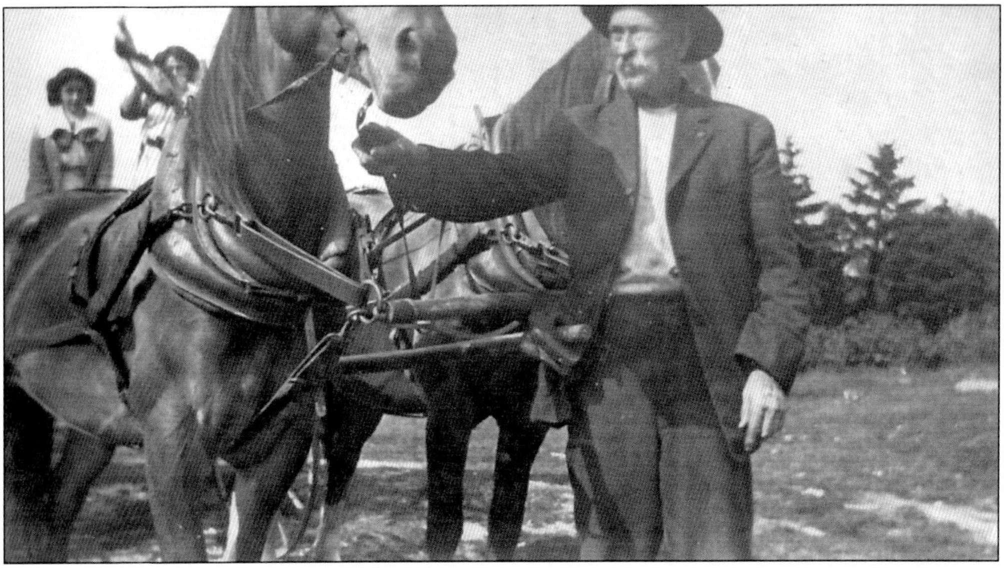

Even after the advent of automobiles, horses continued to serve an important purpose, particularly in farming. Although the number of horses used in farming reached a maximum around 1918, tractors only slowly gained traction. It was not until 1944 that the tractor overtook the horse as the dominant source of farm power in the United States. (MH.)

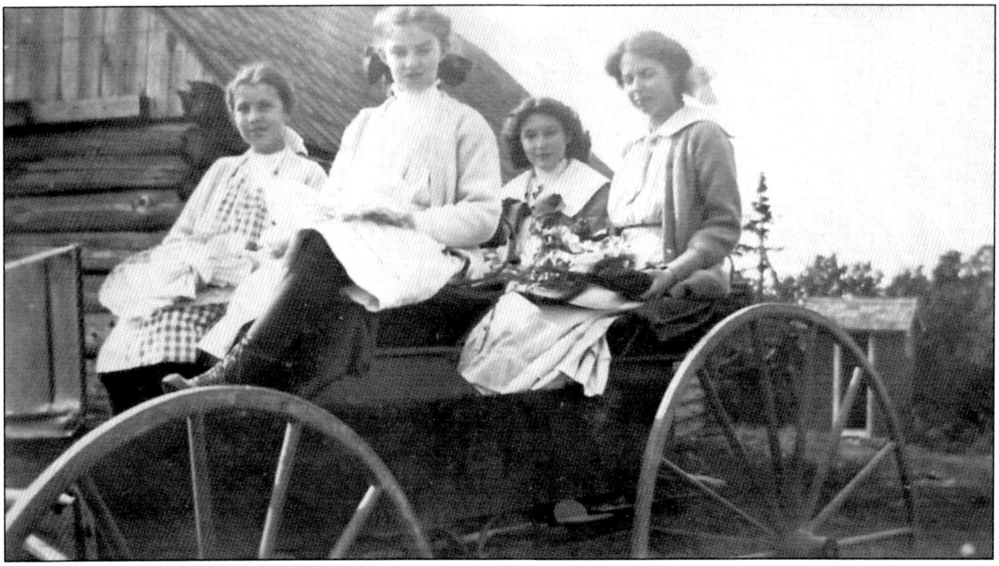

Here, the traditional horse-drawn wagon is used to take these teenage girls for a ride. This is the wagon being pulled by the horses in the previous photograph. Judging by the fancy bonnets that are being held by each of these girls, one might wonder if they are heading out for Easter services. (MH.)

Ed Ryan poses with one of his Holsteins at Elm Spring Farm on Rimmon Hill Road. Elm Spring was one of a half dozen farms along this stretch of road. It operated as a dairy farm through most of the 20th century, and like many dairy farms of the period, it bottled and delivered milk to its customers. (JBW.)

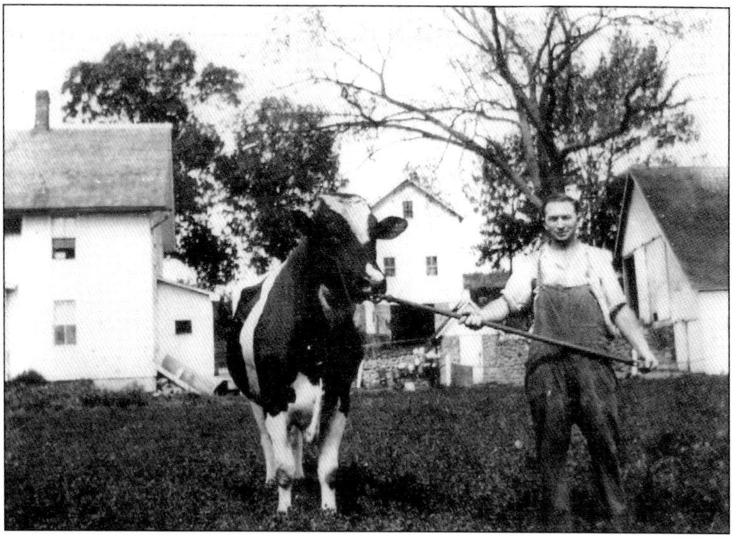

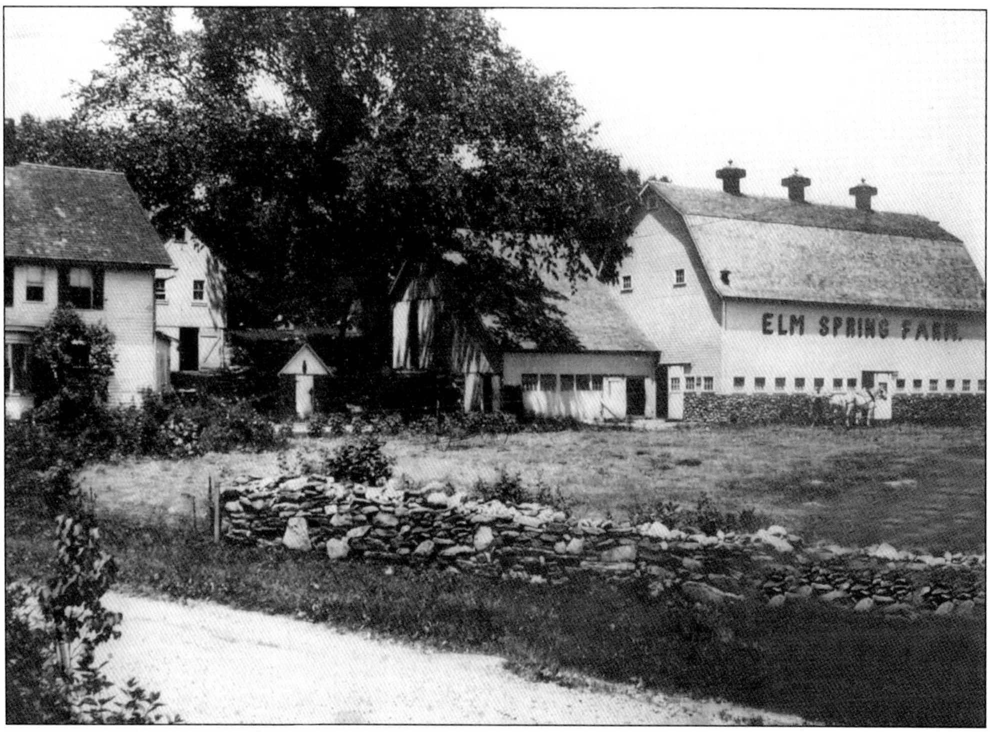

This pastoral scene is in sharp contrast to the daily grind of running a dairy farm. In addition to the twice-a-day ritual of milking all the cows by hand, hay was harvested in the nearby fields for feed, which was stored in the loft of the cow barn (right). Though invented in the late 1800s, automated milking machinery did not come into common use locally until around 1940. (JBW.)

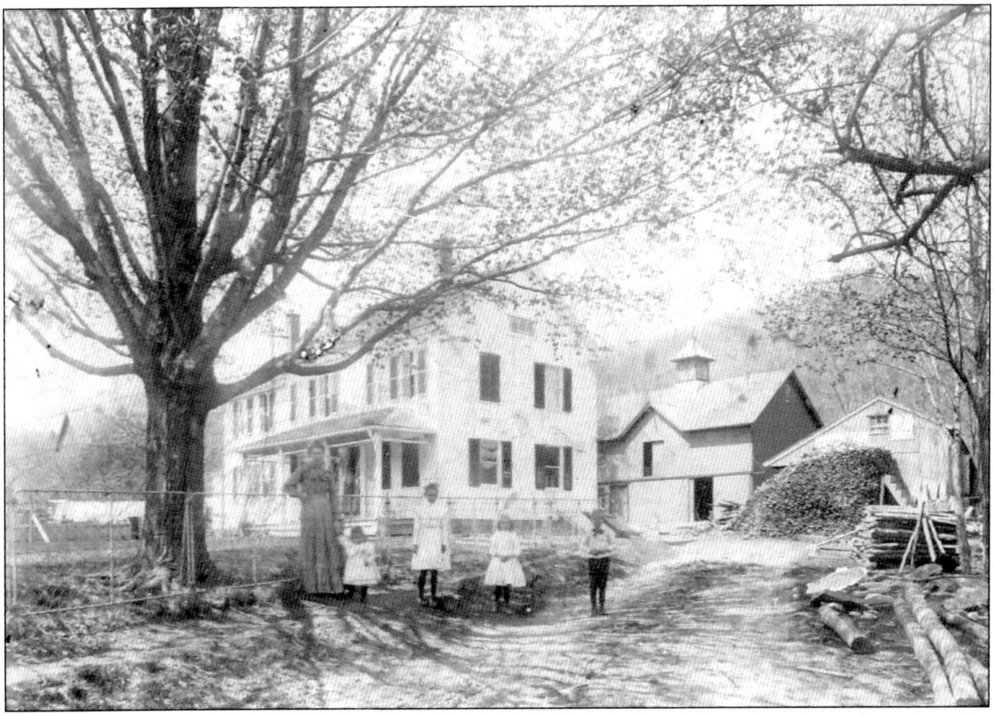

Off of Burton Road was Clark's farm. The Clarks were early settlers of the area and predate the creation of the town. At the time this photograph was taken, George Clark was running this farm set on 150 acres. George married Mary Reffelt in 1886 and had five children: Frank, Eva, George, Ethel, and Rosetta. Mary and four of the children are seen in this photograph. (AT.)

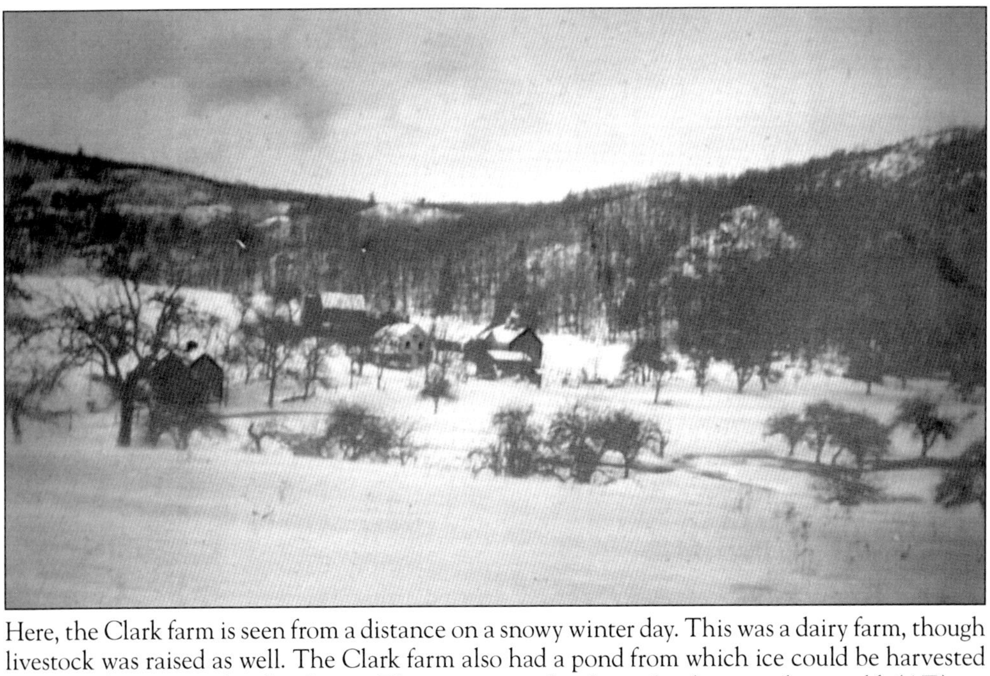

Here, the Clark farm is seen from a distance on a snowy winter day. This was a dairy farm, though livestock was raised as well. The Clark farm also had a pond from which ice could be harvested and stored in an insulated icehouse. The ice was used to keep the dairy products cold. (AT.)

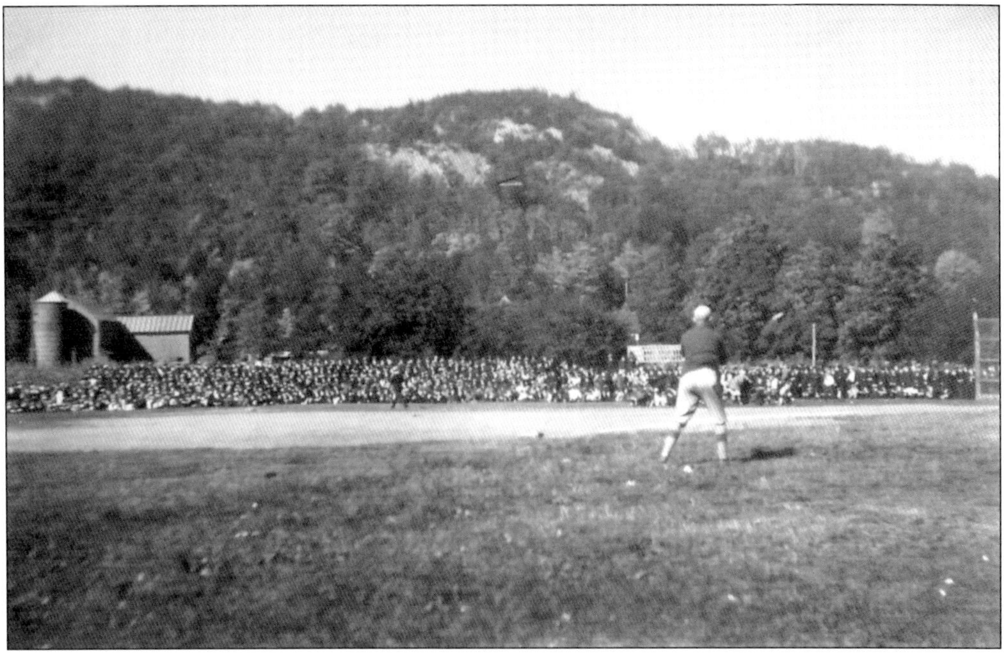

In the 1910s, when the hill section of town was developed by the Beacon Falls Rubber Shoe Company, some of the Clark farmland was utilized for a ball field. The Clark farm barn can be seen in this action shot. Laurel Ledge School sits on this spot today. The Rubber Shoe Company sponsored the Top Notch team, and their games were covered extensively in the company newsletter the *Top Notcher*. (MH.)

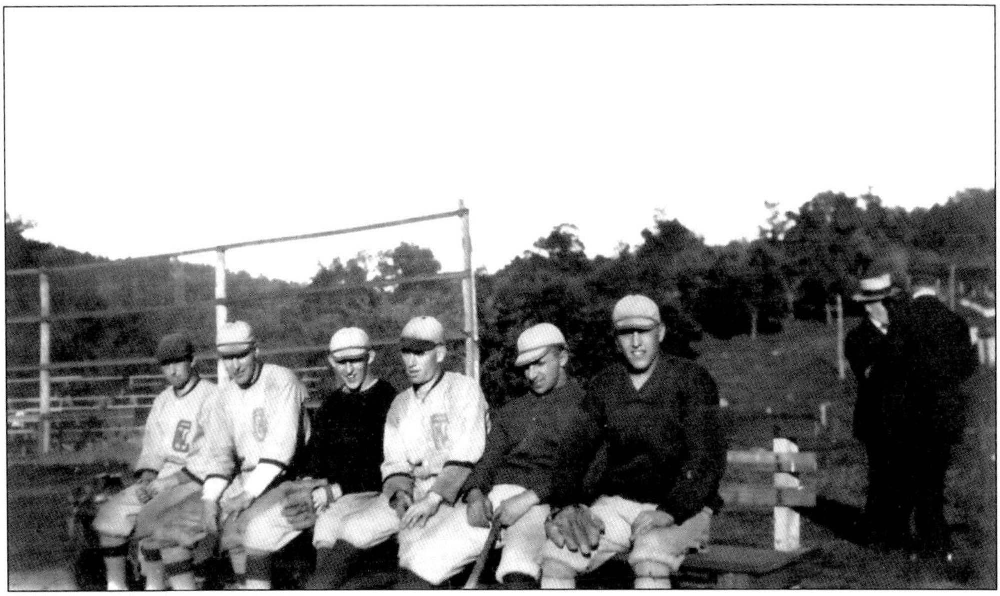

Here, members of the Top Notch baseball team pose for a photograph. In 1920, Charles Kevit gained some notoriety when he pitched a no-hitter. Of note is the Beacon Falls Rubber Shoe Company Top Notch logo sewn into the team uniforms. Other companies in the valley sponsored teams as well; one such adversary was the Rubber Regenerators of Naugatuck. (MH.)

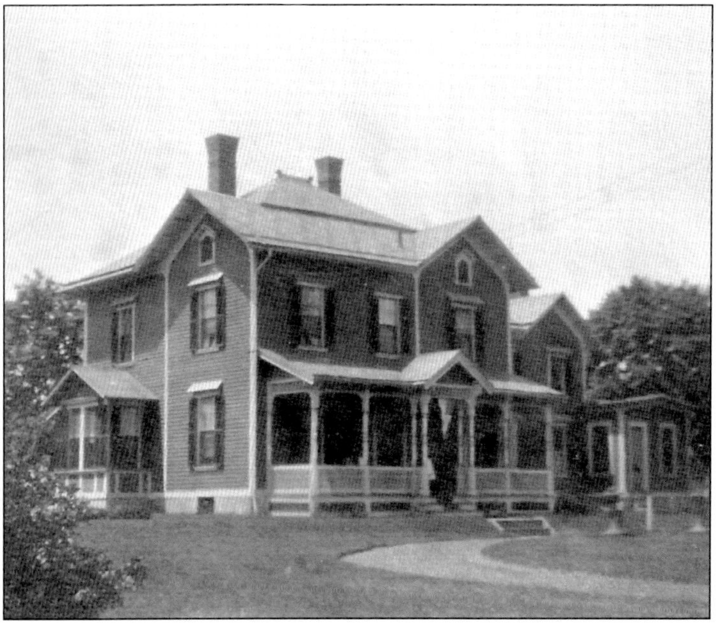

In 1863, John Wolfe became the superintendant of the Home Woolen Mill in Beacon Falls, and he became the owner in 1879. Pictured here in 1910, his home was a mansion by Beacon Falls standards, and the street became known as Wolfe Avenue. When he retired in 1885, Clarence Bodfish took over the mill. It is thought that John Wolfe was a driving force in the formation of the town of Beacon Falls. (JW.)

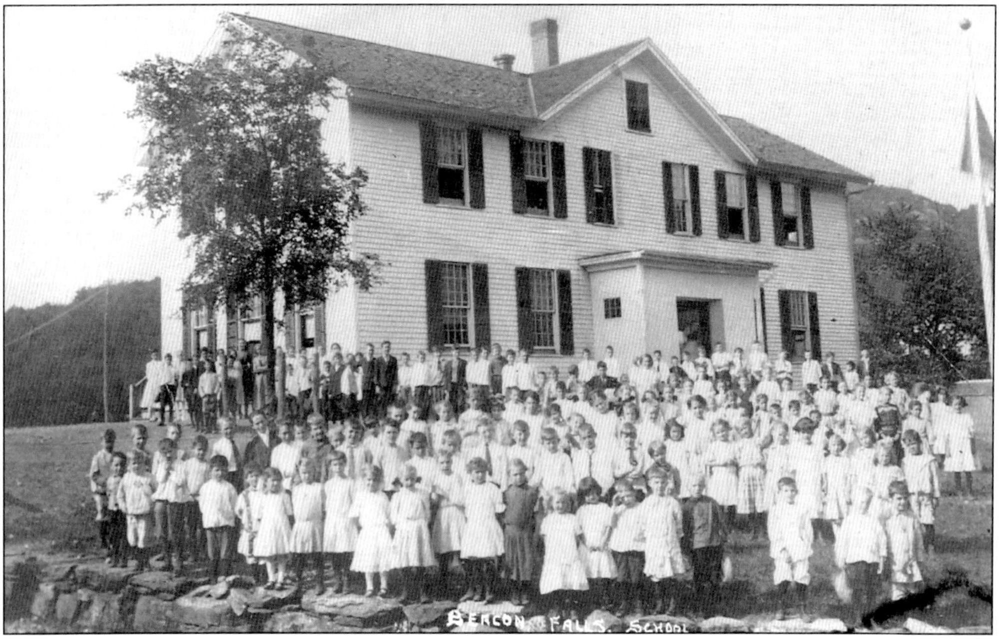

In 1899, Bethany built a schoolhouse with two instruction rooms for $3,100. By 1910, when this postcard was taken, Beacon Falls could boast a four-room schoolhouse, which sat on land next to where town hall sits today. A schoolhouse of this size was justified, considering it sat near the population center of the town. (MK.)

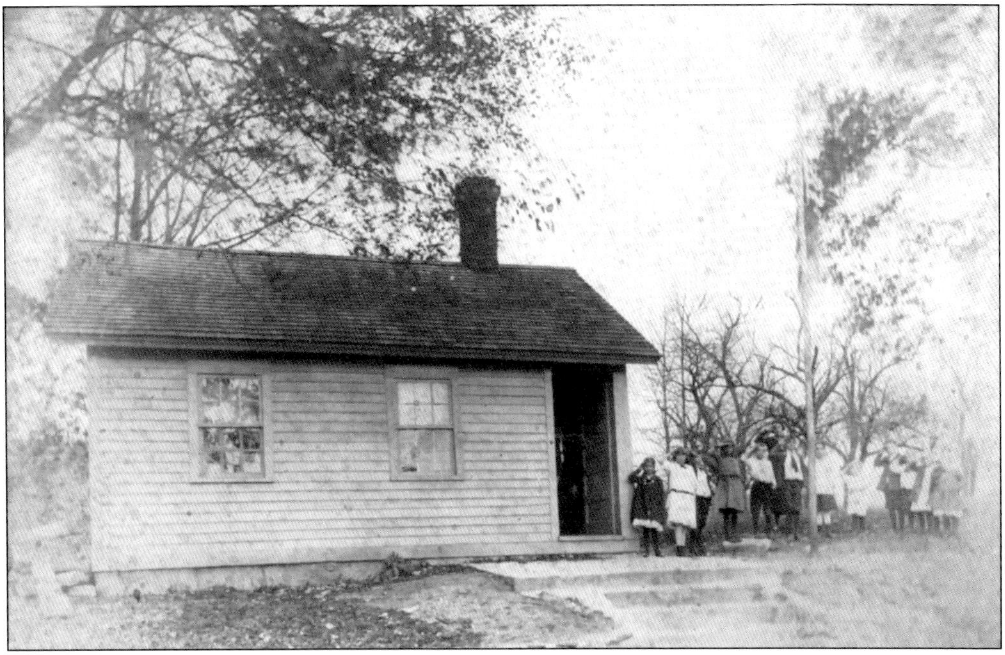

Pictured here is the first Nyumph School on Bethany Road. In Samuel Orcutt's 1880 book *The History of the Old Town of Derby Connecticut*, he defined Nyumph as, "A school district in the town of Beacon Falls about two miles back from the Naugatuck." A new Nyumph School was built on Feldspar Avenue in 1924 where Mable Chatfield taught for 30 years.

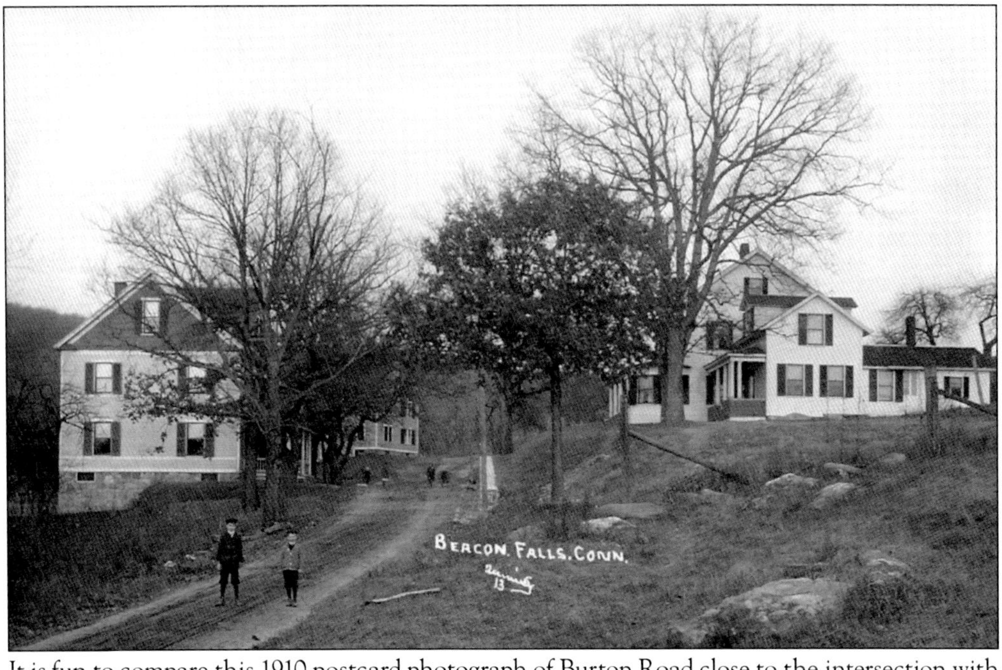

It is fun to compare this 1910 postcard photograph of Burton Road close to the intersection with Highland Avenue to what is seen today. These houses are still here, but Laurel Ledge School now dominates the area. It sits just beyond the left edge of this photograph. The children in the foreground might be the two Cook grandchildren that lived in the house on the right. (MH.)

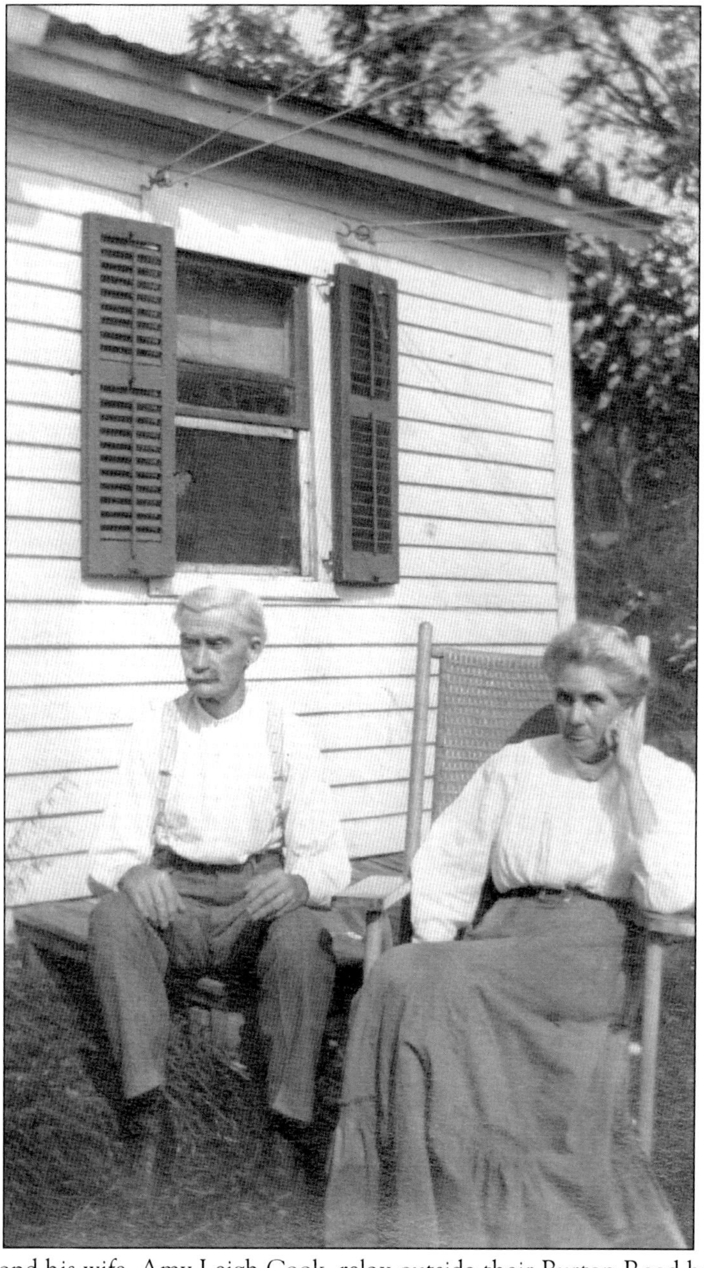

Samuel Cook and his wife, Amy Leigh Cook, relax outside their Burton Road house in 1912. Born in England, Samuel moved to town to work at the Home Woolen Mill after having worked at several woolen mills in Massachusetts. His previous position had been at the Blackinton Mill in Blackinton (North Adams), Massachusetts, where he was the boss weaver for 10 years. In 1900, the trade journal *Fibre & Fabric* reported that Cook returned to Blackinton to visit friends. He worked at the Beacon Falls Rubber Shoe Company after the woolen mill closed here. The Cooks had three children: son John, who became a longtime postmaster of Beacon Falls; daughter Sarah, who married shopkeeper Edward Gruber; and daughter Edith, who married selectman Bradford Wakefield. In retirement, he worked as janitor at the Center School. He passed away in 1918 at age 72.

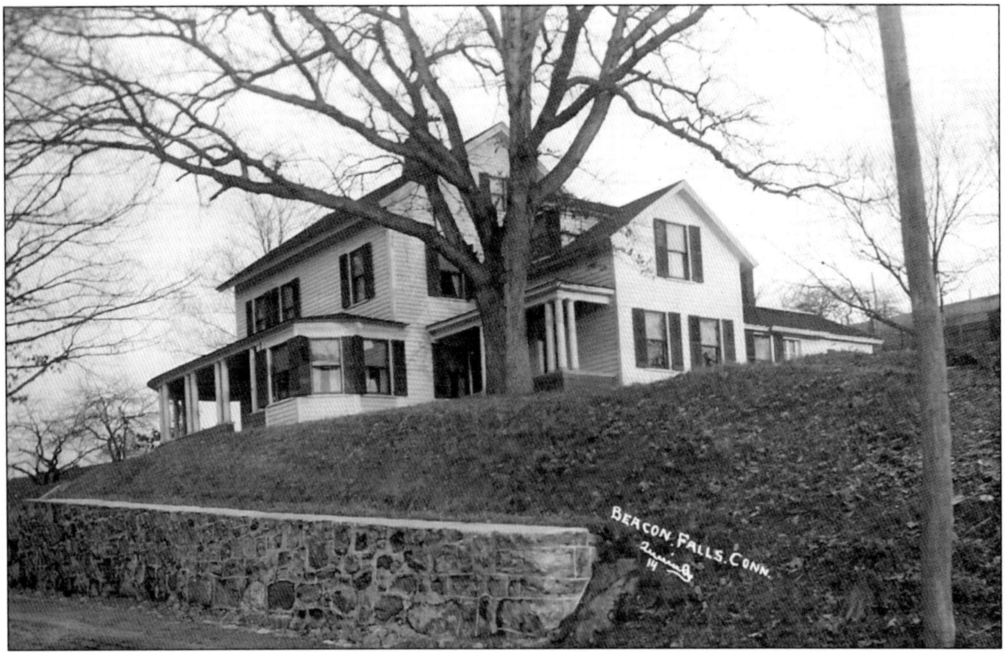

The Cook house looks virtually unchanged today. This stone wall has withstood the test of time and still sits alongside the now paved Burton Road. The porch has a distinctive curved roofline (seen in the photograph below). Irving, one of the Cook grandchildren, would later inherit this house. (MH.)

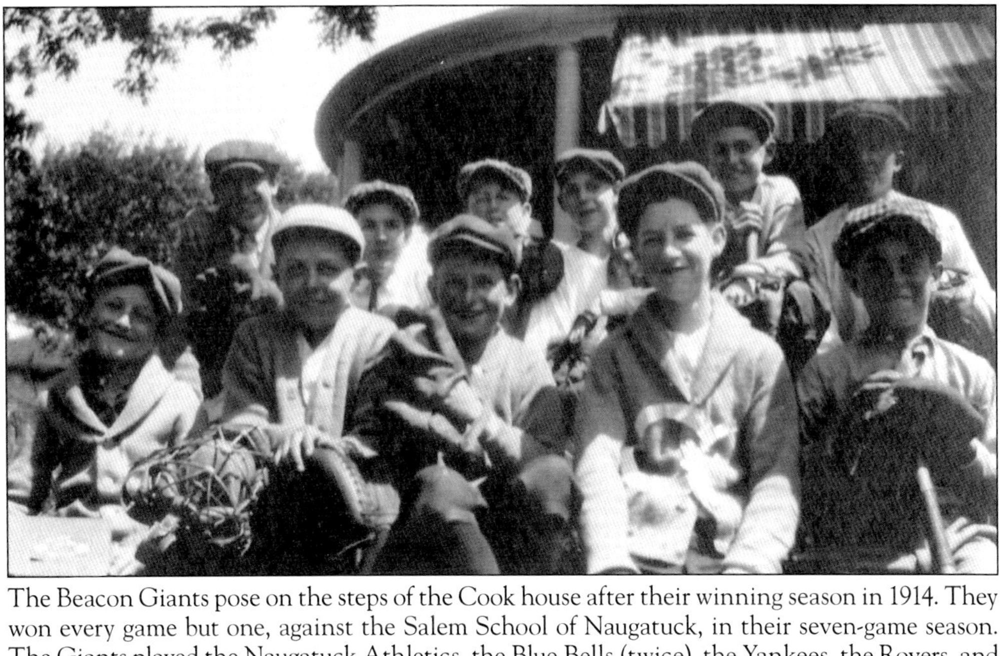

The Beacon Giants pose on the steps of the Cook house after their winning season in 1914. They won every game but one, against the Salem School of Naugatuck, in their seven-game season. The Giants played the Naugatuck Athletics, the Blue Bells (twice), the Yankees, the Rovers, and the Salem School (twice). (MH.)

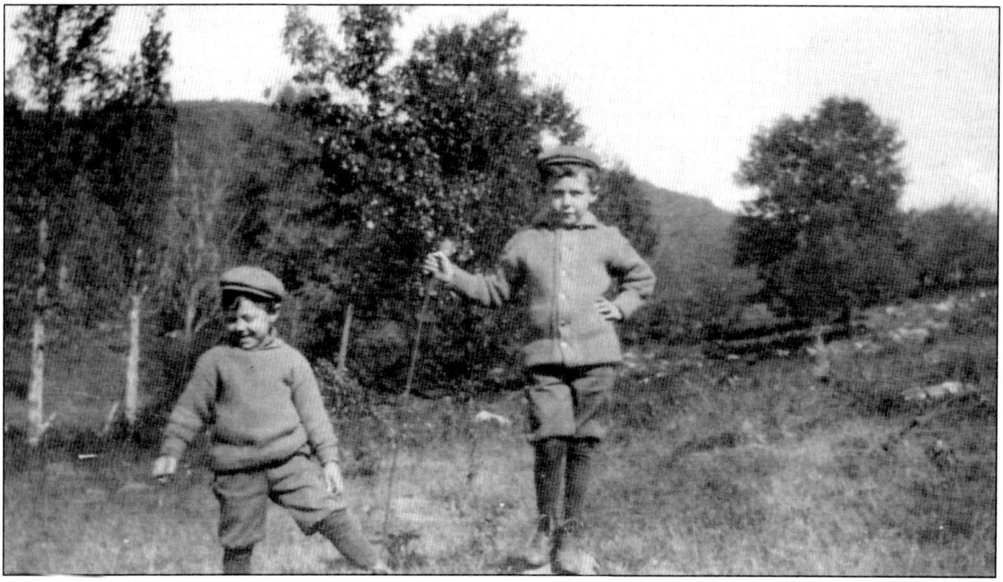

On a hike, Warren (left) and Irving Cook pose for a photographer. In the 1920s, Harris Whittemore, of Naugatuck, began securing land on both sides of the Naugatuck River with plans to donate it to the state. Eventually, the Whittemore family donated 2,000 acres of land to the State of Connecticut Park and Forest Commission, which ultimately grew to 5,000 acres and became the Naugatuck State Forest. (MH.)

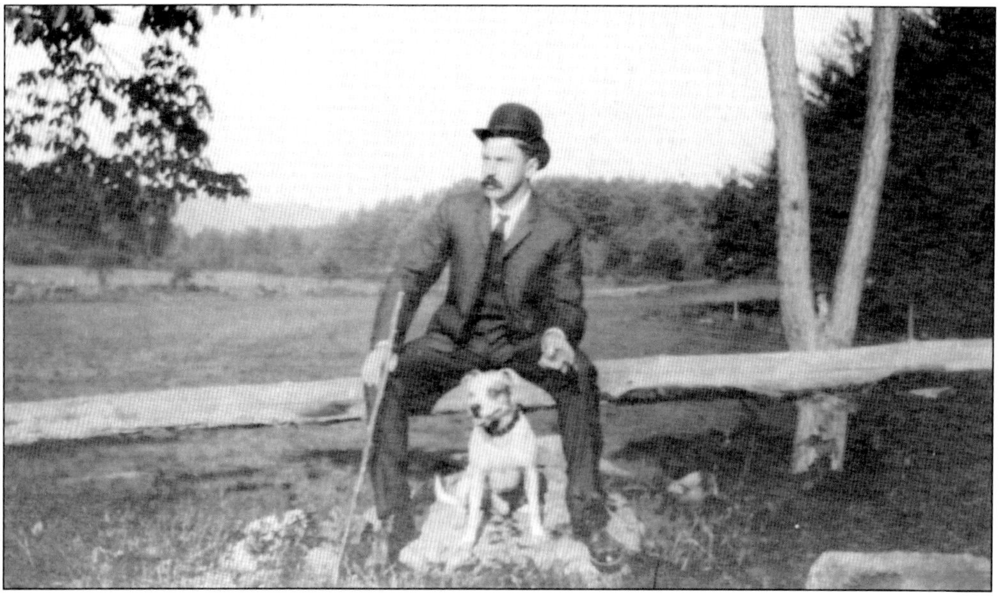

Sadly, the subject and exact location of this photograph are not known. It was taken in Beacon Falls around 1915. The gentleman seems to be somewhat of a dandy, sporting a derby hat and cane. It is included here because this lovely photograph portrays life in Beacon Falls at a simpler time. (MH.)

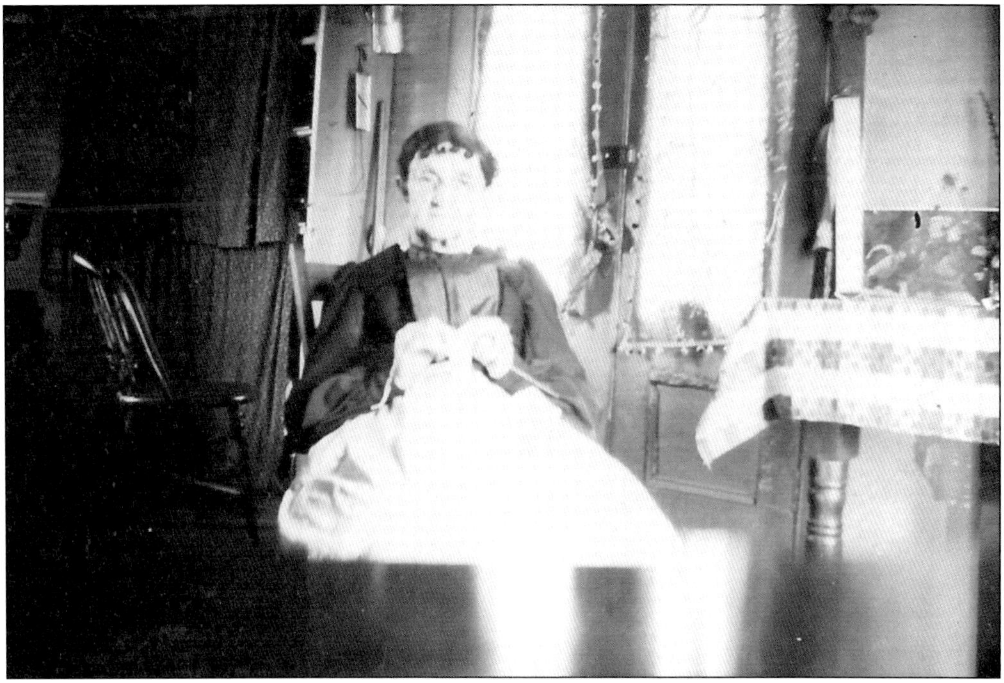

Another unidentified subject is shown knitting. In these days before television, radio, and electricity, knitting provided a useful pastime by creating clothing for family and friends. Indoor photographs are rare during this period in the first decade of the 20th century. Most cameras required bright light, yet they lacked a flash. (MH.)

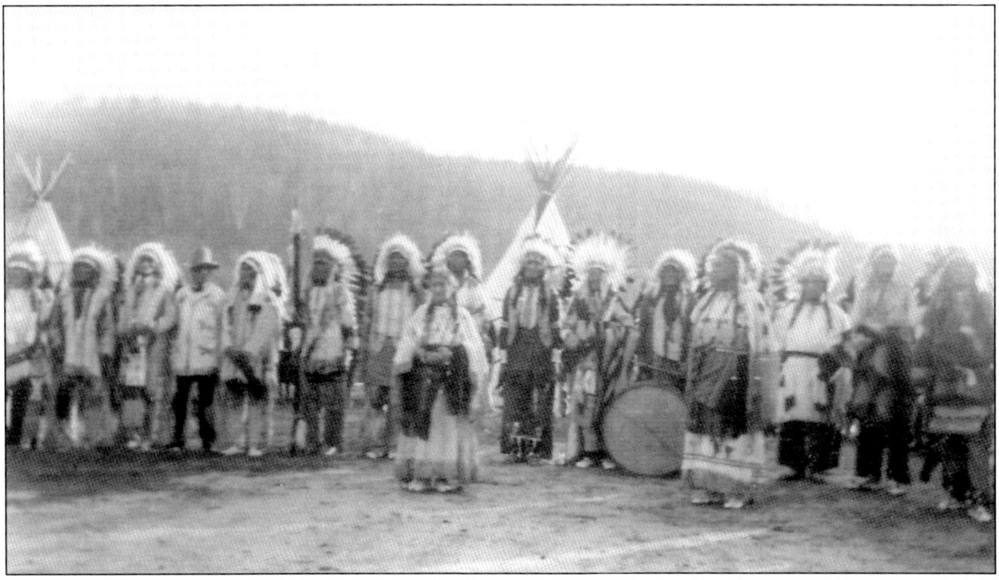

Chico Colon Meridas, also known as Chief Two Moons, claimed to be a full-blooded Pueblo Indian and used his knowledge of ancient Indian herbal medicines to market a line of elixirs to the public. When his credentials were disputed by the State of Connecticut in 1932, he assembled at his own expense 26 actual Indian chiefs on his reservation in the Cotton Hollow section of Beacon Falls to testify to his authenticity.

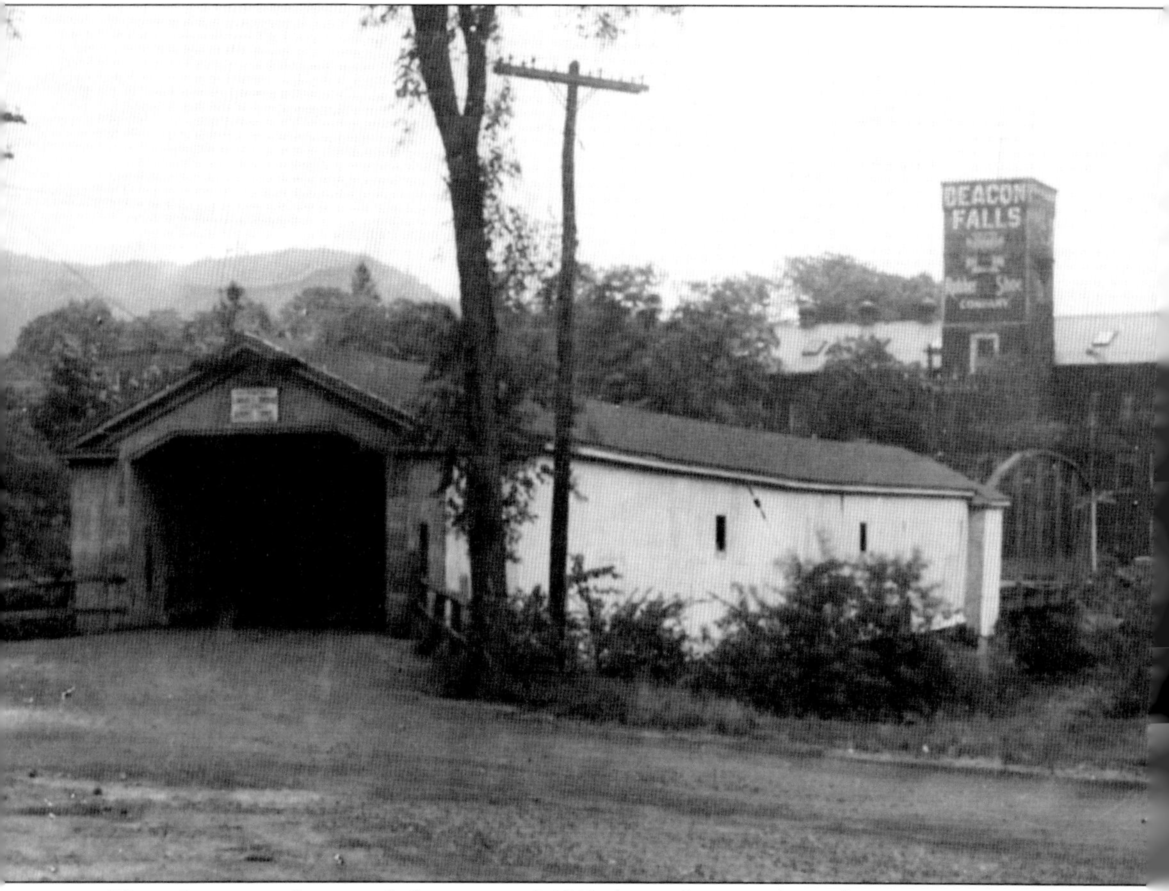

This often-seen photograph from around 1910 shows the view from the Beacon Falls railroad depot toward the center of town. The covered bridge, which was built in 1836, is still performing well. Beyond the covered part of the bridge is a steel section built in 1892 that replaced a section of the bridge that was considered unsafe. The sign above the entrance says, "Attention. Load on the Bridge limited to Eight Tons." By 1931, only two covered bridges remained in all of New Haven County, but none remain today. Beyond the bridge, one of the towers of the Beacon Falls Rubber Shoe Company is seen. Millions of shoes crossed this bridge—but not on feet. These shoes were in boxes en route to freight cars waiting nearby. This bridge played a key part in the development of Beacon Falls by providing a gateway to the world marketplace for products manufactured here. (BK.)

Four

Rubber Shoes and Brass Hinges

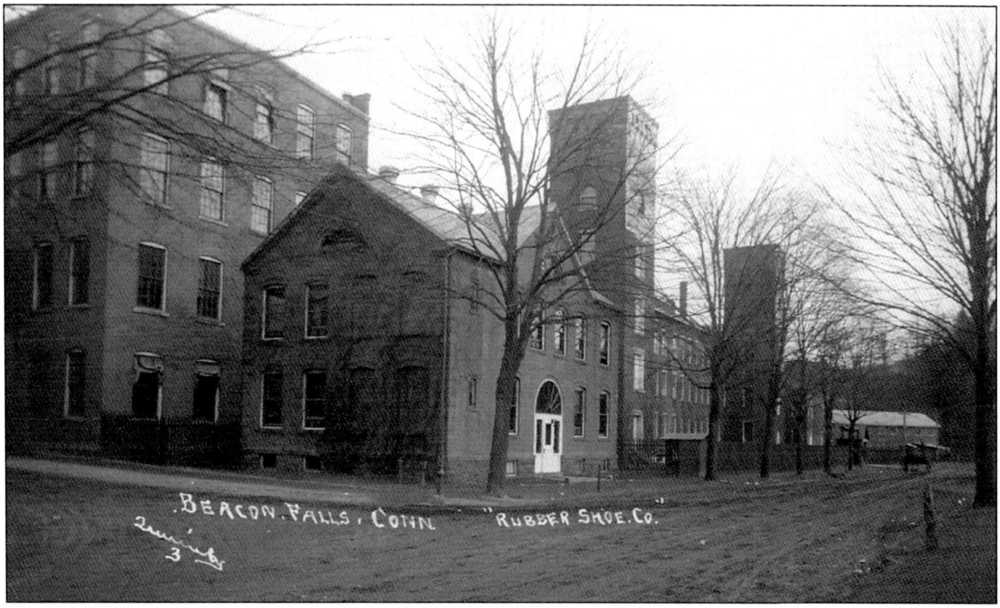

The Beacon Falls Rubber Shoe Company was formed in 1898. Prior to this, these buildings contained the American Hard Rubber Company (1852–1862), the Home Woolen Mill (1864–1887), and the Standard Woolen Mill (1889–1897). Several times over the years, manufacturing halted at this mill, notably in 1897 and 1898 when many homes in town were boarded up. Clearly, the success of Beacon Falls was tied to the success of this factory. (MH.)

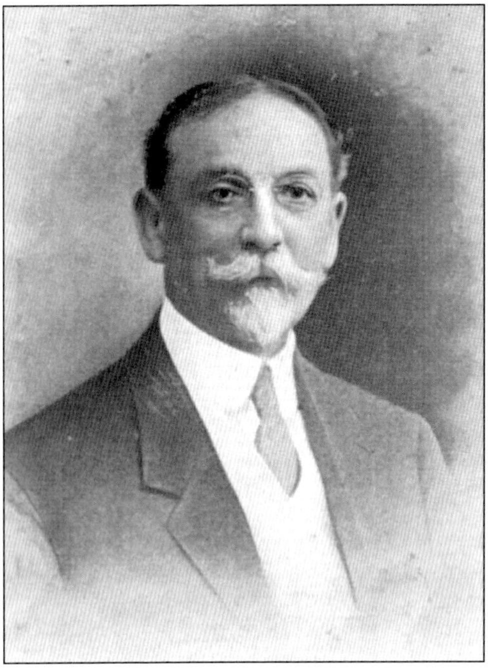

The Lewis family must have had rubber in their blood. Prior to 1898, George A. Lewis (seen here) was president of the Wales-Goodyear Rubber Company, a rubber shoe division of the US Rubber Company in Naugatuck. His father, Samuel Lewis, became a pioneer in rubber shoe manufacturing when he transformed his woolen mill in Naugatuck into a vulcanized rubber shoe company in 1849.

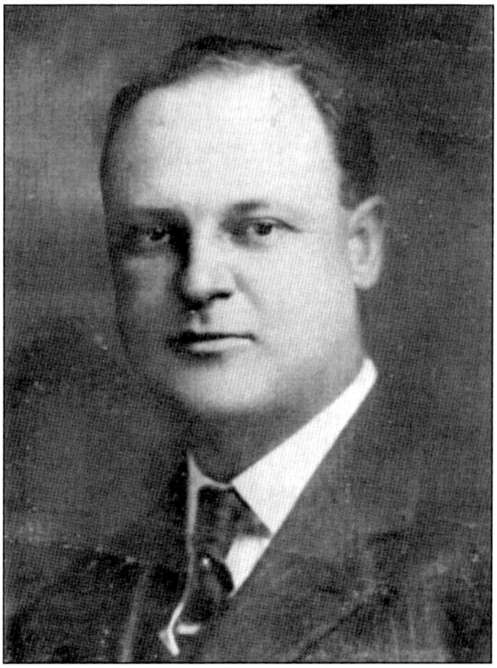

History would repeat itself when George Lewis transformed the former Home Woolen Mill in Beacon Falls into the Beacon Falls Rubber Shoe Company. The property included 200 acres and 30 tenements. Tracy S. Lewis (seen here) took over as president of the Beacon Falls Rubber Shoe Company upon the death of his father on January 26, 1914. Tracy operated the company until his death on April 4, 1921, at age 42.

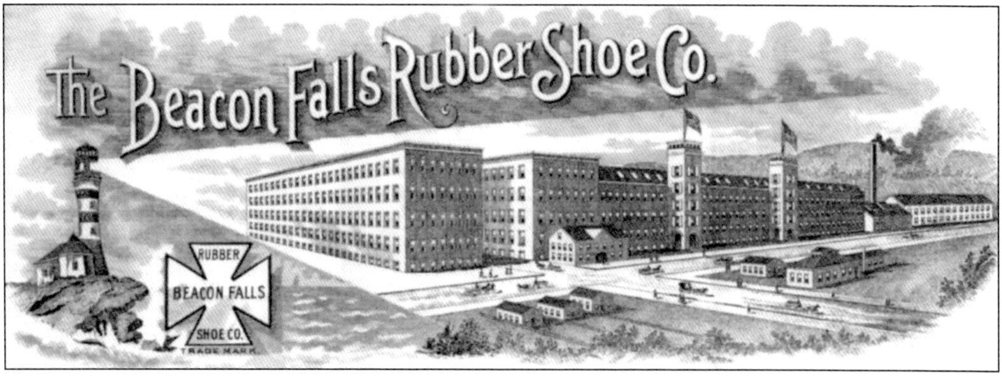

Here, an artist uses a bit of artistic license in his rendering of the Beacon Falls Rubber Shoe Company that appears on the company's stock certificates. Not only does the company seem to tower over the surrounding buildings, but the town of Beacon Falls is shown with overly wide thoroughfares, including one where the covered bridge ought to be. This drawing seemed to predict Main Street becoming a four-lane highway. (MK.)

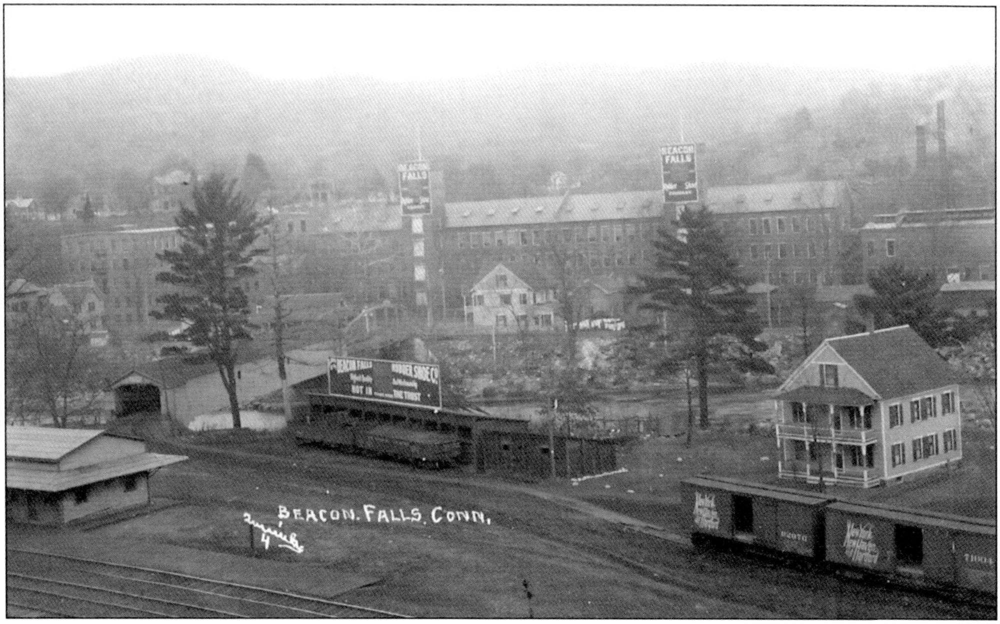

Shown here in 1910, the Beacon Falls Rubber Shoe Company was operating in full swing by 1916 when 1,500 employees turned out 20,000 pairs of shoes a day from this factory. It is no surprise that boxcars are on a siding with the doors open and ready to go. Around this time, a second factory was opened in a leased building in College Point, Long Island, to manufacture the increasingly successful basketball shoes. (BK.)

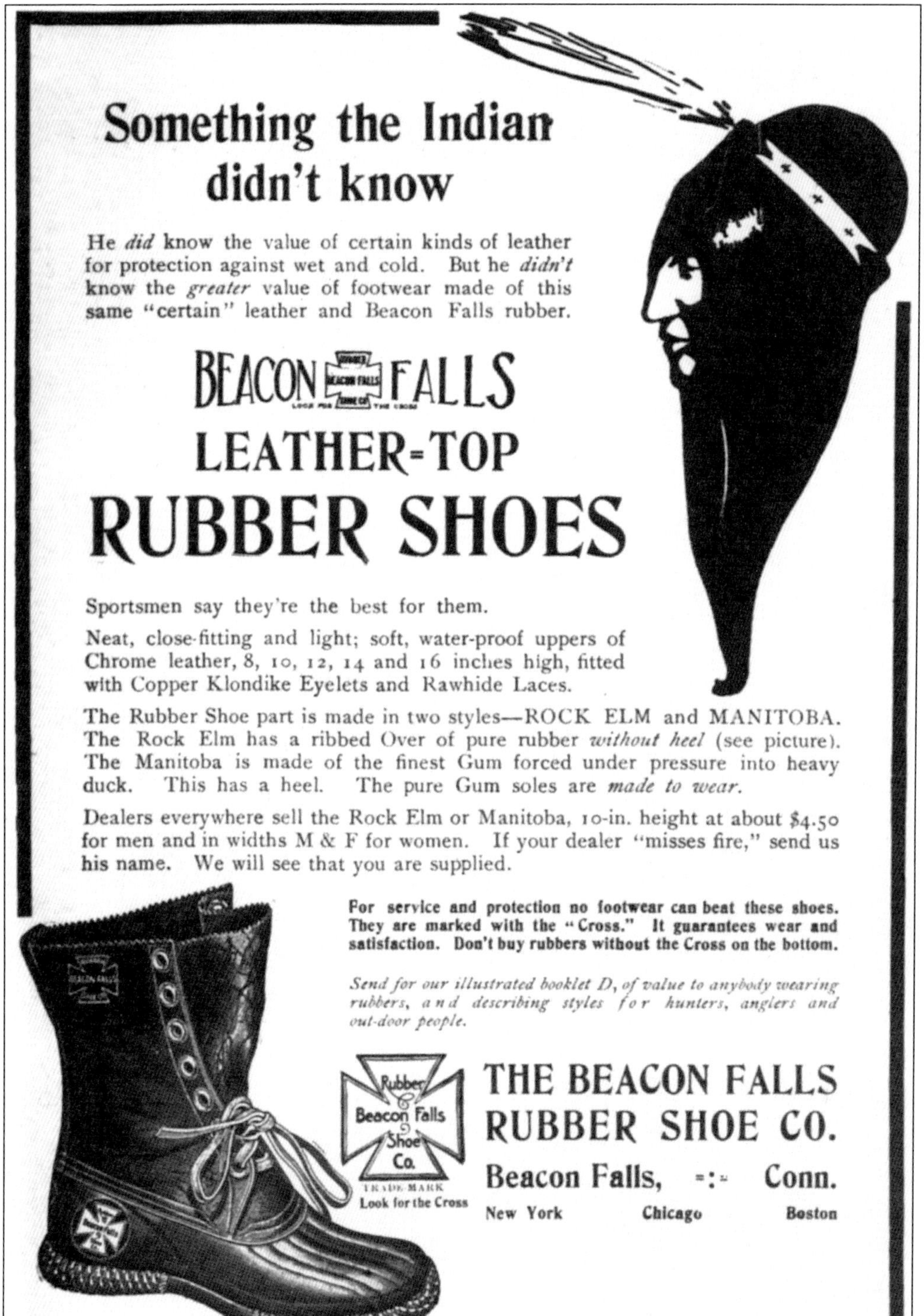

If something works, stick with it. A 1911 magazine advertisement highlights the line of Beacon Falls traditional rubber boots with a molded rubber sole and leather upper that could just as likely be sold in sporting goods stores or online catalogs today.

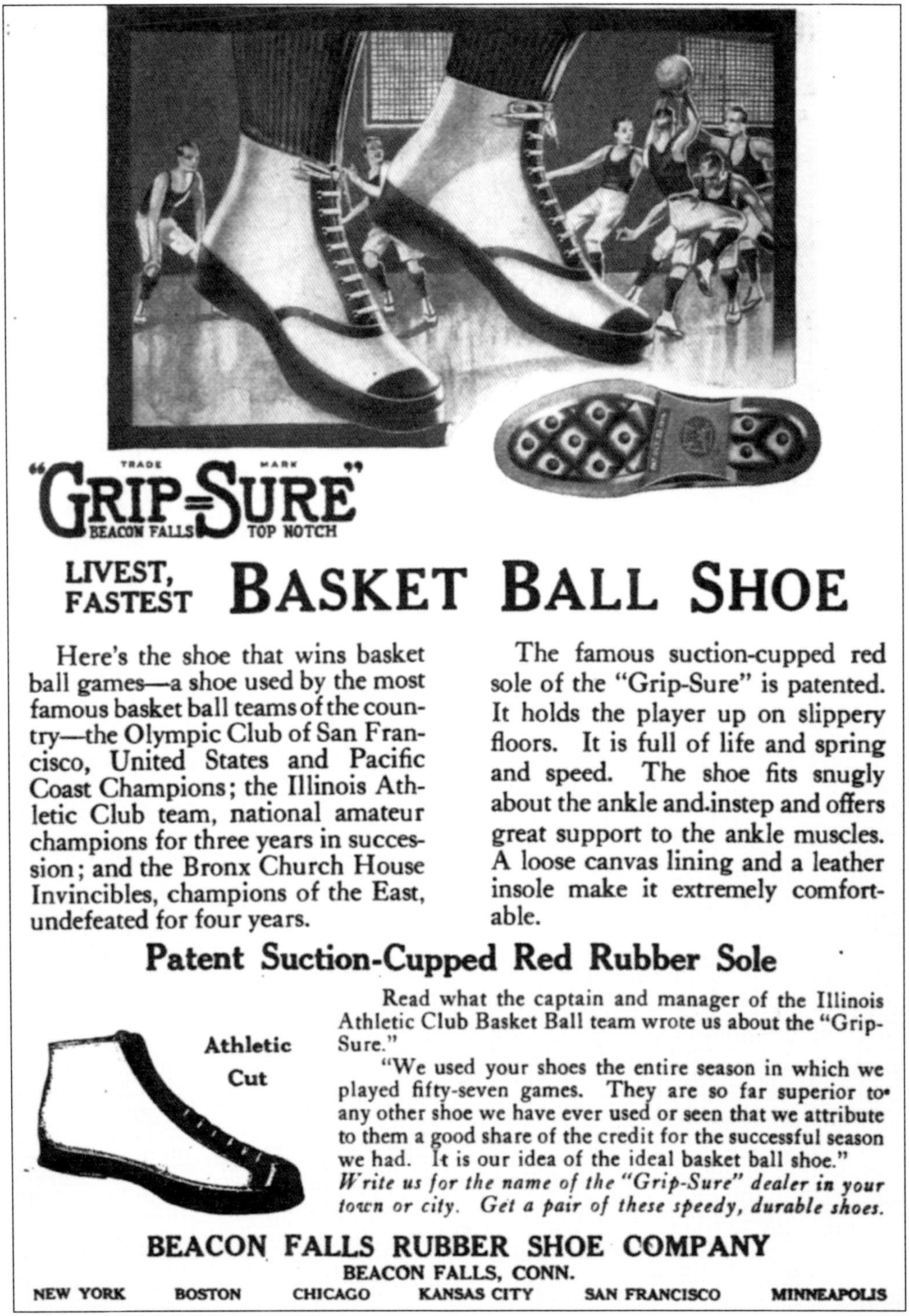

A 1917 magazine advertisement shows the Beacon Falls "Grip-Sure" basketball shoes. The name would later be simplified to "Grips." The term "sneaker," which was not yet commonly used, is thought to have originated from the fact that these rubber soles were quiet, perfect for sneaking around.

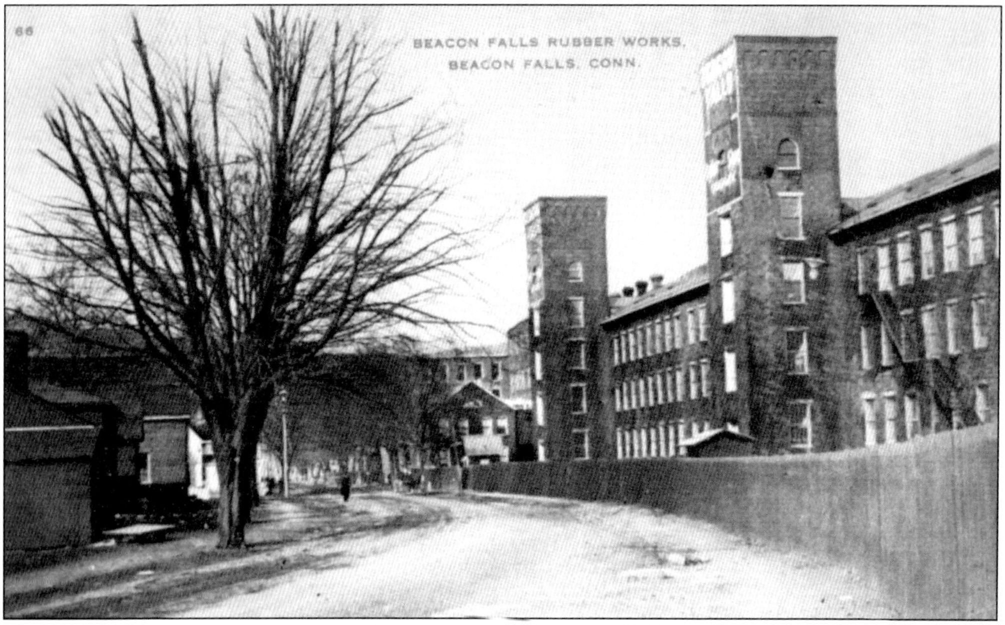

One of George Lewis's motivations for creating the Beacon Falls Rubber Shoe Company was to escape the "Rubber Trust," a monopoly of rubber manufacturers that he himself had earlier helped create. The company grew rapidly in the early 1900s, adding or expanding buildings in 1900, 1902, 1909, 1912, and 1915. Some of these were built across Main Street, alongside the river, as seen here on the left. (MK.)

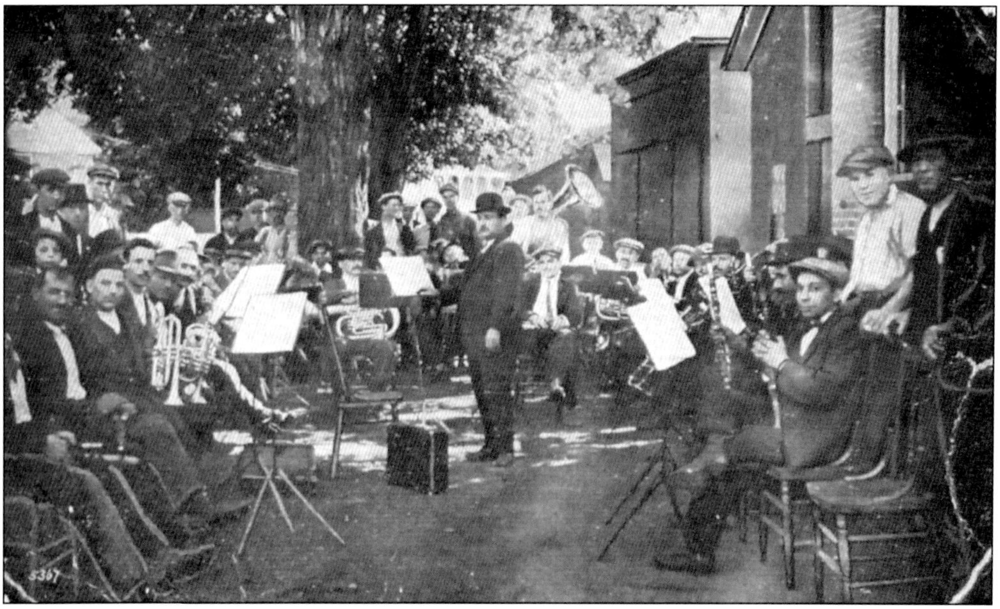

In 1918, William Jamieson Pape wrote in his *History of Waterbury and the Naugatuck Valley*, "The company maintains a band within its organization which plays selections every noon time the year around, in front of the plant, while in the summer months many concerts are given in the cozy little park fronting on the main street, which are thoroughly enjoyed by the townspeople and oftentimes by automobile parties from nearby towns." (MK.)

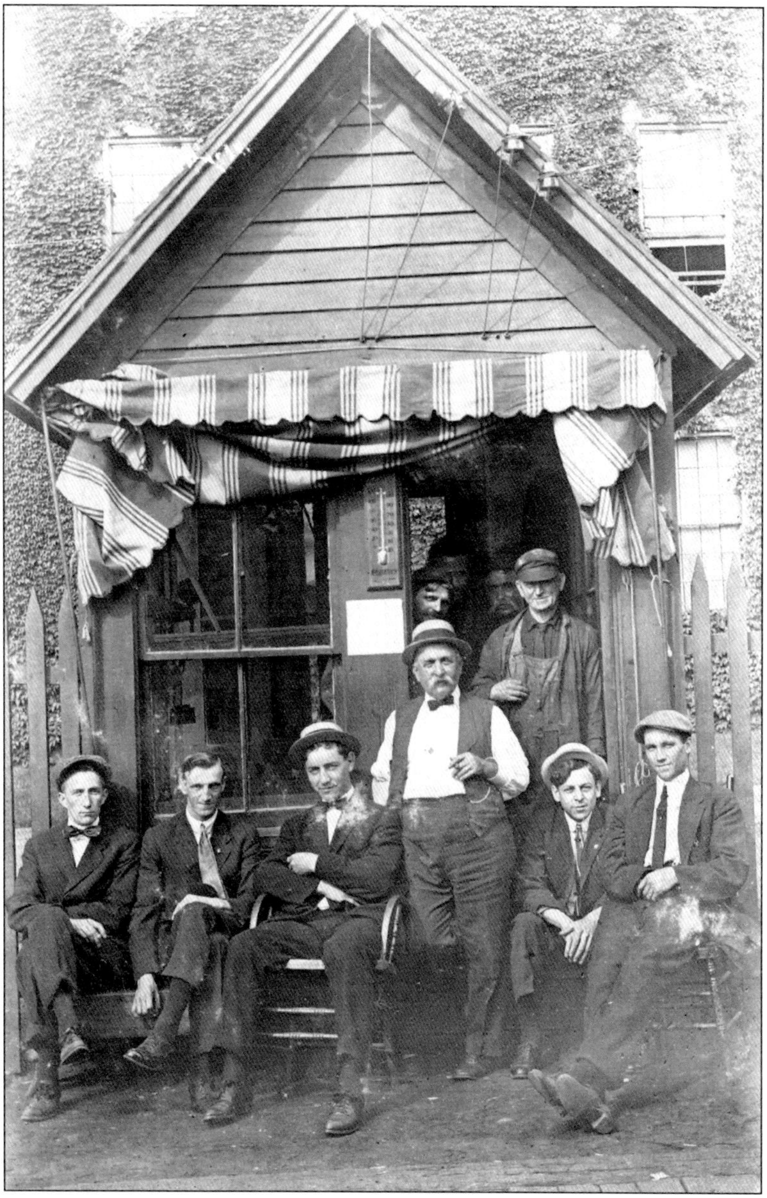

A watchman's booth stands immediately in front of the Beacon Falls Rubber Shoe Company with an interesting assortment of characters present. After the death of company president Tracy Lewis in 1921, control of the Beacon Falls Rubber Shoe Company was taken over by the US Rubber Company. Shoes continued to be manufactured here until 1930 when production was moved to Naugatuck and the Beacon Falls buildings became warehouse space. Marquis Converse, who had worked at the Beacon Falls Rubber Shoe Company office in Boston, left to form the Converse Rubber Shoe Company. Their Chuck Taylor sneakers became a direct competitor to Beacon Falls's Lew Andreas signature sneakers. Converse hired Chuck Taylor, a former a basketball player, to help refine and promote Converse sneakers while Lew Andreas, longtime coach of the Syracuse Orangemen basketball team, endorsed Beacon Falls sneakers. The US Rubber Company and later Uniroyal continued to market the Beacon Falls Grips brand alongside their own Keds brand well into the 1960s. (MK.)

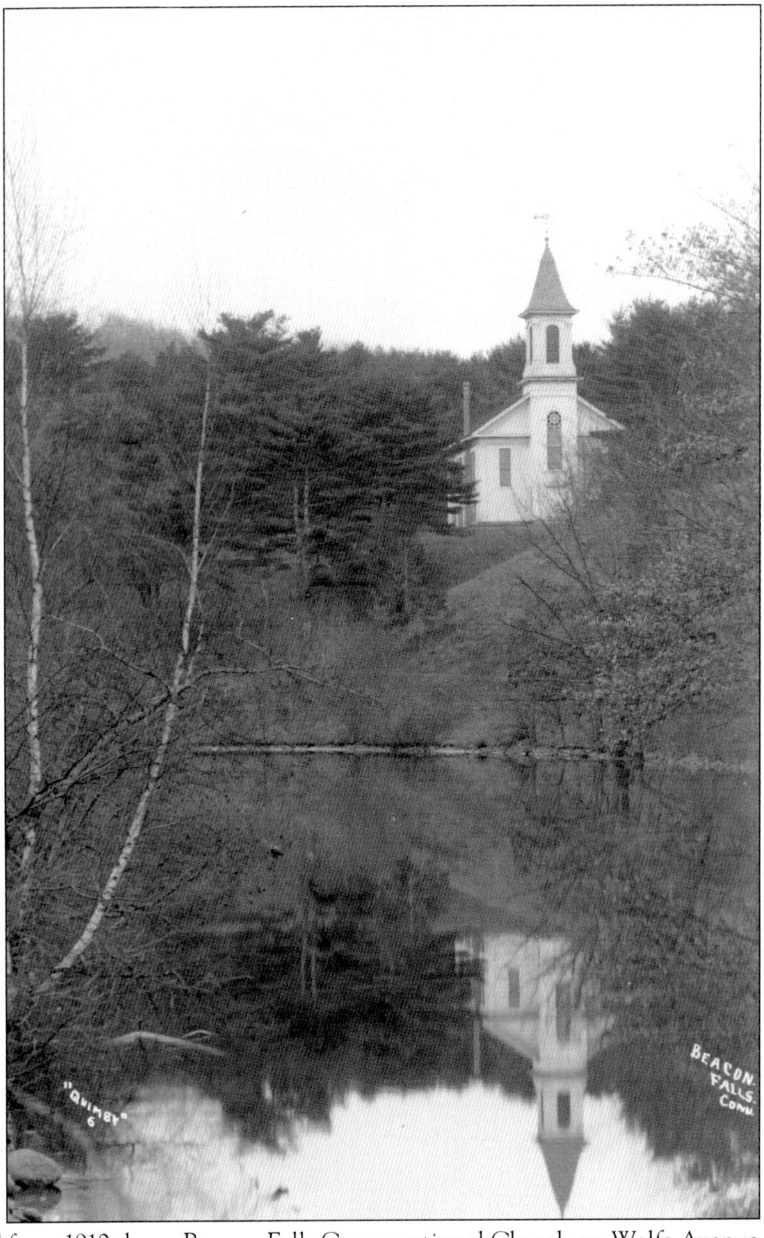

A postcard from 1910 shows Beacon Falls Congregational Church on Wolfe Avenue, which was known as the "Little White Church on the Hill," as seen from behind the Rubber Shoe Company buildings. What appears to be a still lake is, in reality, water in the canal that ran from here through the backyards of the houses on North Main Street. This is the canal that began at the dam on the Naugatuck River near High Rock Grove. There are few photographs of the canal in operation despite its long, productive life. Eventually, the canal was filled in, leaving little evidence that it ever existed. According to William Pape in his *History of Waterbury and the Naugatuck Valley*, another more grand canal project was considered in 1895 when Congress appropriated $25,000 to survey a proposed canal from tidewater at Derby through Beacon Falls to Waterbury, a distance of 18.5 miles. The survey concluded that 11 locks would be needed to raise canal boats 270 feet over that distance, but the project never got started. (MH.)

For a number of years, the Ladies' Aid Society in Beacon Falls prepared an annual fundraising convention in which lunches were offered to employees of the Beacon Falls Rubber Shoe Company for several days. These were held at the church on Wolfe Avenue. The funds were used for improvements on the church and for constructing a parsonage. Here is the 1915 menu, cut to match the company logo. (MH.)

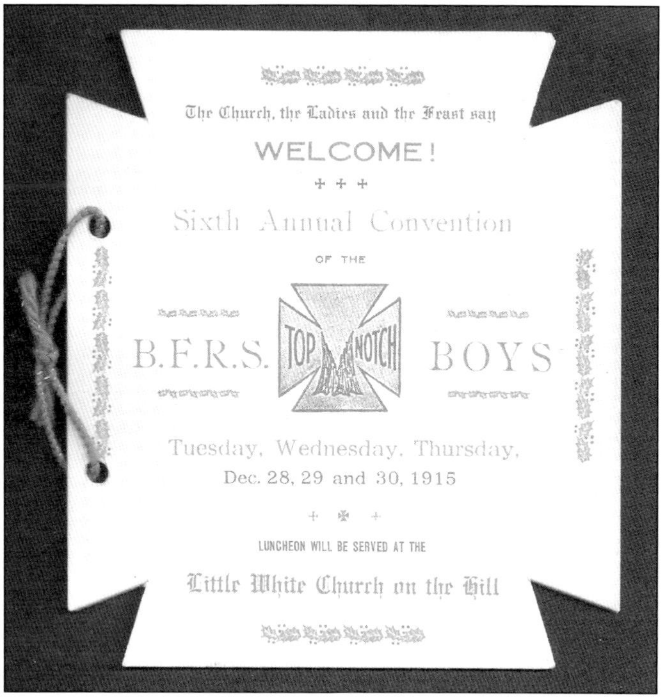

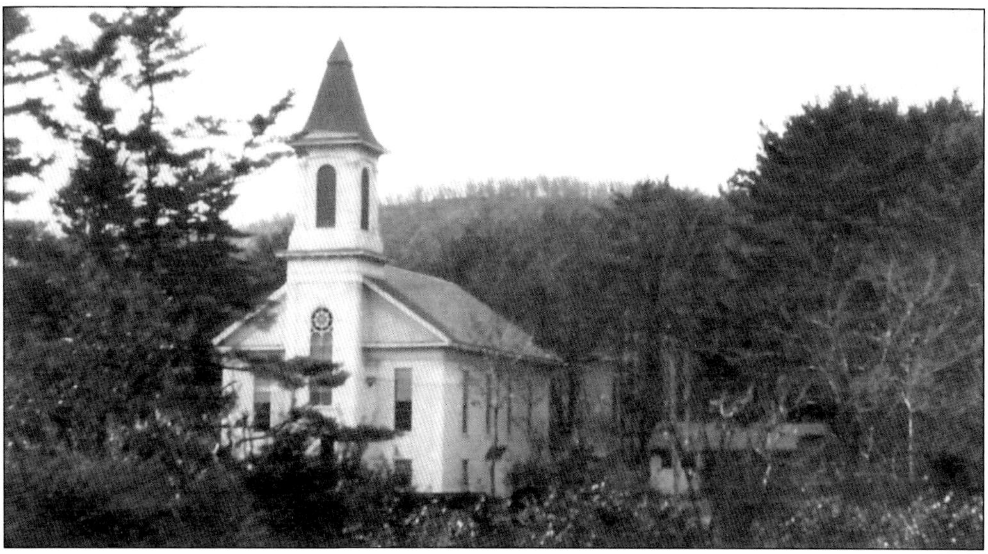

Originally founded as a Methodist Episcopal church in Pines Bridge, the church later moved to a building on Main Street (now Beacon Falls Pizza Palace). When the Home Woolen Mill donated land in a pine grove off Wolfe Avenue, the current church building was erected. Its doors opened in 1871. In 1900, the church became an independent ecclesiastical society and Congregational in 1919.

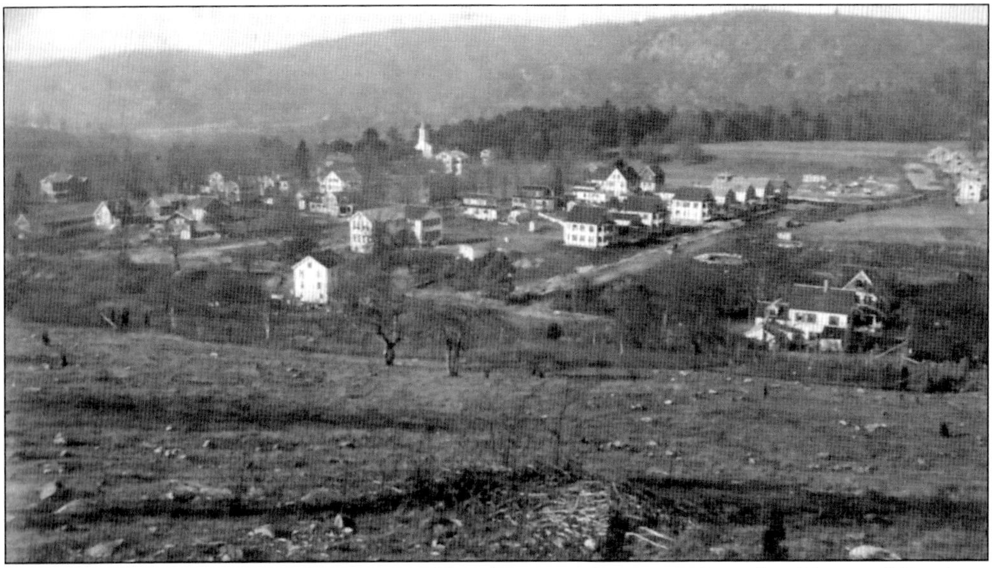

In 1916, Tracy Lewis hired the renowned landscape architecture firm the Olmstead Brothers to develop the hill area of Beacon Falls, seen here. The Olmstead brothers had inherited the business from their father, Frederick Law Olmstead, who is recognized as the founder of American landscape architecture. His sons continued the family business, developing the landscapes for many hospitals, universities, libraries, state capitols, and neighborhoods. (MK.)

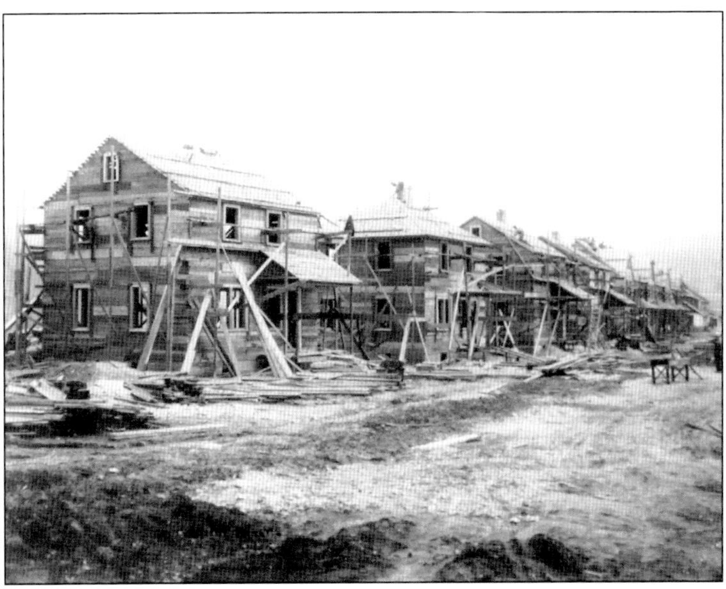

This photograph shows the construction of homes on Highland Avenue in 1915. As part of the plan for development, some existing homes on the eastern side of Highland Avenue near Burton Road were moved across the street to make room for a ball field where Laurel Ledge School would later be built. (LHD.)

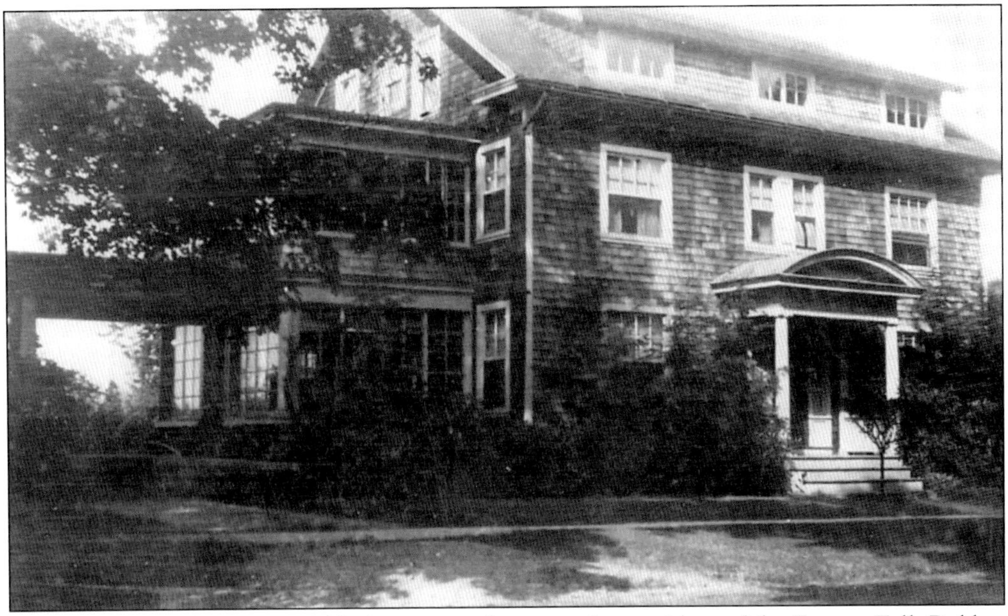

The Tracy Lewis house on Wolfe Avenue was home to the president of the Beacon Falls Rubber Shoe Company during the latter years of his tenure there. Befitting his status as a successful businessman, the three-story house, which sat on one and a half acres overlooking the Naugatuck Valley, contained 16 rooms and 7 baths. This photograph of the house, which was built in 1916, was taken in 1932. (RDV.)

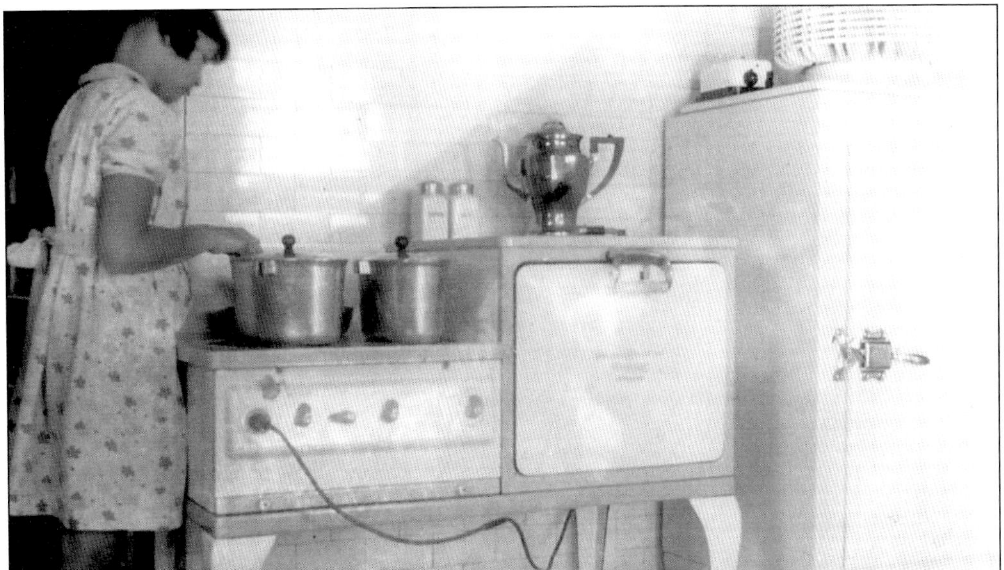

In 1932, the Tracy Lewis house featured this state-of-the-art kitchen, complete with an electric stove and "monitor-top" refrigerator. Unfortunately, Tracy Lewis was not able to enjoy this house for very long. He died in 1921, only a year after the birth of his daughter Cynthia. His death left the Beacon Falls Rubber Shoe Company in financial trouble and with no obvious successor. (RDV.)

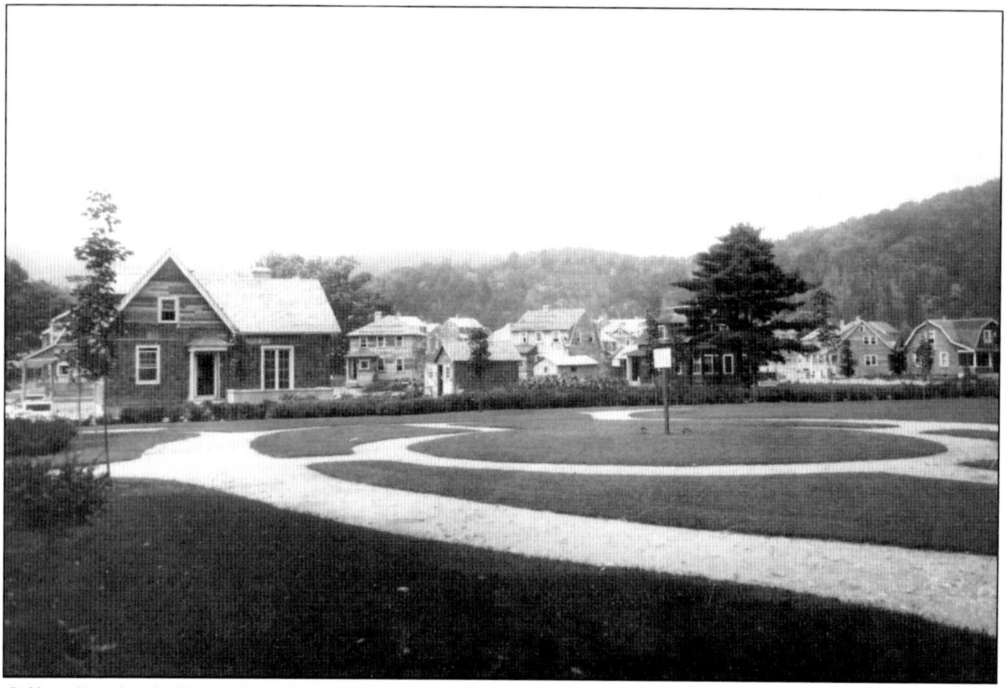

Officially, the hill neighborhood was financed by the Beacon Falls Rubber Shoe Company, but Tracy Lewis also hired the Olmstead Brothers to design the landscape for his own estate on Wolfe Avenue. The design included a park with a small pond. The park was completed but without the pond. Here is the park at a time when houses were still being constructed. (LHD.)

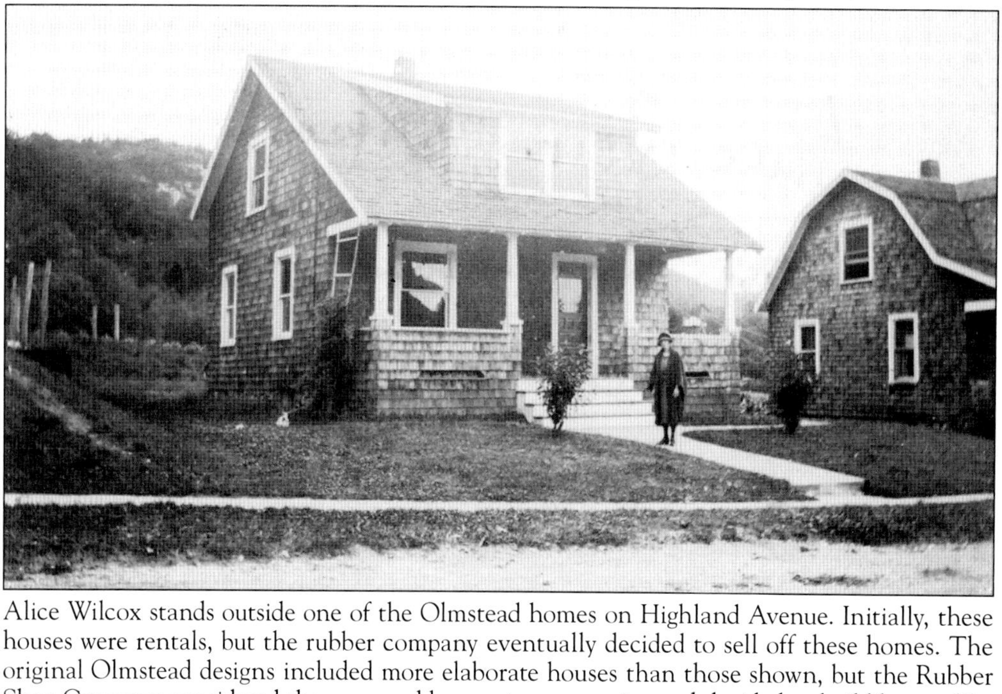

Alice Wilcox stands outside one of the Olmstead homes on Highland Avenue. Initially, these houses were rentals, but the rubber company eventually decided to sell off these homes. The original Olmstead designs included more elaborate houses than those shown, but the Rubber Shoe Company considered the proposed houses too expensive and decided to build homes like these instead. (BK.)

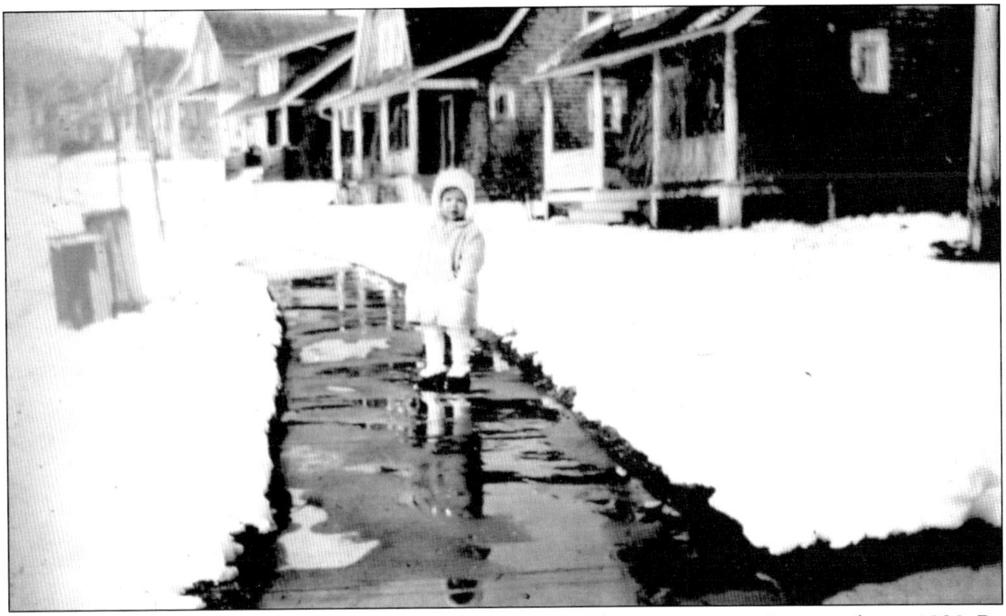

This view looking northward up Highland Avenue was taken on a snowy January day in 1930. By now, the hill area was well developed. As part of the Olmstead plan, the house styles alternated: first, a traditional roofline, then a Dutch-style roofline, then repeated. The Dutch-style homes even had a Dutch front door with independent upper and lower sections. All of the houses had a spacious front porch. (MH.)

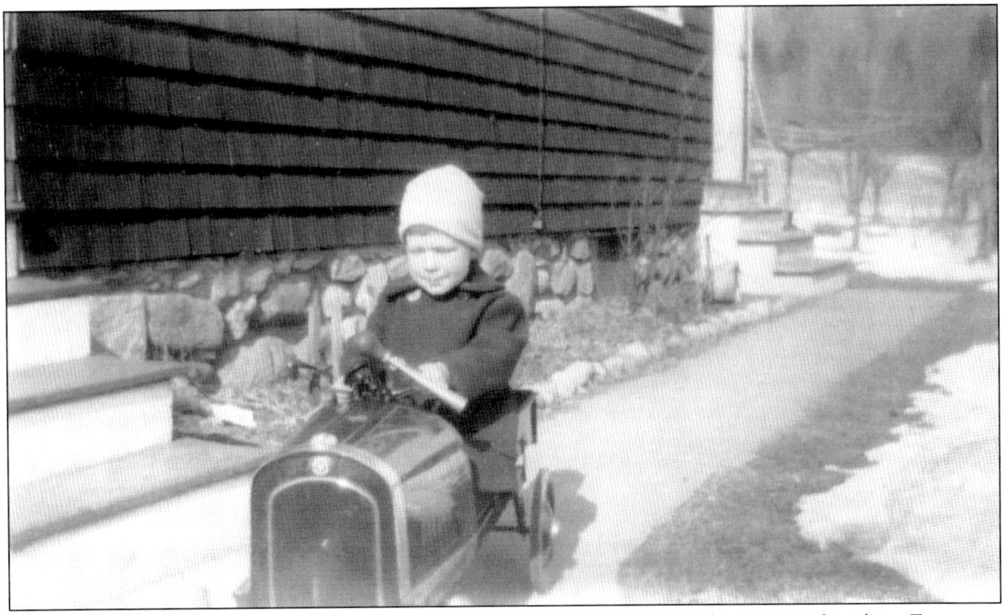

Just as the Olmstead plan had intended, the hill section was ideal for raising families. Enjoying his Christmas present in his Highland Avenue driveway is Gordon Heiss. A fourth-generation resident, he was born here in 1929 and spent his adult career working nearby at the Homer D. Bronson Company. This photograph was taken in January 1933. (MH.)

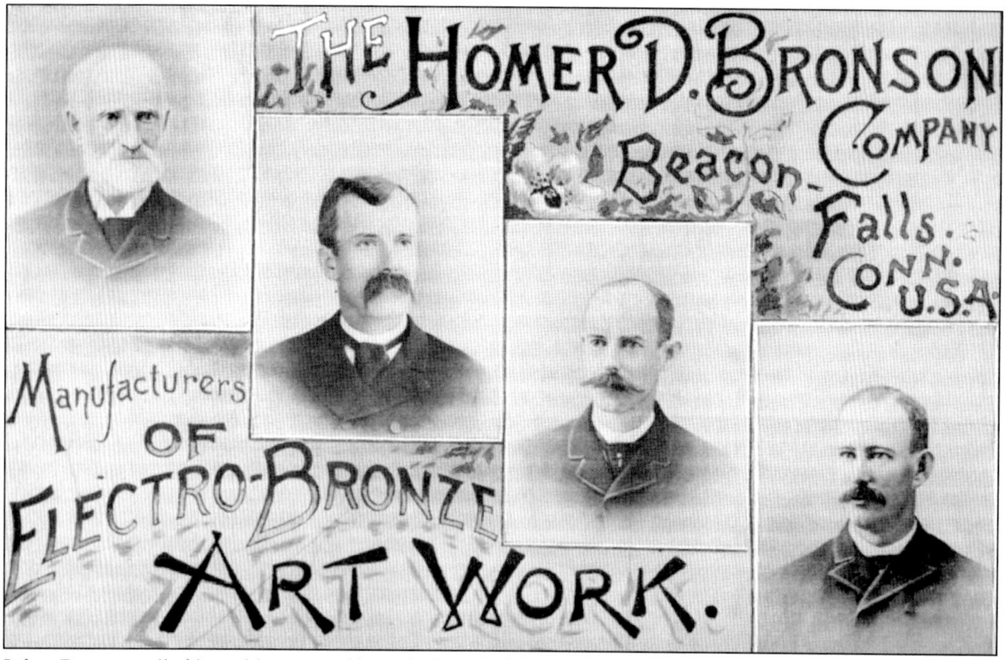

John Bronson (left) and his sons (from left to right) Homer, George, and Luther are seen in this very early advertisement for the Homer D. Bronson Company. Originally founded in Waterbury in 1839, John Bronson and his sons moved to Beacon Falls in 1882 after swapping their property in Waterbury for John Coe's tannery property in Beacon Falls. Initially, they produced brass novelties as well as artwork in brass and copper using waterpower from Lebanon Brook.

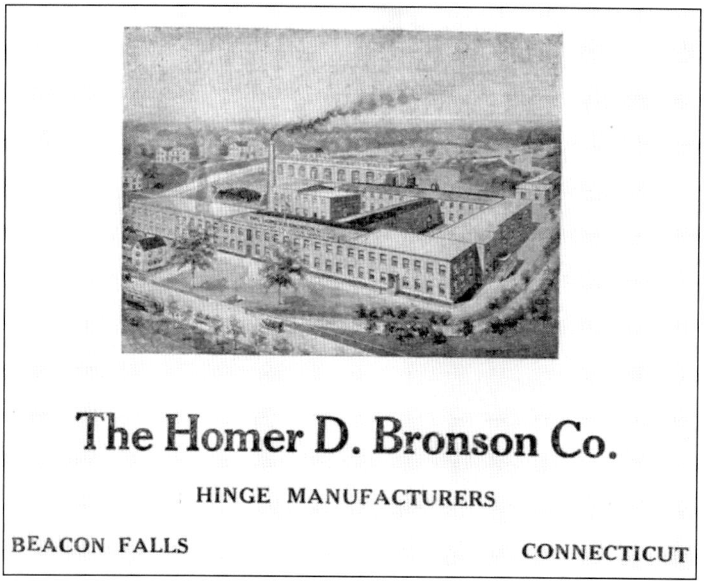

Eventually, the Bronson Company settled upon the manufacture of hinges. In this advertisement from 1935, the Bronson company factory has reached an impressive size. The brick headquarters building has not yet been built. It would replace the wood-frame structure seen in the bottom-left corner. Although they certainly made conventional door hinges, or butts, they were better known for their custom work.

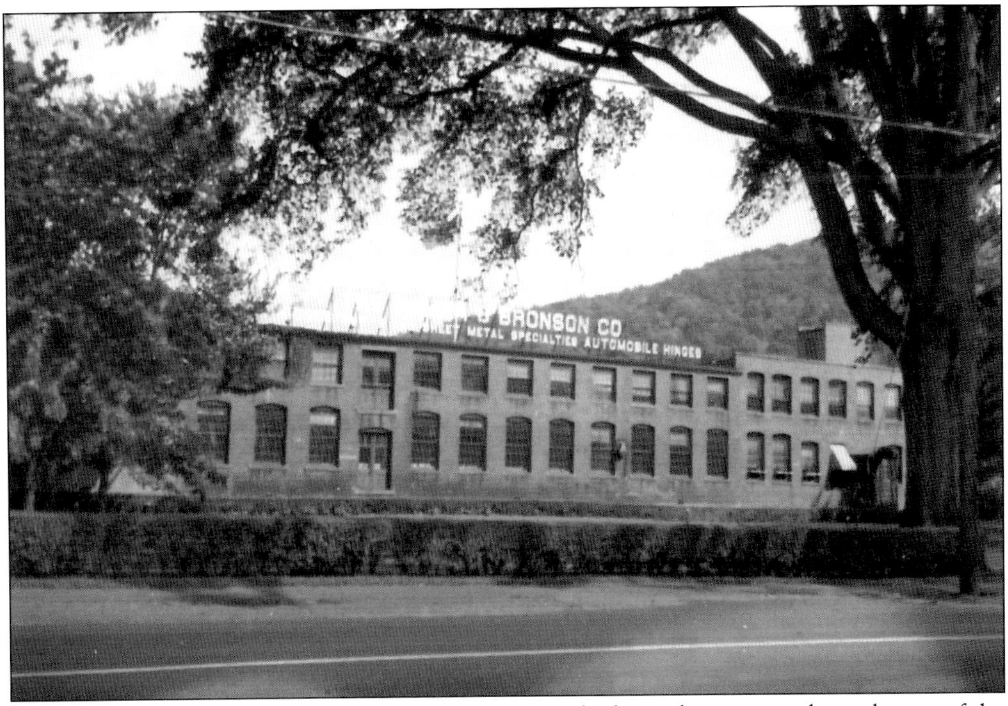

The popularity of the automobile provided a boost to the hinge business in the early part of the last century. The Bronson Company specialized in custom-made hinges, and automobile hood hinges quickly became one of their specialties. This is highlighted in their sign that reads, "Hinges, Butts, Sheet Metal Specialties and Automobile Hinges." The Bronson Company continued to operate out of these buildings in Beacon Falls until moving to Winsted in the 1980s.

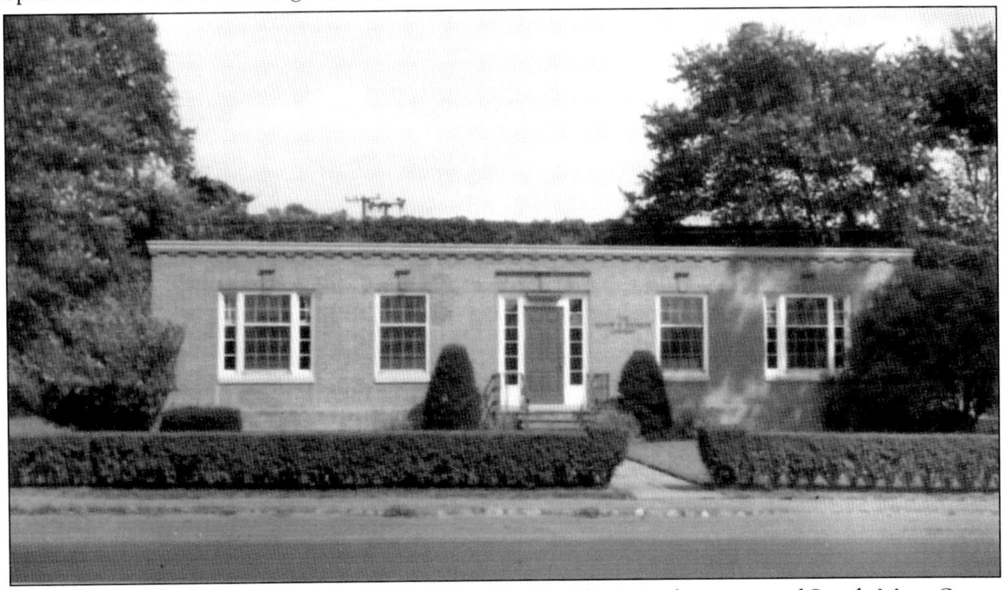

Here is the Bronson Company's new headquarters building on the corner of South Main Street and Bethany Road. A second story would be added in 1955. Just to the right of this building, the Bronson Company maintained a fountain that created gigantic ice formations in the wintertime. It was illuminated with colored lights each Christmas.

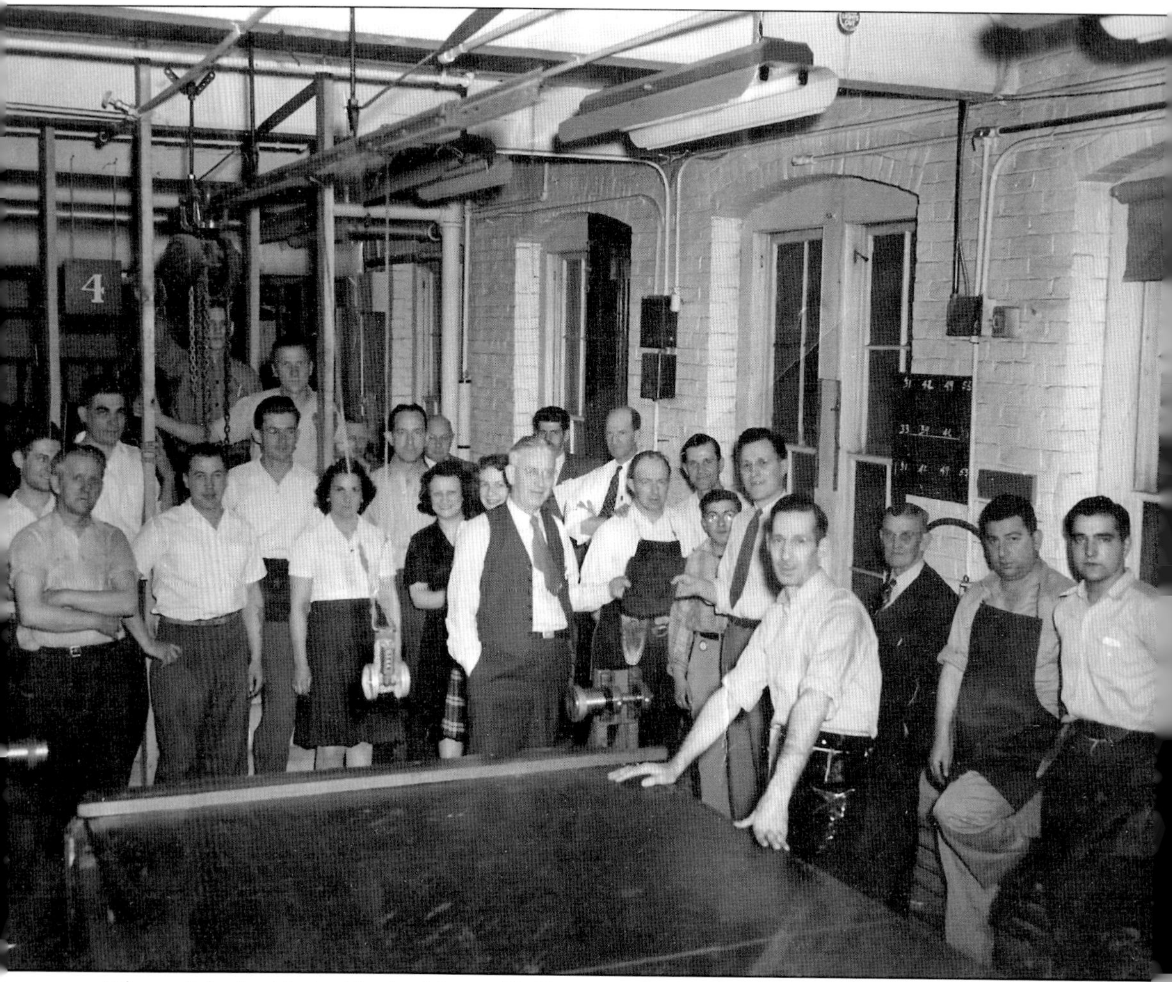

The polished table inside the Homer D. Bronson Company was critical to working with long hinges where maintaining an absolutely straight knuckle is crucial to ensure that the hinge does not bind during operation. The Bronson Company operated a novel machine that took in coils of sheet brass stock and brass wire, notched out the brass sheet, and curled it around the brass wire to create a "continuous" hinge that could be cut to any desired length. The company's association with automobile hinges began with hood hinges, which were used on automobiles of the 1910s and 1920s. They allowed the panels that covered the engine to lift away and fold for easy access. In addition to continuous hinges, which are often referred to as piano hinges, Bronson manufactured the decorative butt hinges seen on the lid of an opened grand piano. These ornamental hinges with delicate scrollwork were plated in Bronson's own plating room and polished to a mirror finish.

Five

MARCHING ON

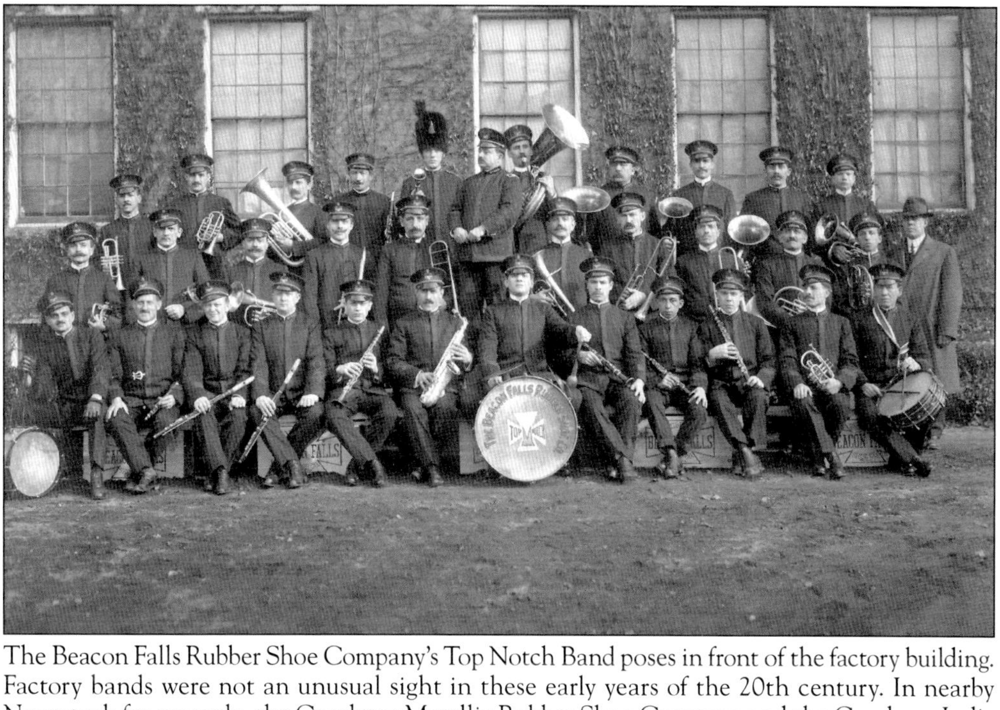

The Beacon Falls Rubber Shoe Company's Top Notch Band poses in front of the factory building. Factory bands were not an unusual sight in these early years of the 20th century. In nearby Naugatuck for example, the Goodyear Metallic Rubber Shoe Company and the Goodyear India Rubber Glove Company both had house bands. (BK.)

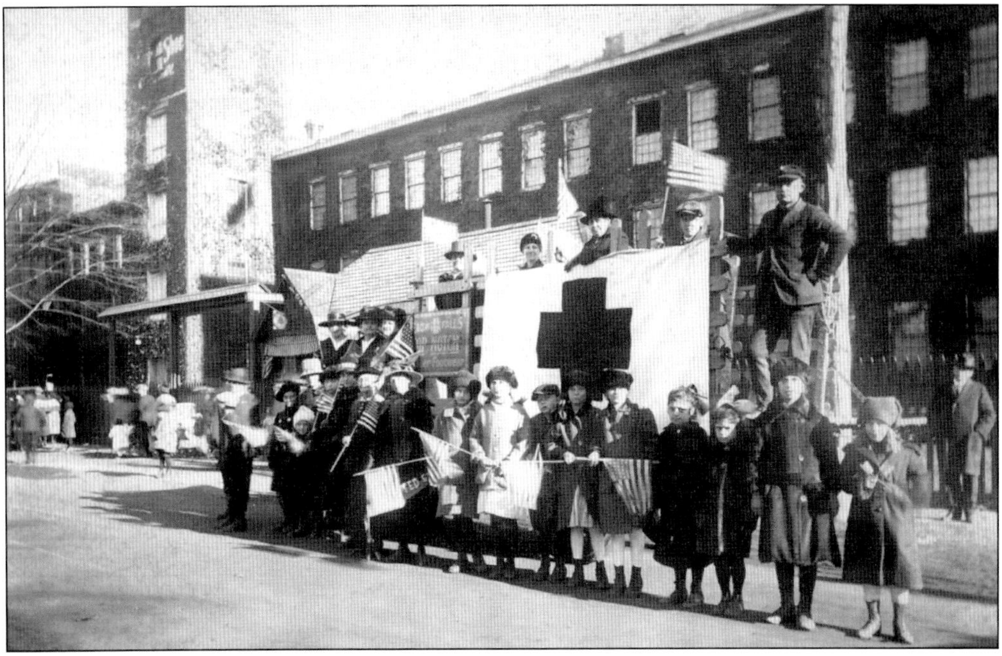

Although the origin of this photograph is not documented, it is almost certainly related to World War I. One can speculate that this wintertime rally utilizing a truck from the Beacon Falls Rubber Shoe Company and displaying the Red Cross flag took place in November 1918 when Kaiser Wilhelm II abdicated. The end of the war was at hand. (MH.)

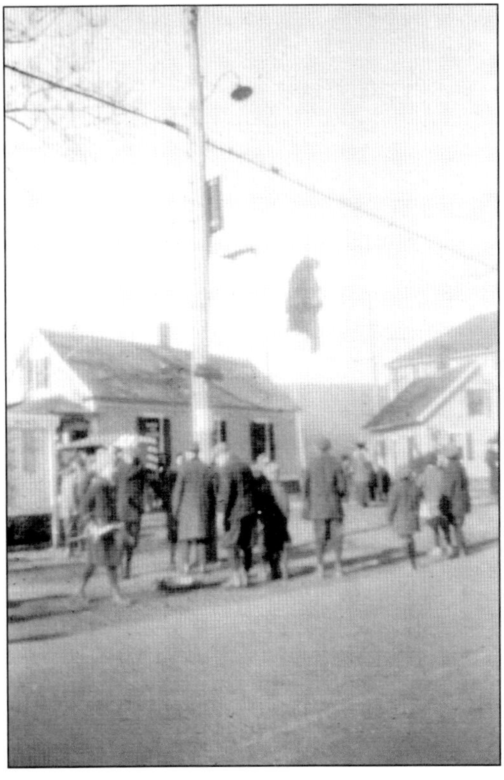

If this event occurred in November 1918, this could be a celebration of "the eleventh hour of the eleventh day of the eleventh month" when a cease fire came into effect and Germany signed the Armistice of Compiègne. The November date would account for the leafless trees and bundled participants. The black object seen above the crowd has often been referred to by locals as the kaiser hanging in effigy. (BK.)

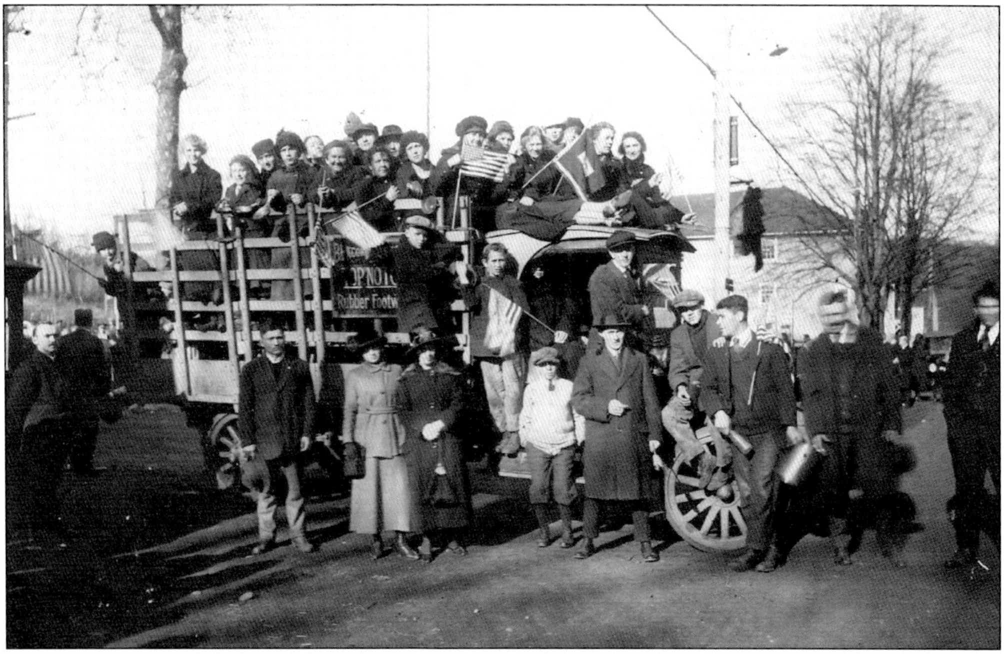

The Beacon Falls Rubber Shoe Company truck is repositioned for this photograph. Beyond the truck looking north, the Top Notch movie theater building is visible. A front-page article in the *Hartford Courant* on Monday November 11, 1918, said, "Hartford begins wild celebration in honor of ending of the war: Whistles blowing arouses sleepy town." Beacon Falls may have followed suit. (BK.)

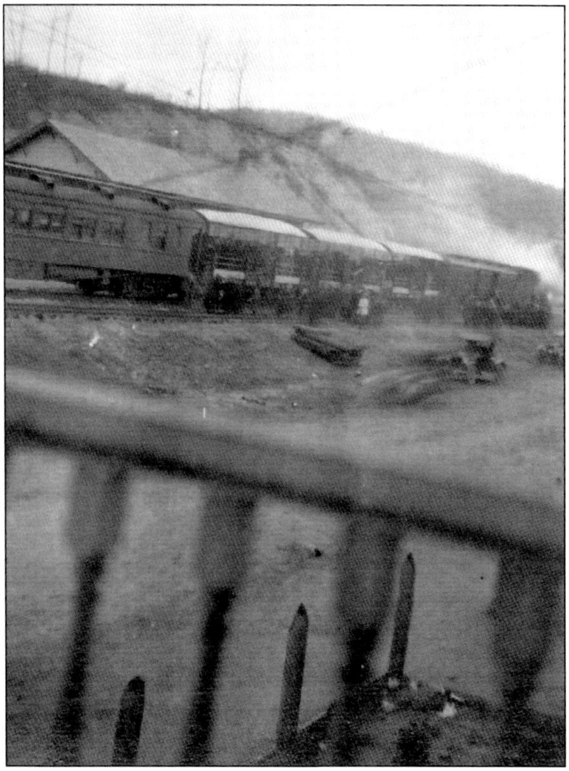

On April 24, 1917, the US government passed the Emergency Loan Act, which authorized the issuing of Liberty Bonds as a means to help pay for involvement in World War I. This was followed by a second bond issue in 1917, two in 1918, and one in 1919. Here, special flatcars arrive in Beacon Falls for a bond rally. (MH.)

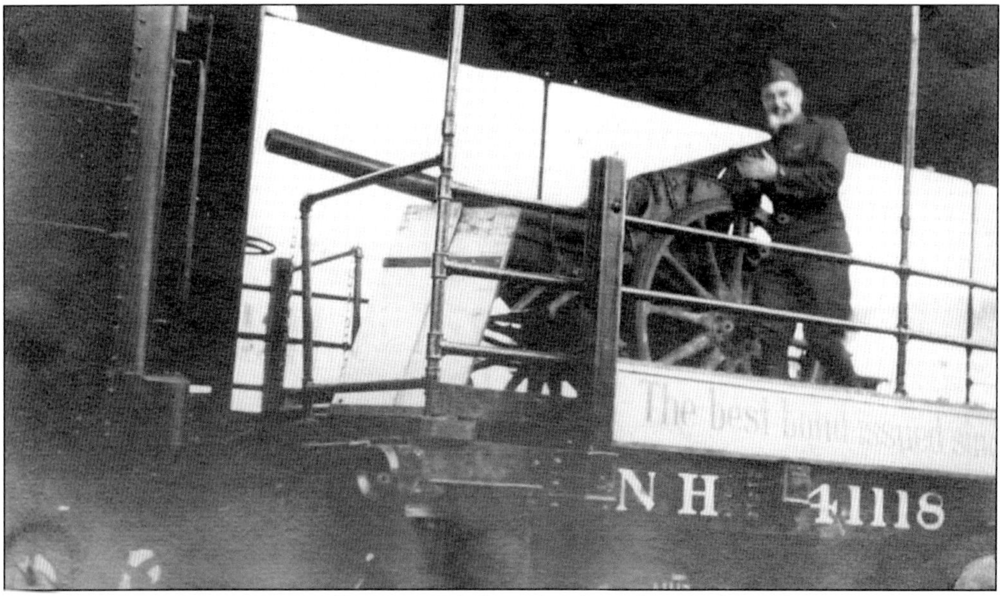

The US government aggressively promoted the sale of war bonds through public events that often featured celebrities. In these photographs, the New York, New Haven & Hartford Railroad delivered customized flatcars with decorative awnings and carrying modern weapons as displays to attract a crowd. (MH.)

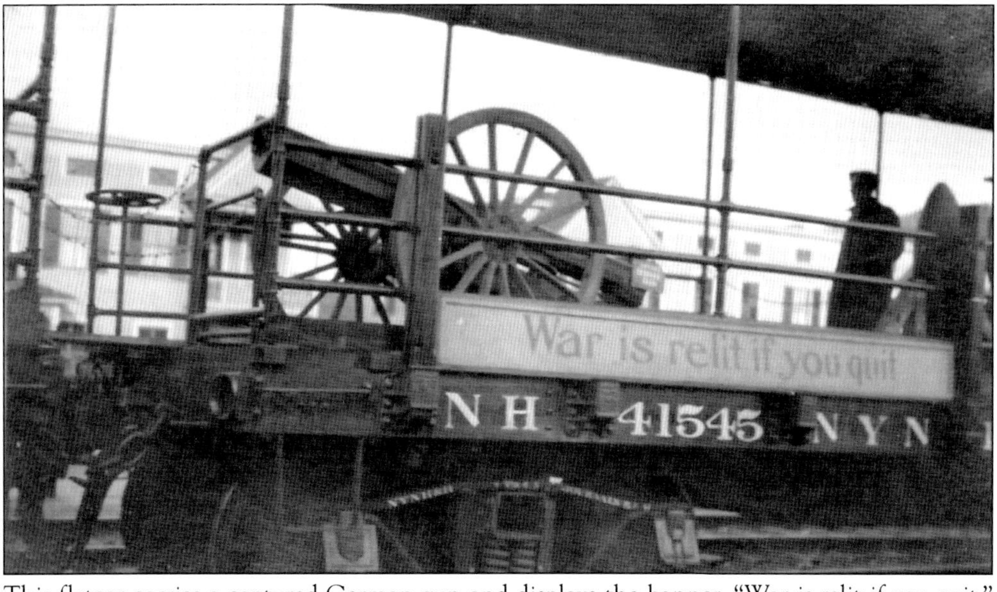

This flatcar carries a captured German gun and displays the banner, "War is relit if you quit." This rally is likely from 1919, as the war was over by then, hence the reference to the war being "relit." No doubt the gentlemen in military garb are extolling the virtues of investing in Liberty Bonds to help eliminate the debt caused by the war effort. (MH.)

The bond rally appears to be drawing a crowd, not surprising in a small town like Beacon Falls where a special exhibition such as this must have been unusual indeed. Totaling $437 million, more of these bonds were sold here in Connecticut than in any other state. The homes along Railroad Avenue can be seen behind the railroad cars. (MH.)

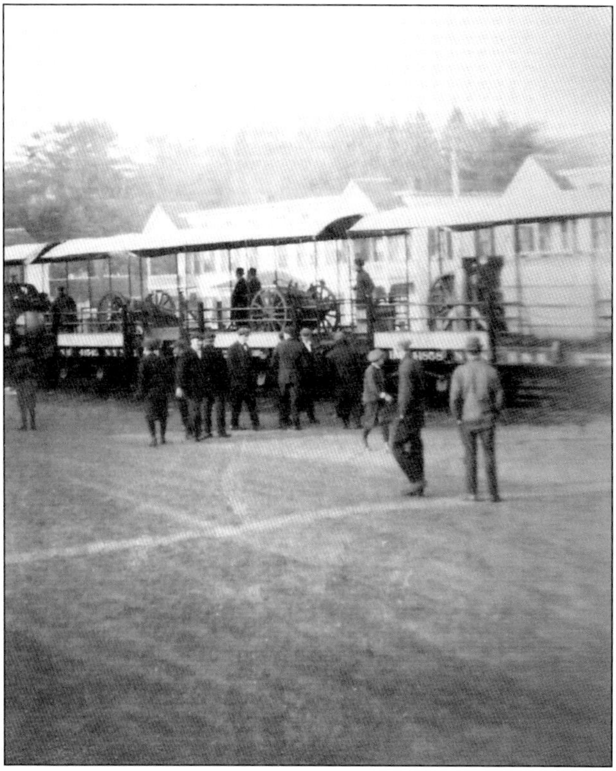

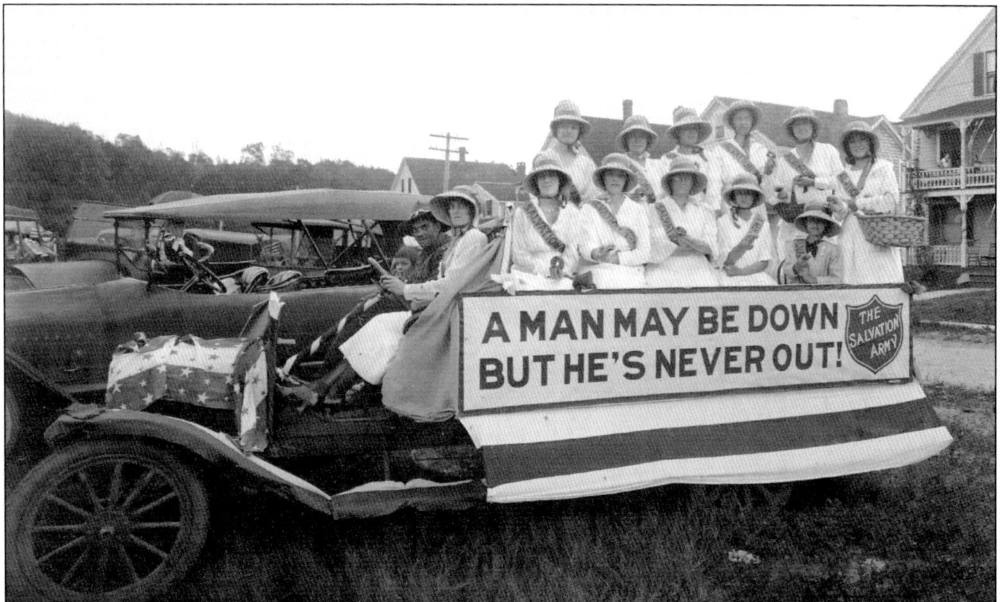

On August 9, 1919, the *Naugatuck Daily News* ran the article, "Greatest Day in History of Beacon Falls Celebrated." The article was in reference to the welcome home celebration the town organized as a tribute to returning soldiers from World War I. Here, a suitably decorated truck carrying members of the Salvation Army parks off Highland Avenue.

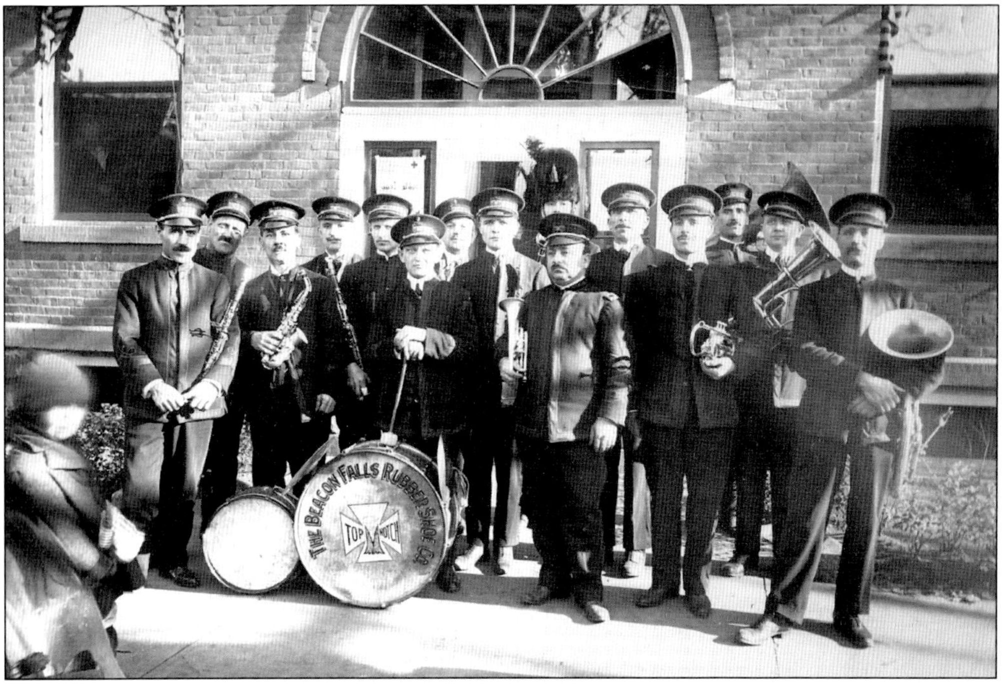

The main feature of the welcome home celebration was the parade that formed on Railroad Avenue and started at 1:30 p.m. It was broken into two divisions. The first division was lead by veterans and town officials, followed by the Beacon Falls Rubber Shoe Company's Top Notch Band seen here.

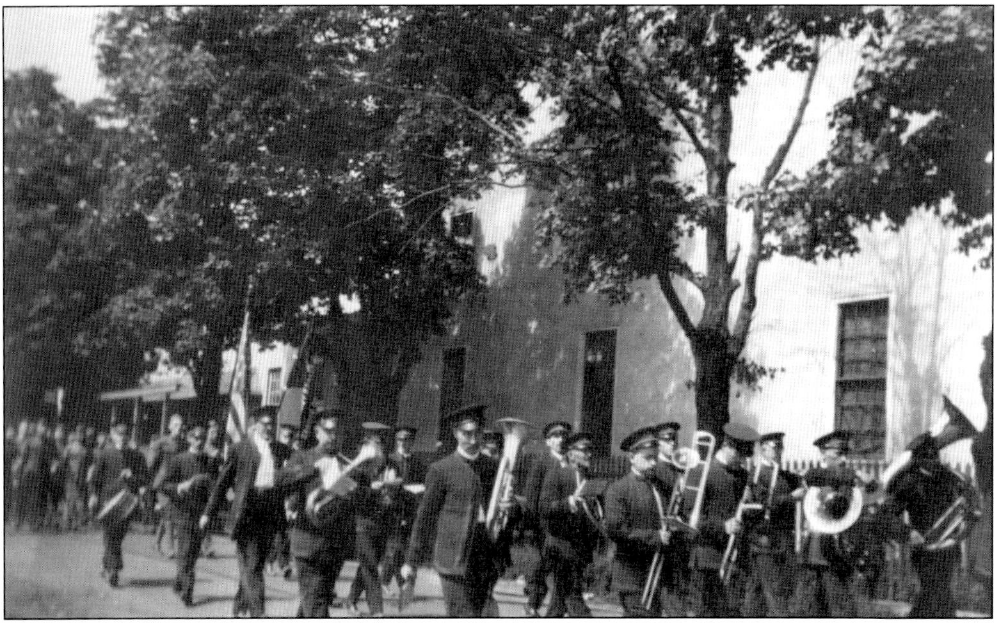

The Top Notch Band is pictured marching in front of a Rubber Shoe Company warehouse where the Beacon Falls Pharmacy sits today. The Goodyear Metallic Rubber Shoe Company Band, the Goodyear India Rubber Glove Company Band, and the Union City Drum Corps appeared later in the parade. (MH.)

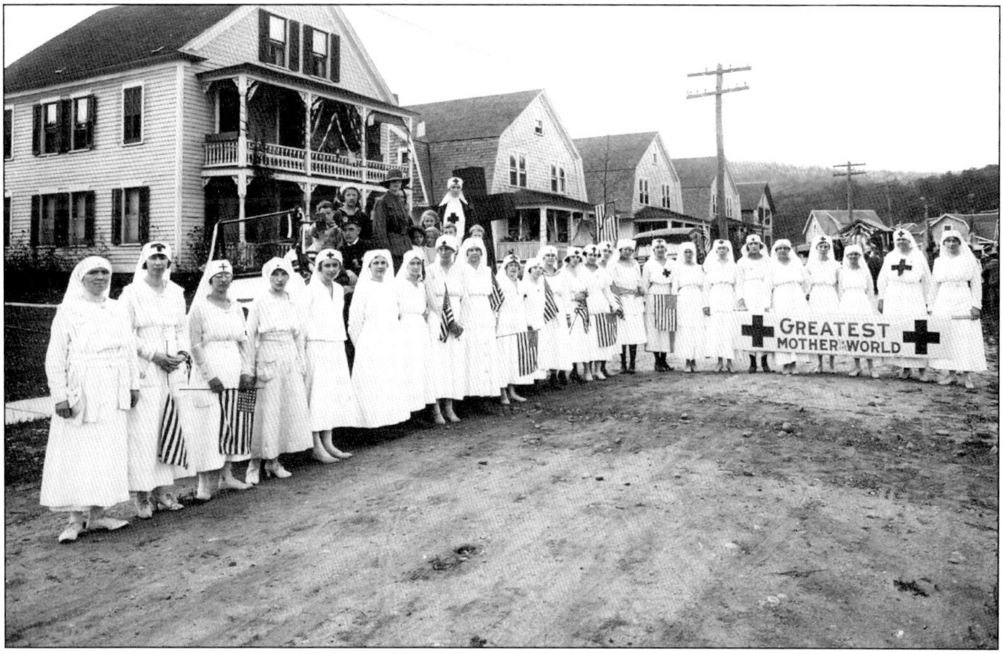

The American National Red Cross can be traced back to the work of Clara Barton during the Civil War. The Red Cross engaged in fundraising activities throughout World War I to provide disaster relief abroad. Here, members of the Red Cross pose on Highland Avenue holding a banner that carries the Red Cross slogan, "Greatest Mother in the World." (BK.)

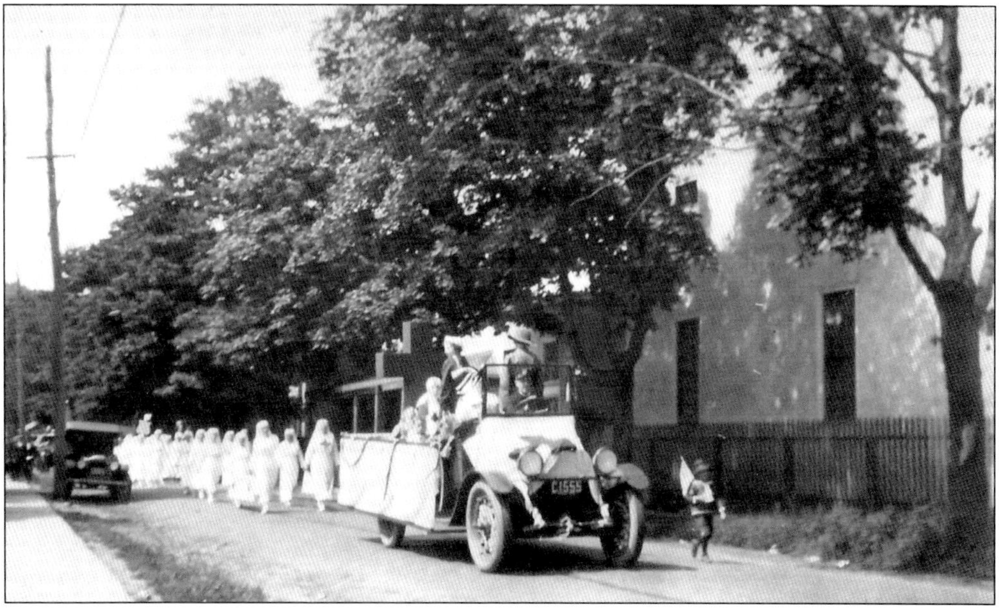

Earlier in the day, the Red Cross marched in the welcome home parade, shown here on Main Street. The outfits are likely influenced by a painting that was used extensively by the Red Cross on printed promotional material at the time. The 1918 painting by Alonzo Earl Foringer depicted a woman in flowing, white robes referred to as a "modern Madonna." (MH.)

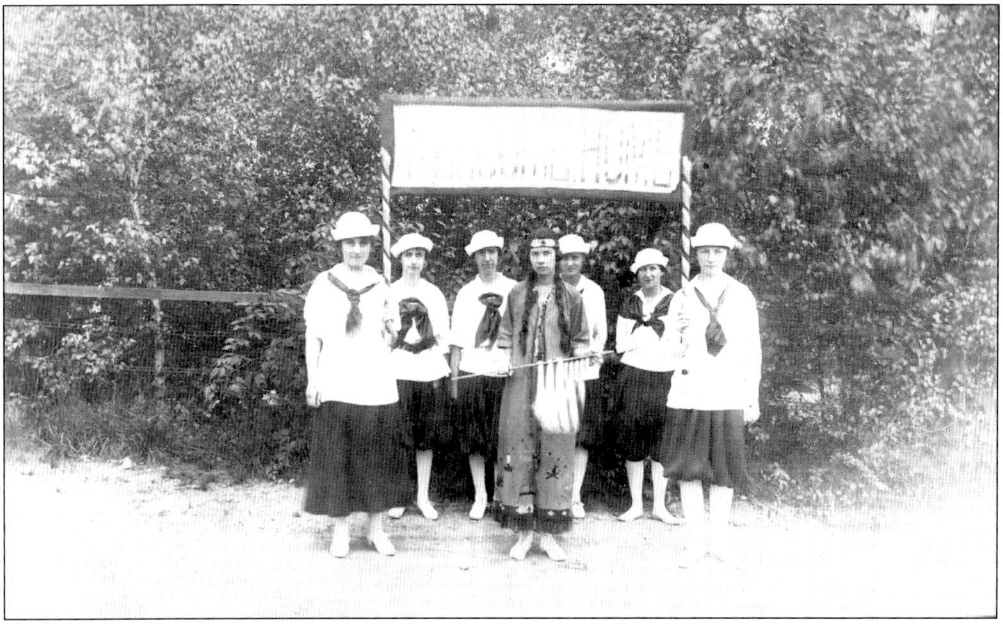

Members of the Beacon Falls Camp Fire Girls pose for the photographer with their sign that greets the returning servicemen with a hearty "Welcome Home." Seen here, from left to right, are May Bow, Agnes Bow, unidentified, Mildred Bronson Woodward, Anna Astrom, unidentified, and Estrid Morrits Campbell. The Indian costume is quite appropriate for a Beacon Falls parade. The history of the town often emphasizes its Indian heritage.

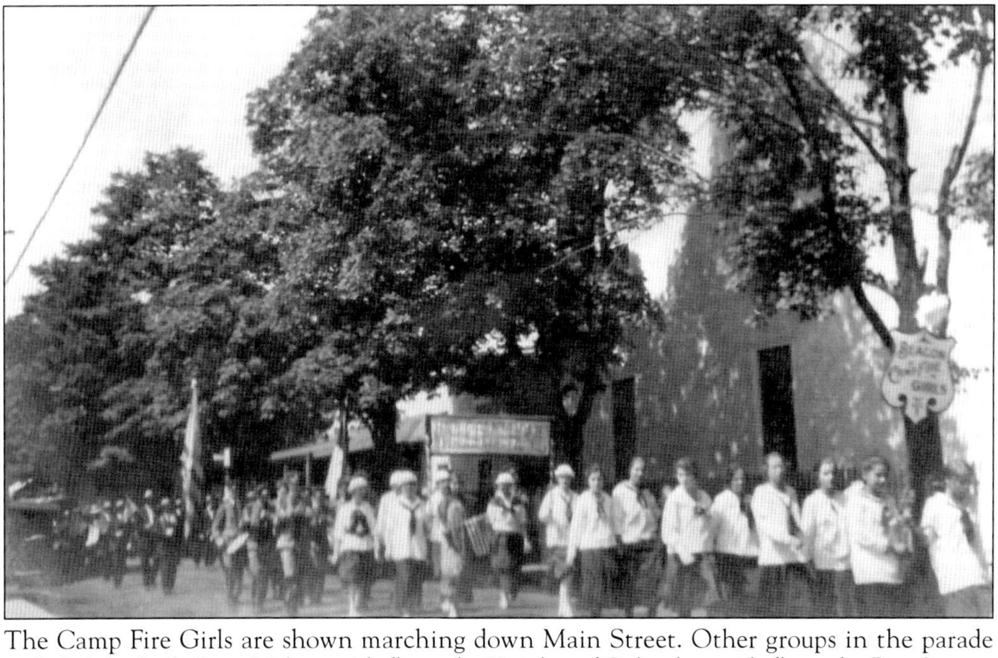

The Camp Fire Girls are shown marching down Main Street. Other groups in the parade included the Lady Boot Makers with float, the Knights of Columbus with float, the Boy Scouts, the Knights of Pythias with float, St. Mary's Polish Society with float, the Top Notch Club, and the Christian Endeavor float. Employees from the Beacon Falls Rubber Shoe Company and the Homer D. Bronson Company also marched in the parade. (MH.)

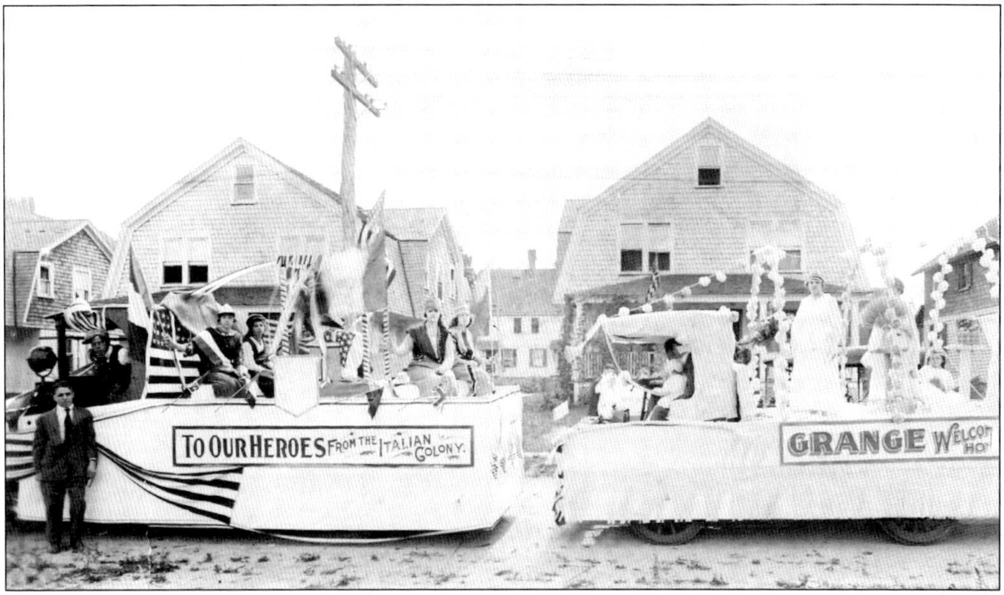

Reporting on the parade, the *Naugatuck Daily News* commented, "Virtually the entire membership of every fraternal organization in the town was in line." Here, the Italian Colony float and the Rock Rimmon Grange float are seen parked on Highland Avenue. The Beacon Falls Rubber Shoe Company allowed their trucks to be used as the platforms for the floats.

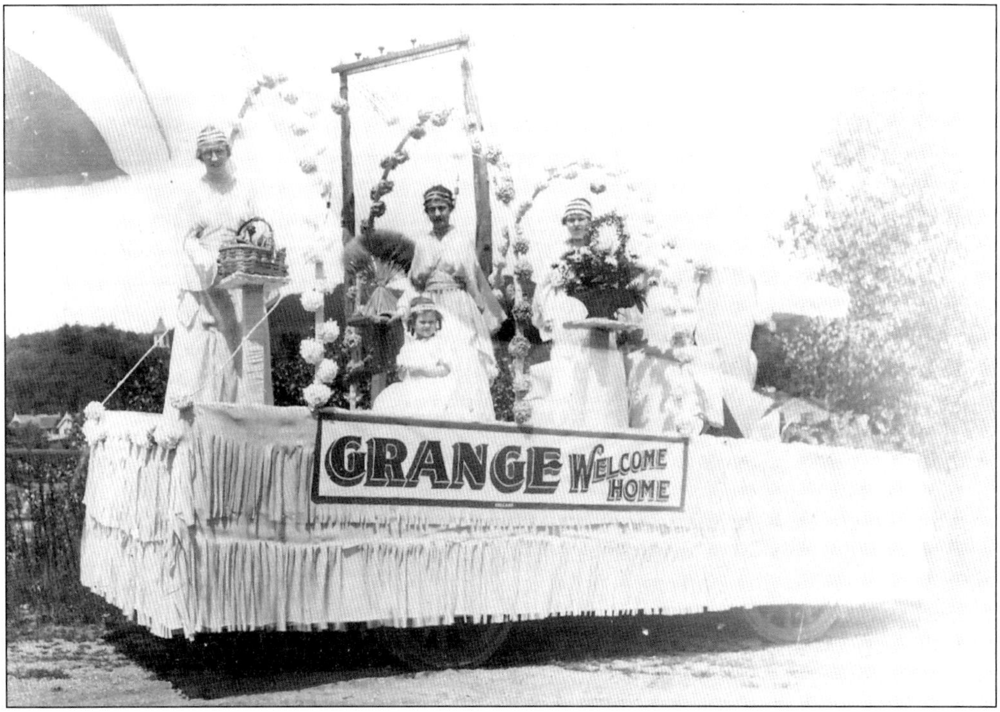

According to the *National Grange*, "granges were formed in the years following the American Civil War to unite private citizens in improving the economic and social position of the nation's farm population." Most towns in Connecticut had a Grange hall that was used not only for agricultural purposes but also for social events.

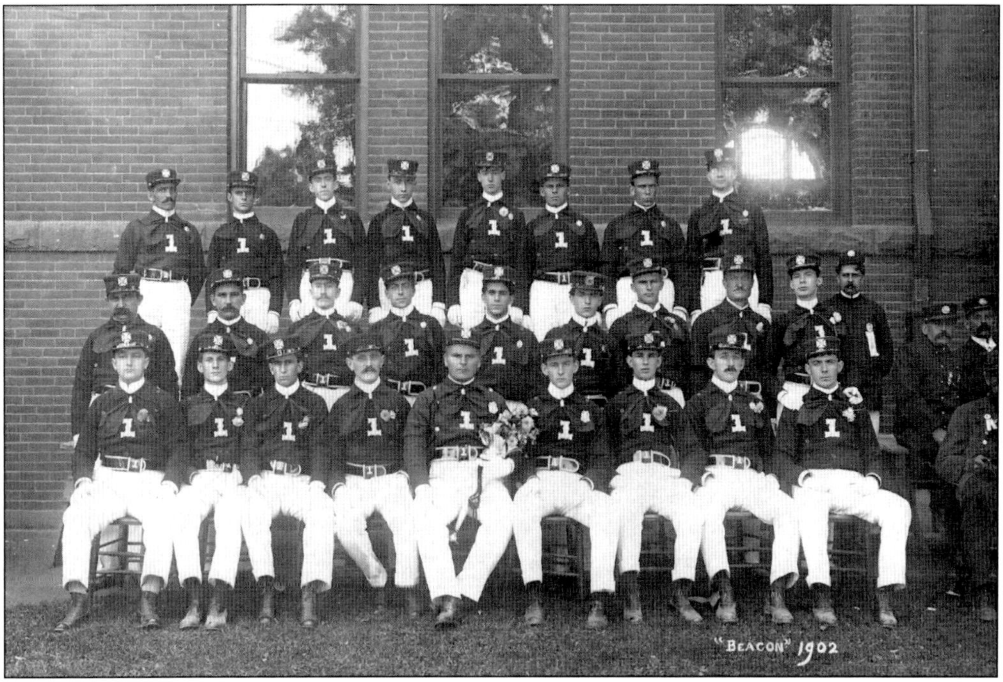

No parade is complete without the fire department. The Beacon Falls Fire Department is shown here in a photograph from 1902. In April 1904, a fire was discovered in the Beacon Falls Rubber Shoe Company factory office. Though heavily damaged, it was rebuilt. Quick action by the Beacon Falls Fire Department prevented the fire from spreading to the other buildings.

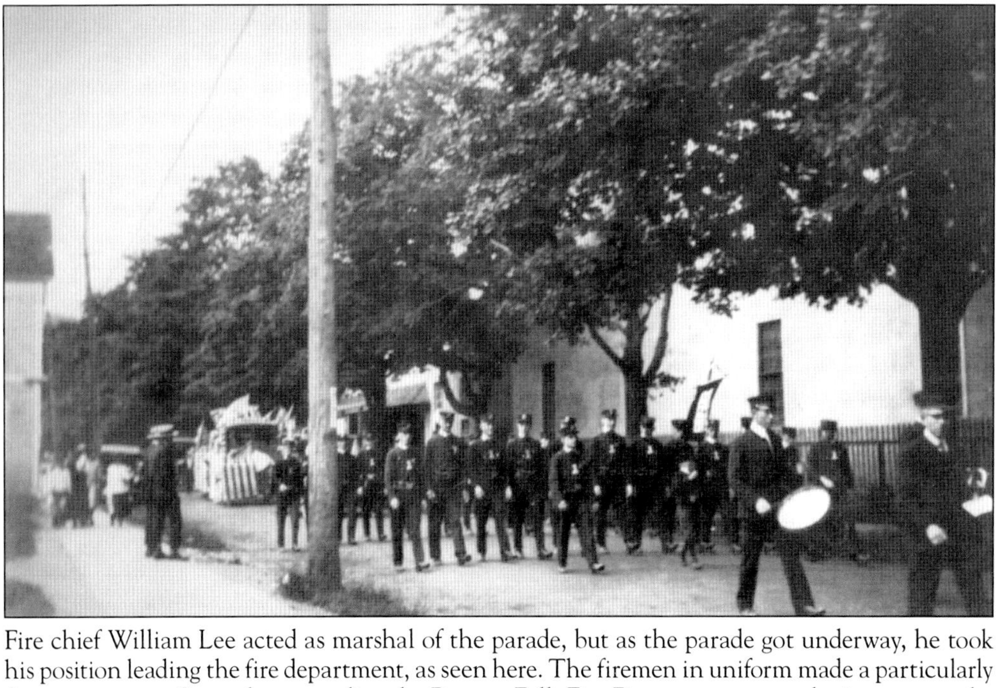

Fire chief William Lee acted as marshal of the parade, but as the parade got underway, he took his position leading the fire department, as seen here. The firemen in uniform made a particularly fine appearance. Several years earlier, the Beacon Falls Fire Department won a loving-cup trophy at a firemen's convention as the neatest-appearing fire department in the state. (MH.)

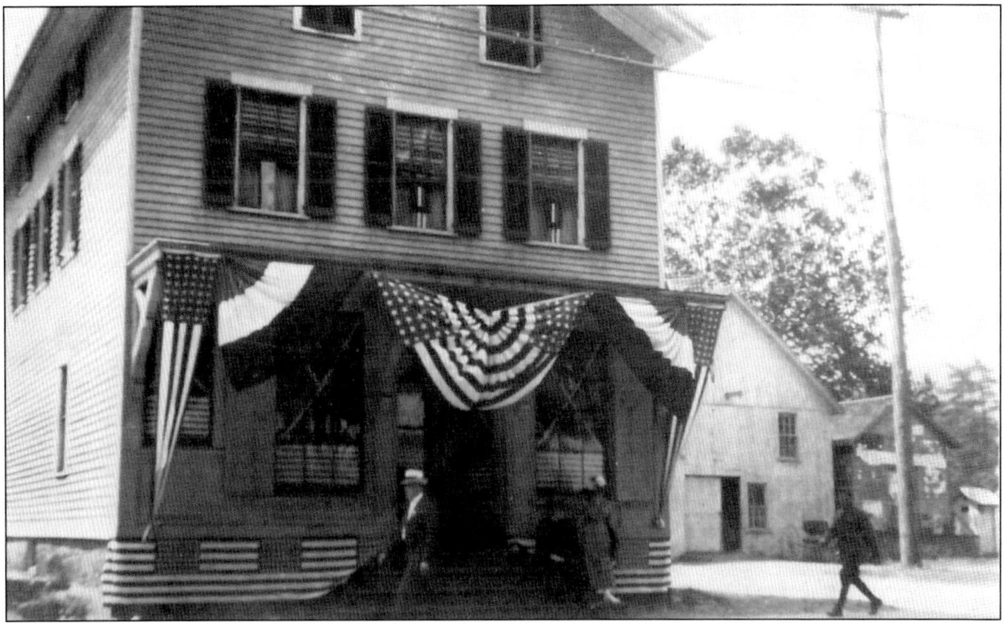

The parade began on Railroad Avenue and proceeded over the bridge to Main Street, then to Bethany Road, Malone Avenue, Feldspar Avenue, back to Main Street, then to St. Michael's Roman Catholic Church, back to College Street, to Wolfe Avenue, Century Avenue, Maple Avenue, Division Street, Highland Avenue, and ending at the ball field. Here, Gruber's Store is suitably decorated, and a soldier approaches from the north. (MH.)

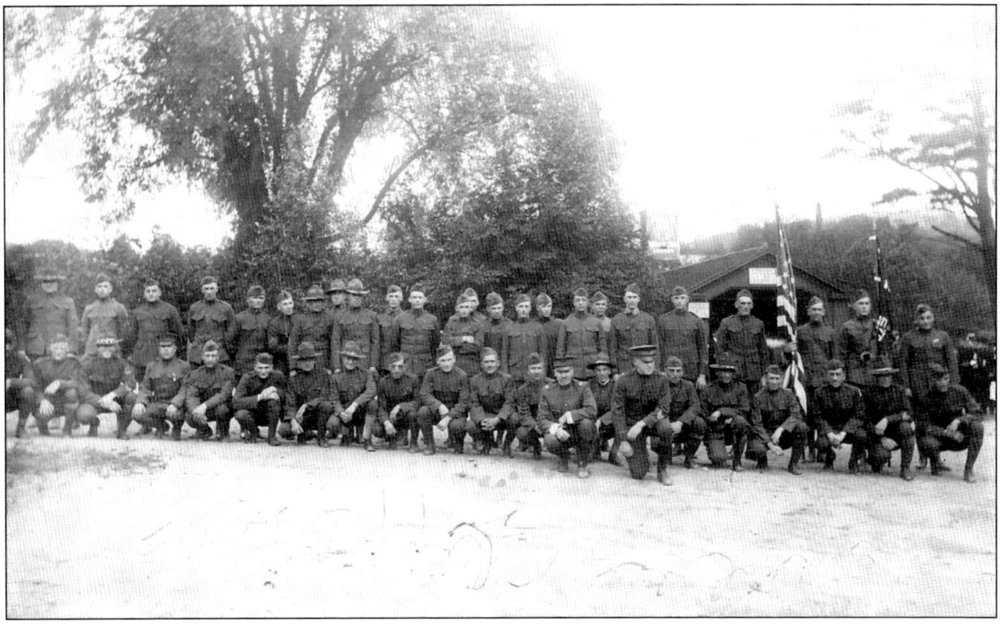

Shown is a photograph of the honorees before the parade. The *Naugatuck Daily News* eloquently stated, "Never, perhaps, in the history of this staid, old New England town, has a greater, more enthusiastic celebration been held here, than that of today. It will go down in the township's history emblazoned in gold, as will the feats of the Beacon Falls boys who played a valiant role in the world war." (BK.)

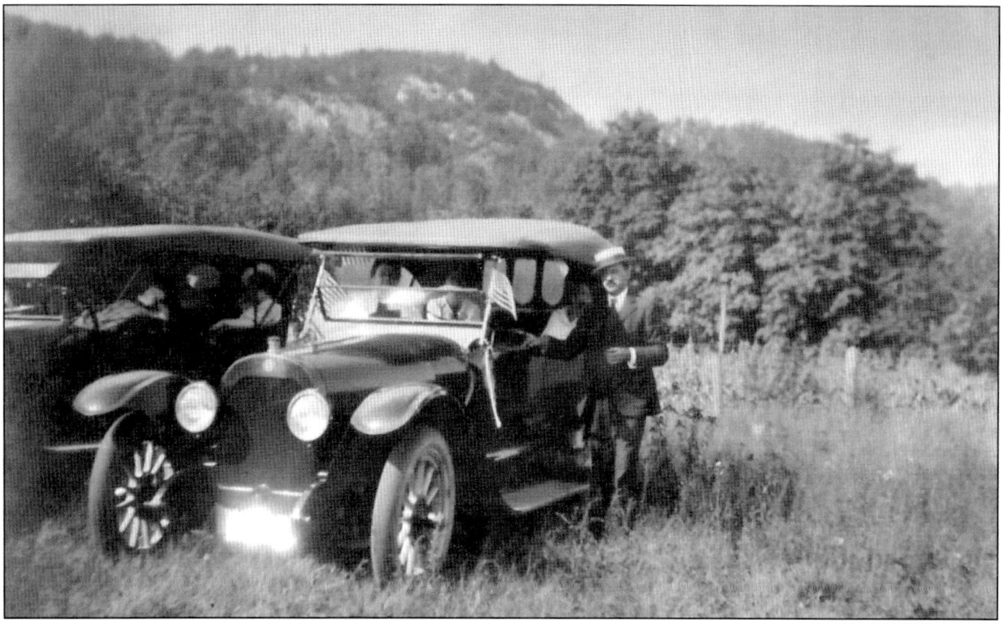

Automobiles were provided to transport the mothers of servicemen in the parade. Here, Edward Gruber stands beside his Dodge Brothers automobile, which is parked in the field off Highland Avenue. After the parade, an athletic meet was held here with prizes awarded. This was followed by a baseball game. In the evening, the servicemen were treated to a banquet at the Top Notch Hotel where a chicken supper was served. (MH.)

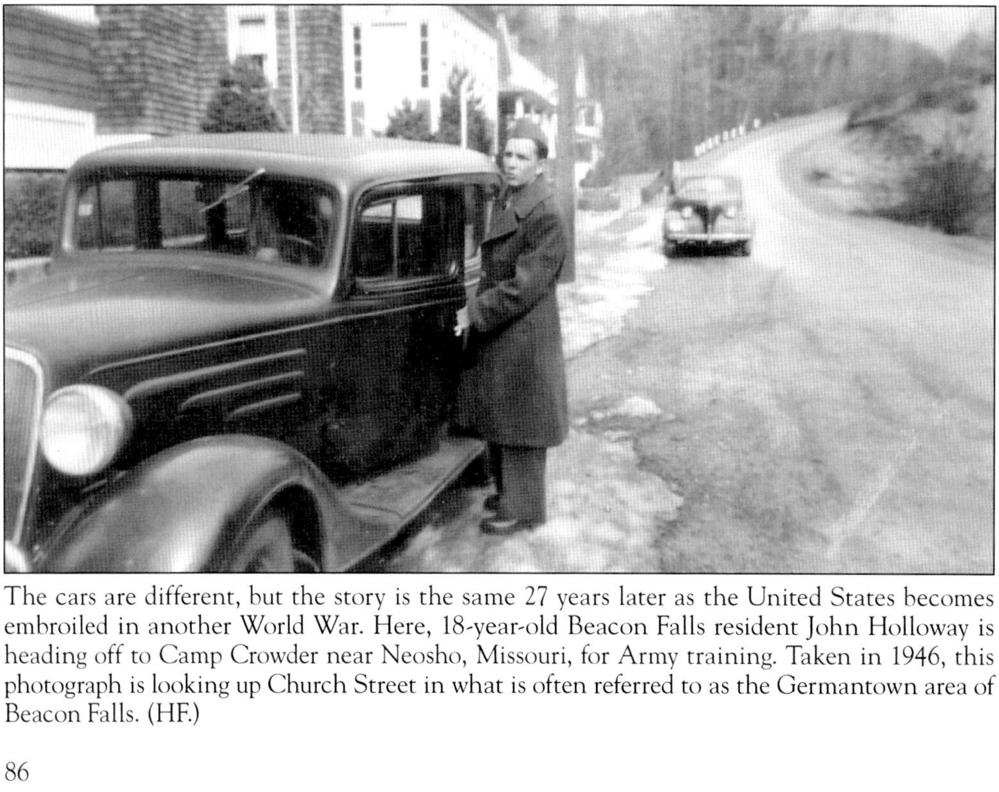

The cars are different, but the story is the same 27 years later as the United States becomes embroiled in another World War. Here, 18-year-old Beacon Falls resident John Holloway is heading off to Camp Crowder near Neosho, Missouri, for Army training. Taken in 1946, this photograph is looking up Church Street in what is often referred to as the Germantown area of Beacon Falls. (HF.)

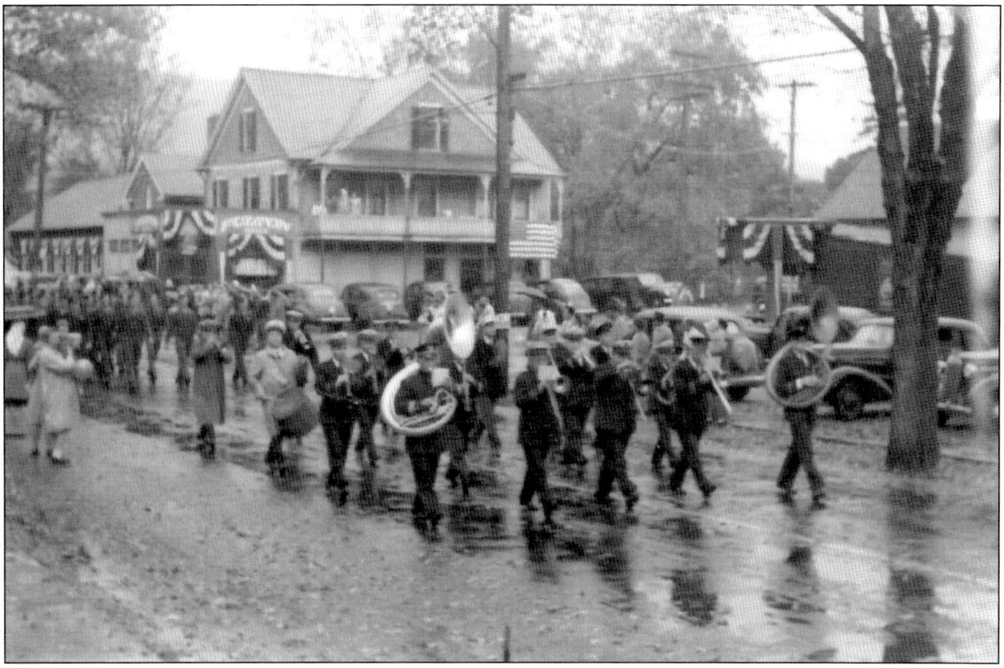

Much as it did for World War I soldiers in 1919, Beacon Falls welcomes home the soldiers from World War II in 1946. This time, the weather is not cooperating as the soldiers march down Main Street past the Fulton Market at the intersection with Depot Street. The building on the right edge of the photograph is Al's Package Store.

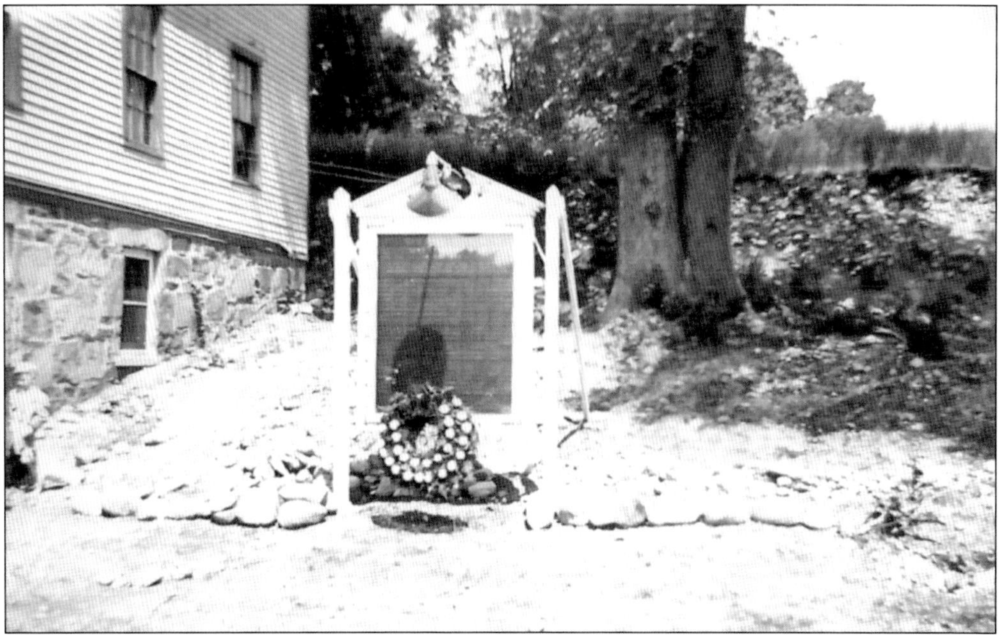

On May 31, 1949, Beacon Falls unveiled this plaque honoring soldiers who fought in both World Wars. The plaque was placed on Main Street next to what would later become Beacon Falls Pizza Palace. Sadly, this plaque did not survive the 1955 flood. A new memorial plaque was later placed near the town hall off Burton Road. (BK.)

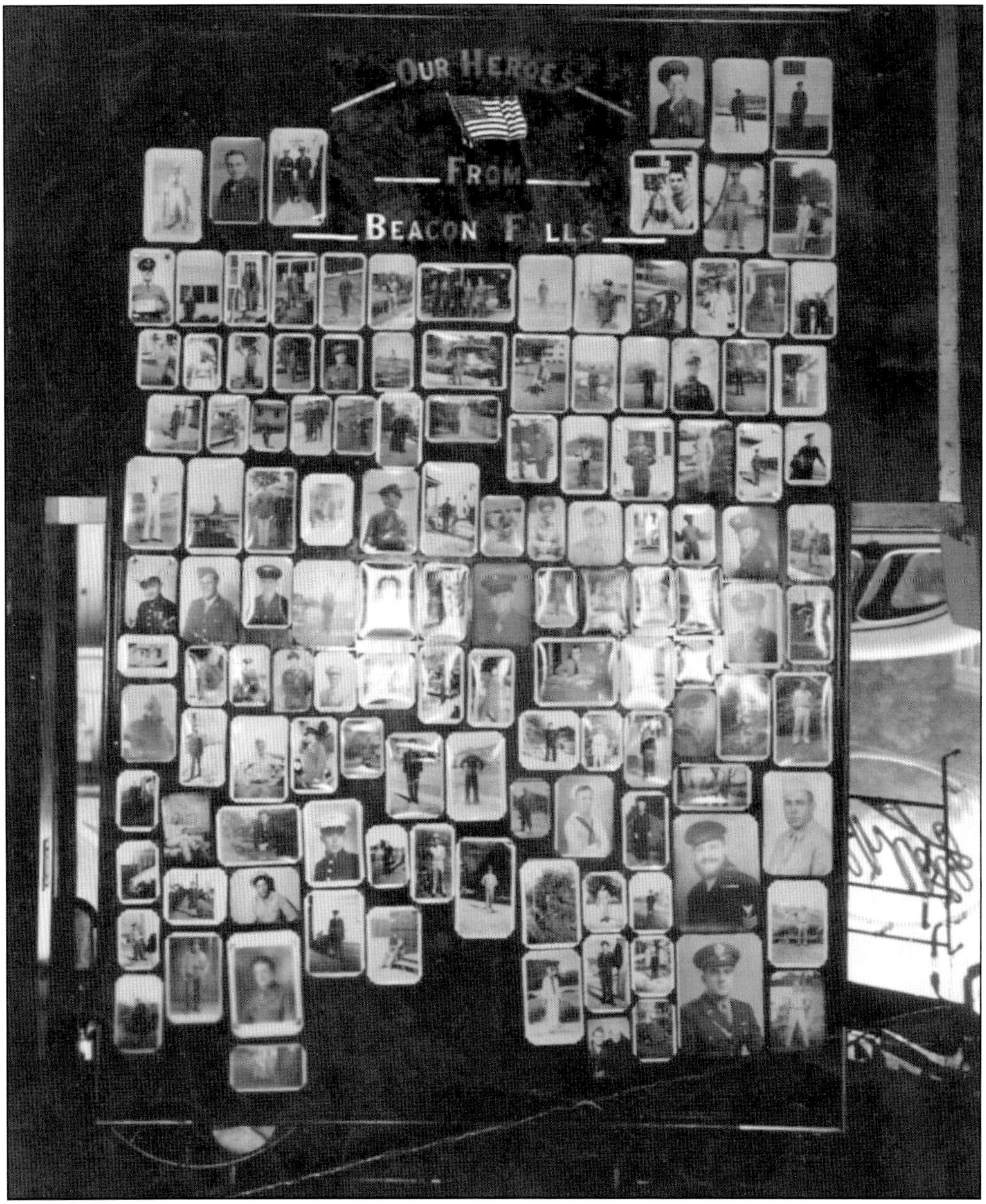

In honor of "Our Heroes from Beacon Falls," Al Mennillo's Package Store on the corner of Depot and Main Streets displayed this collage of photographs of local servicemen during World War II. Only a small sample of the 250 men and women from Beacon Falls that answered the call are represented here. Even the folks back home were active participants in the war effort. Food and gas were rationed. War ration coupon books containing tickets for sugar, coffee, and other staples were distributed. Recycling was encouraged and included newspaper, boxes, magazines, rubber, tin foil, aluminum, iron, copper, rags, and corrugated board. Civil defense drills were held, as were air-raid drills in which a locally designated air-raid warden would make sure that everyone covered their windows and doors to eliminate any escaping light. Even the rubber shoe manufacturing—now in Naugatuck—switched over to making canvas-top, rubber-soled "jungle boots" for soldiers in tropical environments.

Six

Evolution

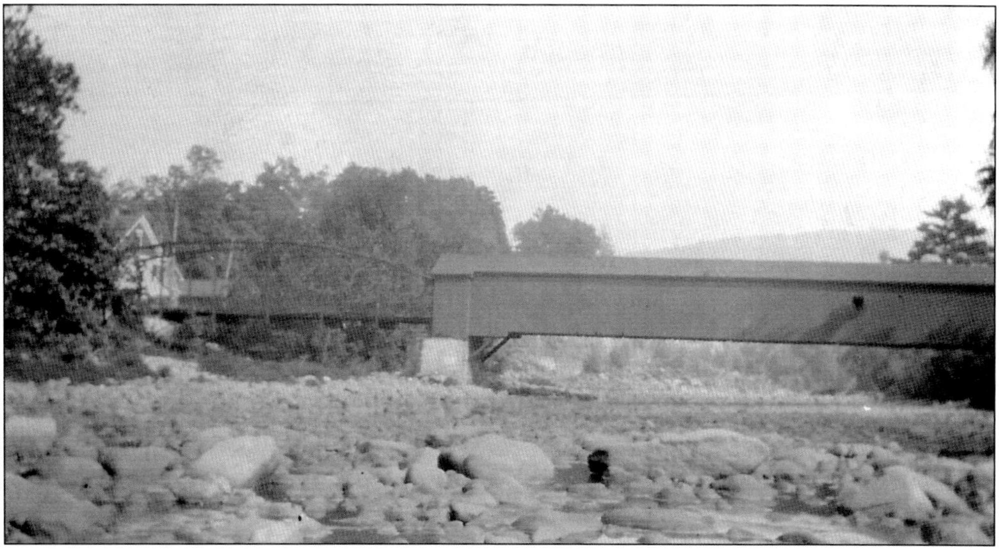

The period from the mid-1930s to the mid-1950s saw a number of changes that altered the look and feel of Beacon Falls. In 1936, the venerable covered bridge in the center of town, which had served the town since 1865, was replaced with the steel girder bridge that is present today. By the early1930s, high maintenance costs doomed the old bridge.

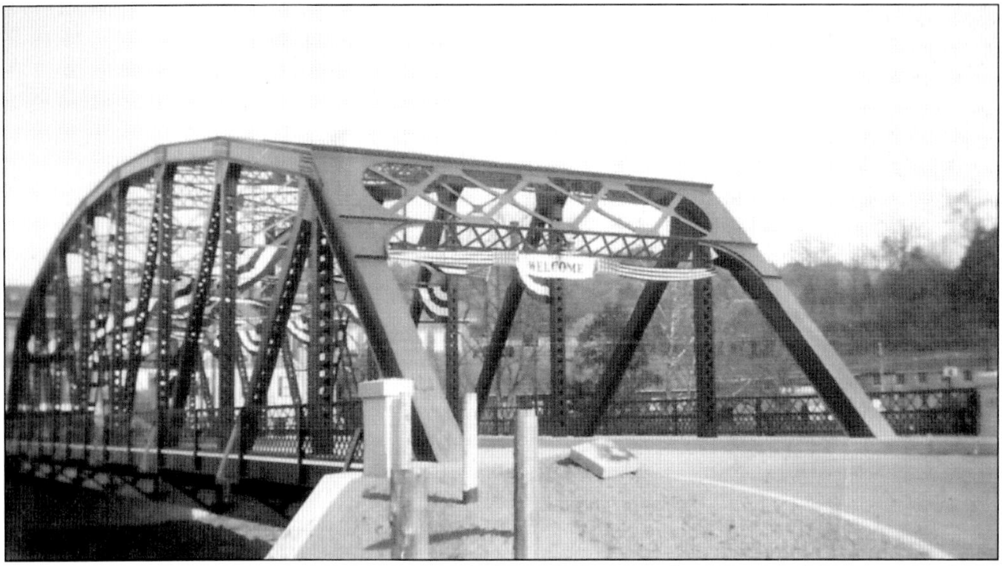

On Saturday, October 26, 1935, the town dedicated the new $75,000 steel bridge, seen here decorated in patriotic ornamentation. The new bridge stood 212 feet long and 45 feet wide and was considered to be "of the most up-to-date mechanical design obtainable." Rep. William B. Bradley provided the introductory address, and Beacon Falls first selectman Christian Heiss acted as master of ceremonies.

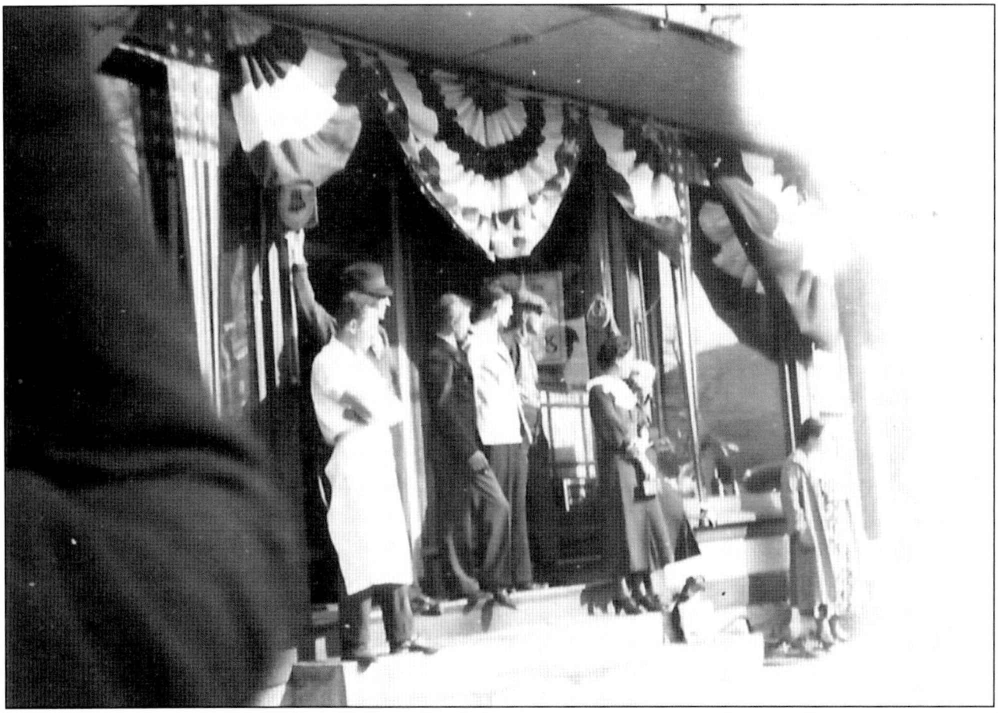

The bridge dedication was followed by a parade. Here, a group watches the parade from the steps of the White Swan Grill. Work on the new bridge began in April 1935. The Gammino Construction Company of Providence, Rhode Island, was awarded the contract. The steel construction was performed by the Leake-Nelson Company of Bridgeport, Connecticut.

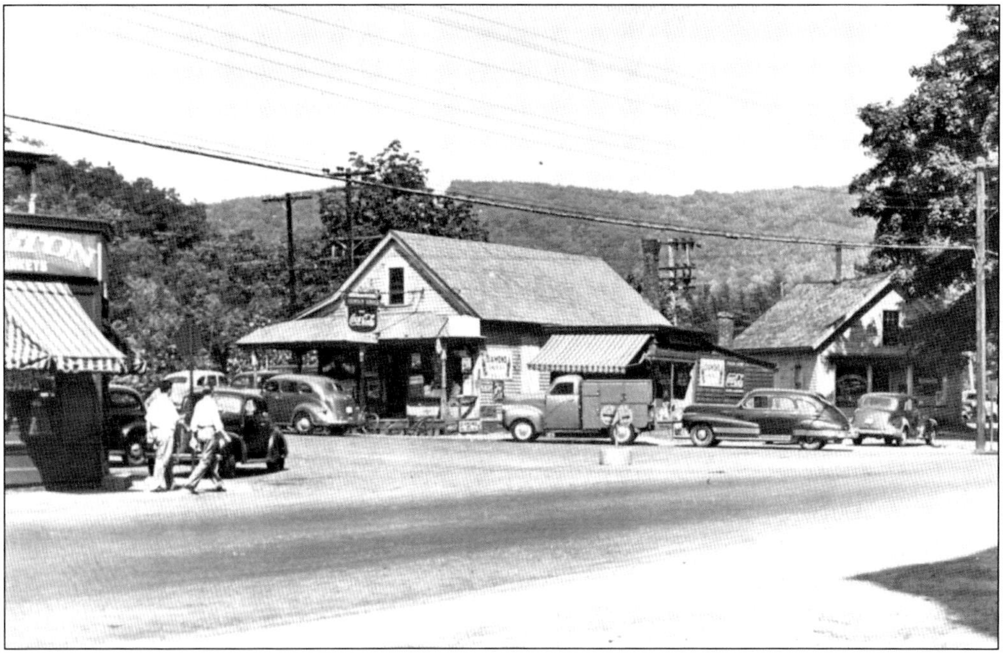

Here, two gentlemen walk past the awning of the Fulton Market on Main Street. The market was located in the building that formerly housed the Crescent Lunch Room but was now expanded to reach out to the Main Street curb. Close examination of the interior, seen below, reveals the enviable prices in the late 1930s; most canned goods are two or three cans for 25¢.

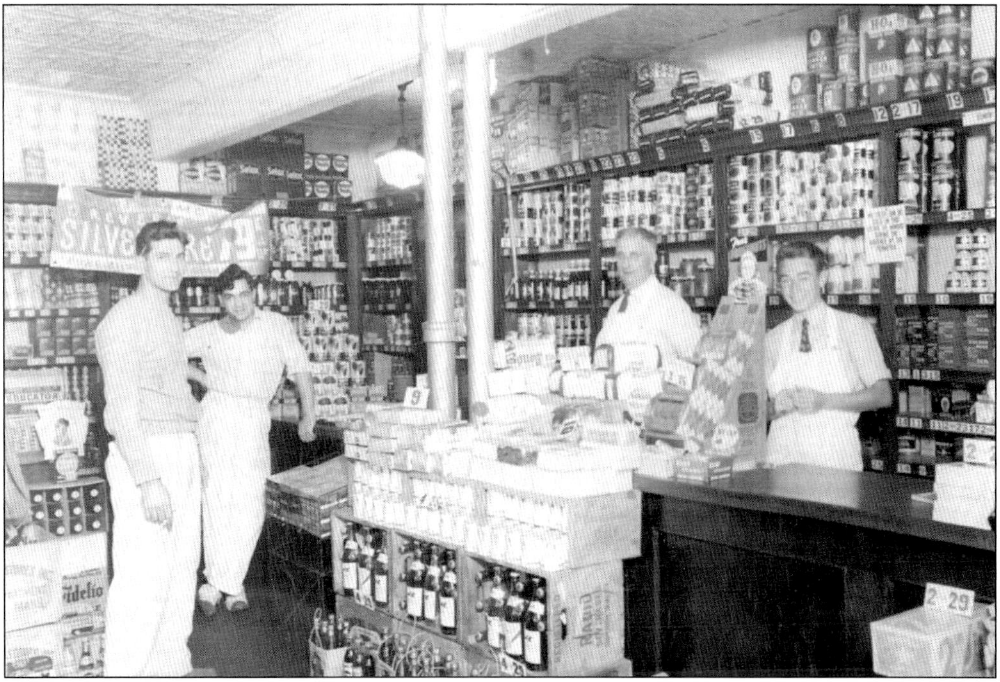

Inside the Fulton Market are (from left to right) Joe Mennillo Sr., Benny Zollo, Elmer Wedge, and clerk Michael Krenesky. Mike delivered groceries for owner Elmer Wedge, who paid him 25¢ an hour. Mike later recalled that he made more on tips than he earned a day in salary. (BK.)

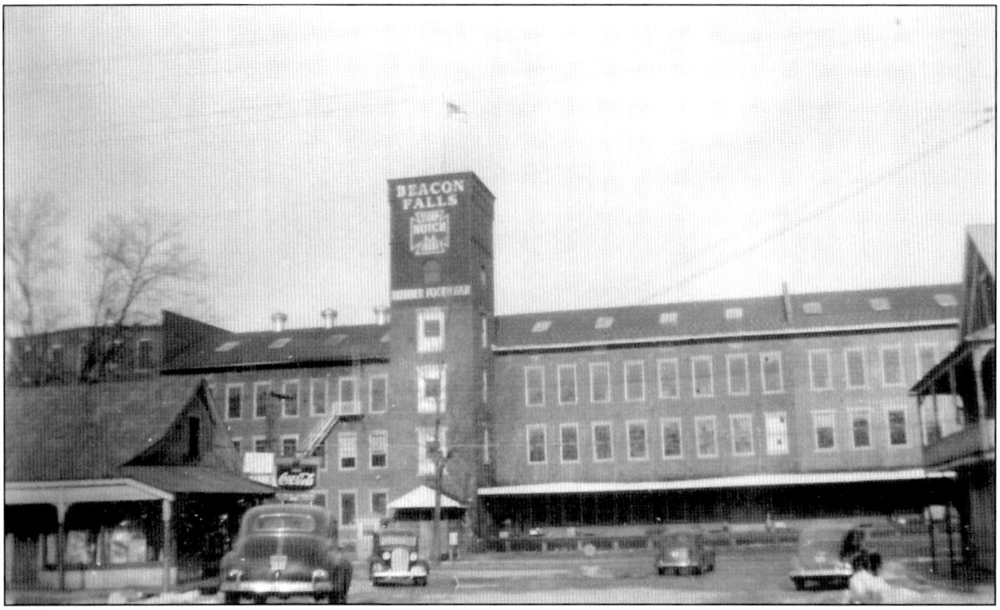

Coming over the bridge around 1940, the venerable Rubber Shoe Company towers stand tall. The old factory was now a warehouse with a loading dock and awning stretching between the towers. Cars pulling out of this intersection flanked by the drugstore on the left and the Fulton Market on the right had to use extra caution turning onto Route 8 because there was no traffic light.

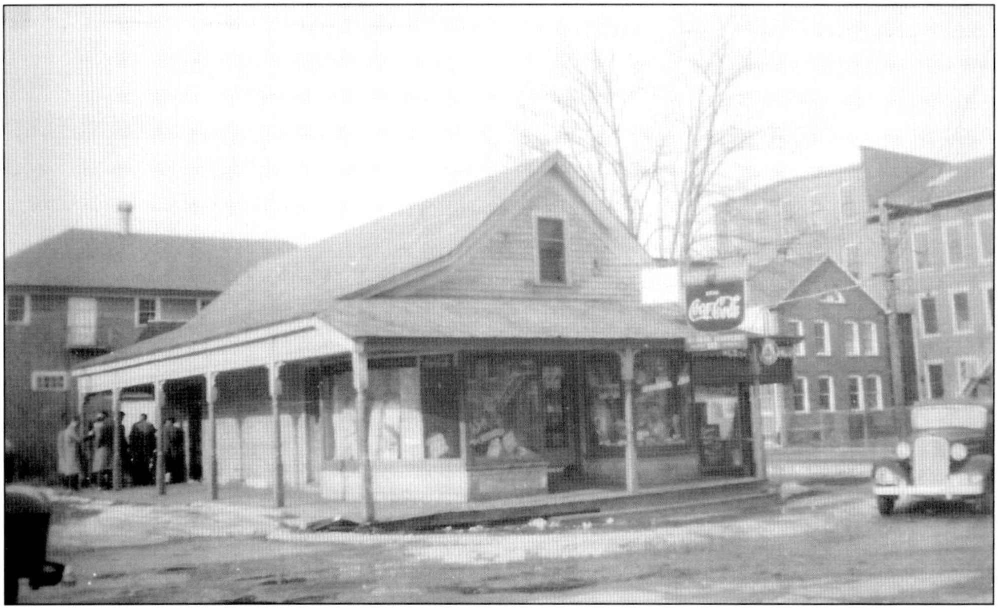

Gone are the trolley tracks alongside the drugstore. But the overhang is still a popular spot. Here, a group of men participate in a game of craps, a gambling game using dice that frequently occurred here. The drugstore contained a soda fountain and advertises ice cream sandwiches for 10¢.

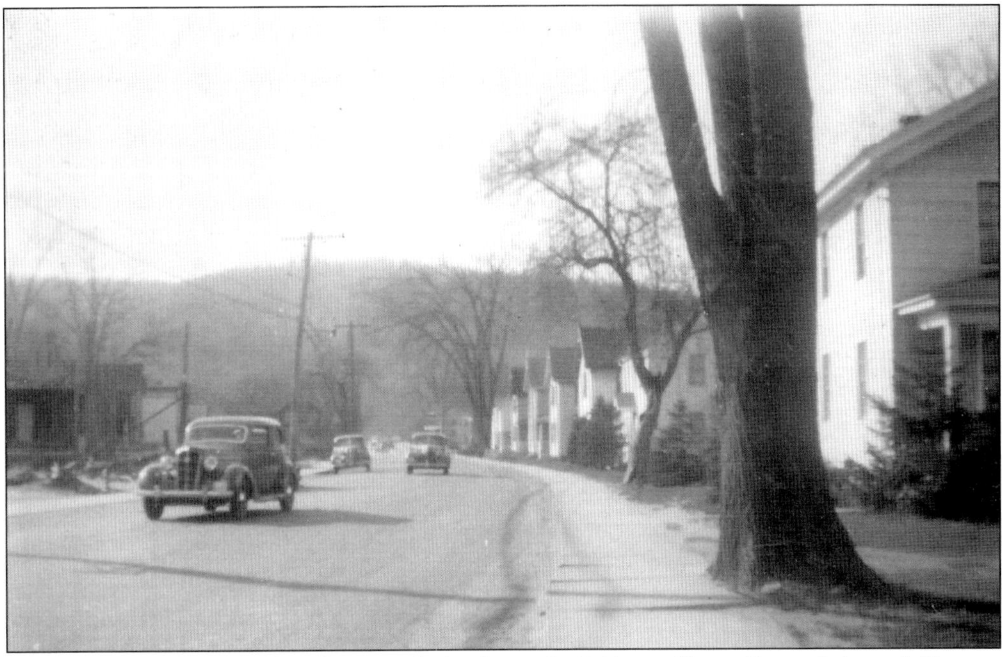

Thought not obvious by this photograph, by the early 1940s, traffic on Route 8 through Beacon Falls was becoming a problem. It was a deadly mix of increased traffic and increased speeds on what was essentially a residential street. Something had to be done. The State of Connecticut began buying up land with the intention of widening Main Street into a four-lane highway.

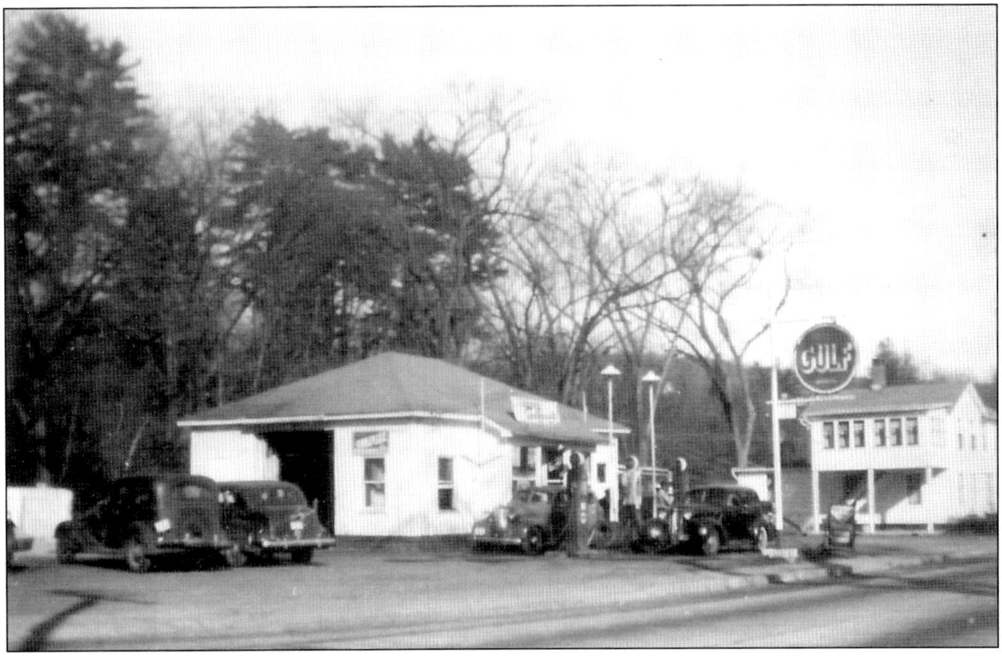

The service station was one business that prospered with all the increased traffic through Beacon Falls. Here, Gary Fuoco's Gulf station is shown on North Main Street. This was when the term "service station" really meant service. It was not uncommon for an attendant to pump the gas, wash the windshield, and check the tires, water, and oil—all for 20¢ a gallon.

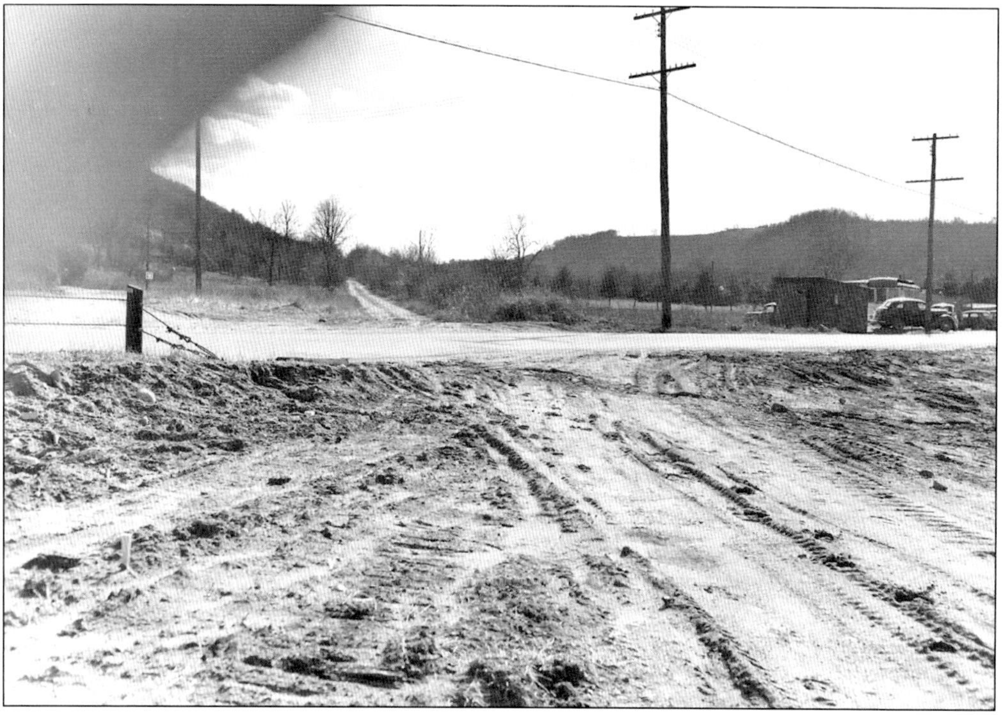

In 1949, the State of Connecticut completed an upgrade to the section of Route 8 through Beacon Falls converting it into a four-lane highway. The following views show Beacon Falls as it looked during the early stages of work. From south of town, Route 8 would head toward Seymour.

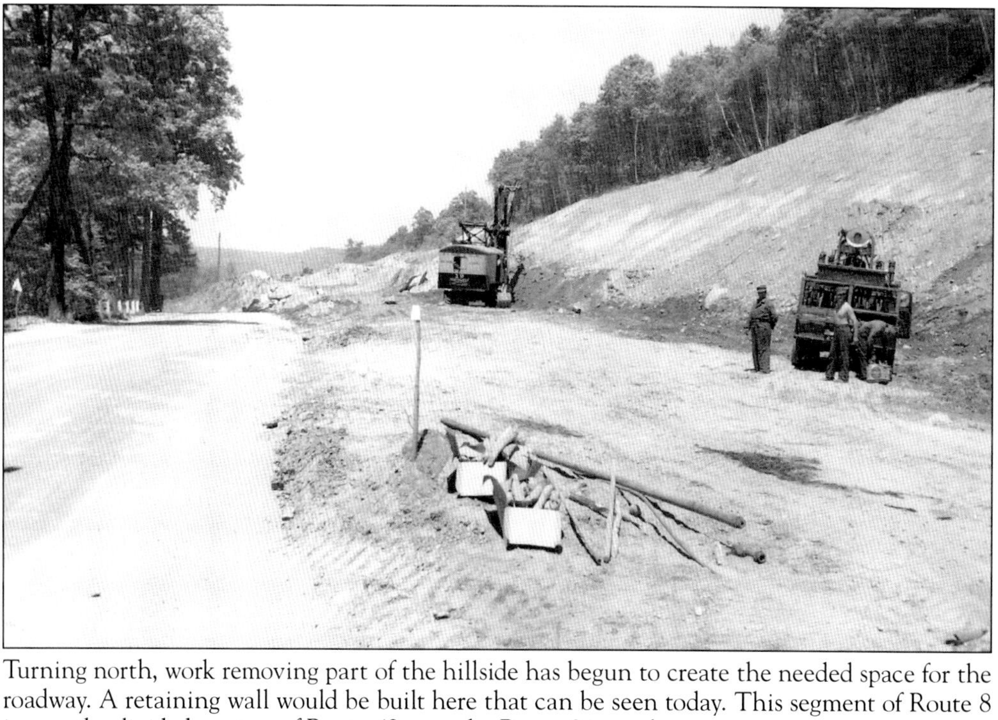

Turning north, work removing part of the hillside has begun to create the needed space for the roadway. A retaining wall would be built here that can be seen today. This segment of Route 8 is now the divided portion of Route 42 near the Route 8 interchange.

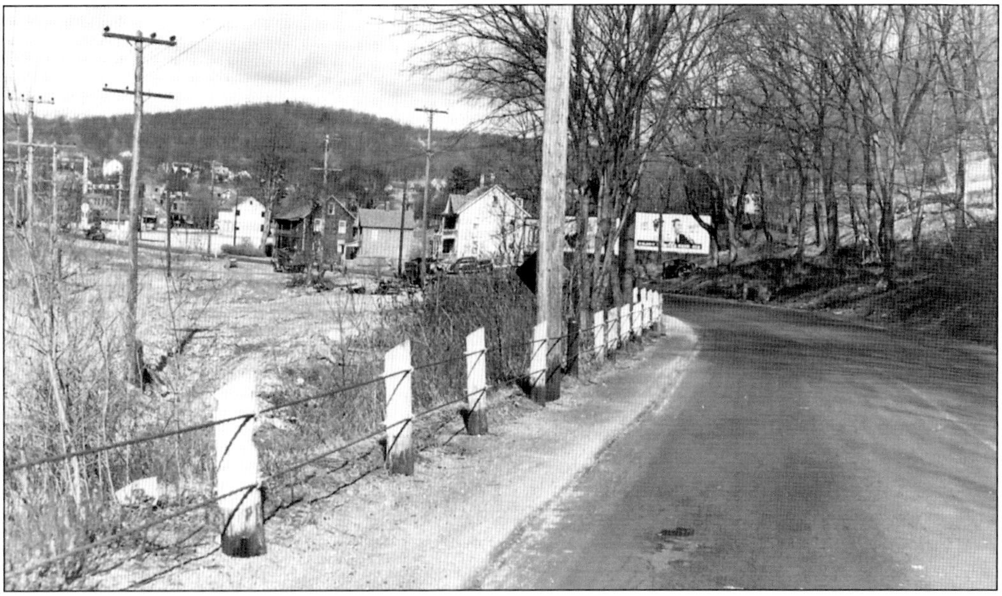

Not much has changed from this vantage point closer to town. This view is from South Main Street looking north. To expand the roadway here, the state will need to dig into the hillside on the left as in the previous photograph. The Bronson Company is at the distant left. (MK.)

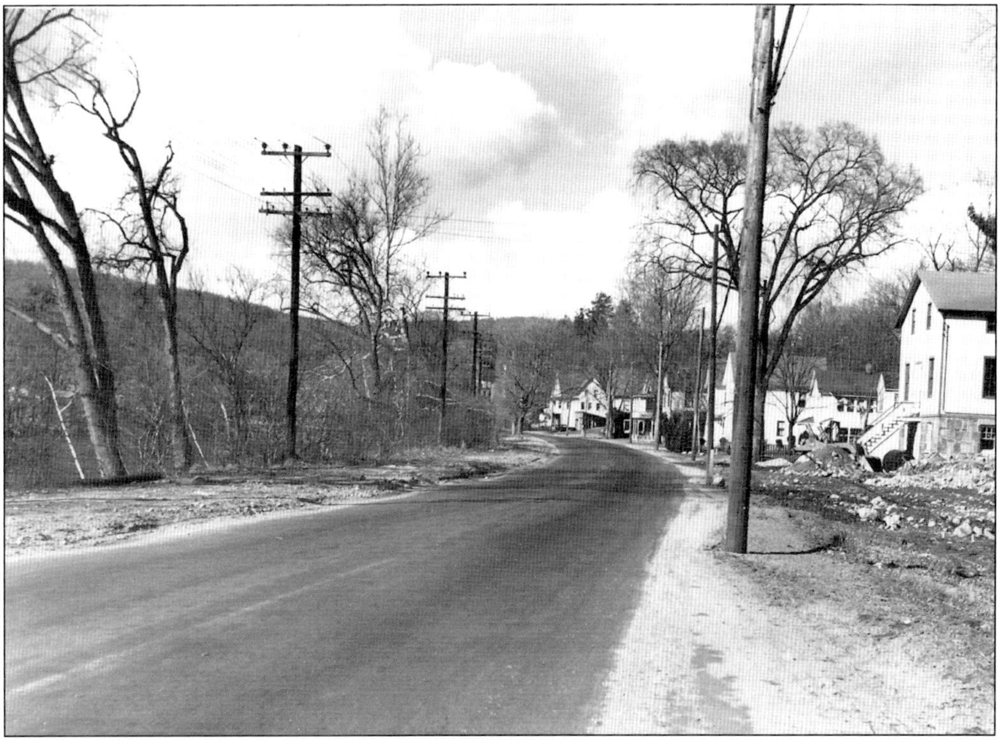

The trolley tracks that once ran down the river side of Main Street on the left are long gone and the land, along with the front yards given up on the right side, provided the necessary real estate to create separate northbound and southbound lanes. The building on the right with the distinctive stone foundation is home to the Beacon Falls Pizza Palace today. (MK.)

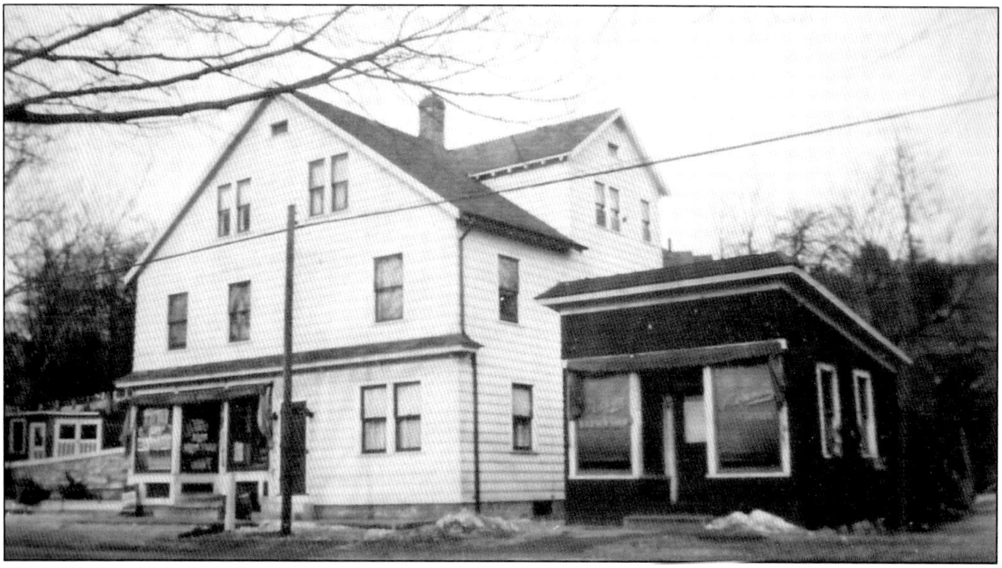

Chicoski's Market is shown on the corner of South Main Street and Feldspar Avenue. The market was started in the early 1930s by Leopold and Bertha Chicoski. The Chicoski family continued to operate the market until the late 1980s. Although now under different management, it continues to operate today as the Beacon Falls Market. The building on the right housed Patsy Mennillo's barbershop.

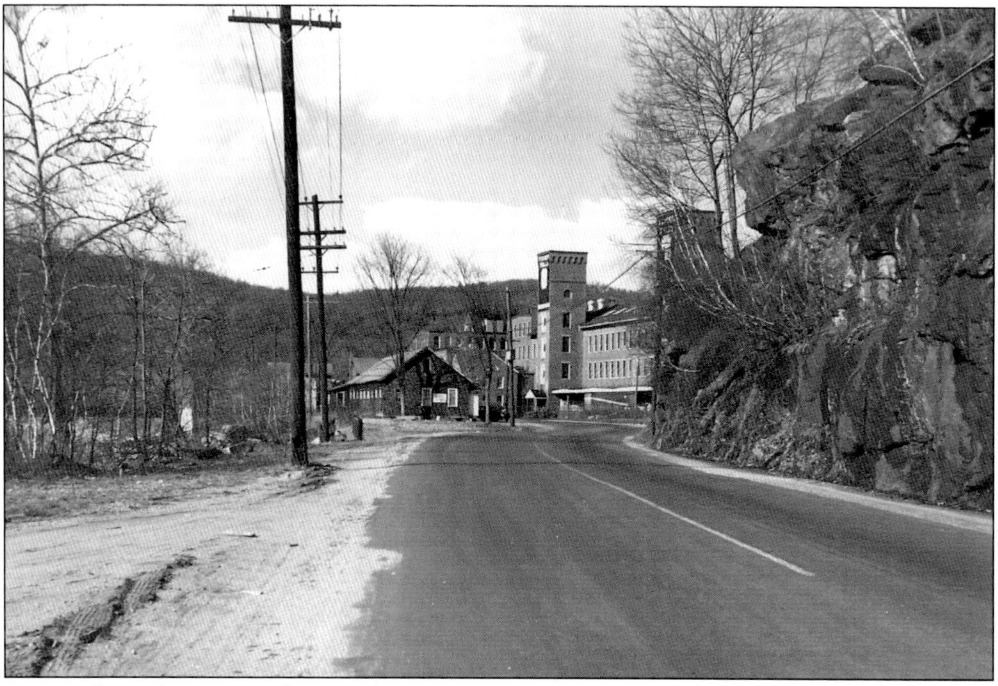

Approaching the center of town, the state was presented with a problem. With rocks on the right and a river and buildings on the left, the original road required an S-curve. To widen and straighten the road, the buildings on the west side of Main Street, seen near the center of this photograph, were moved or demolished, after which no buildings remained alongside the river south of the bridge.

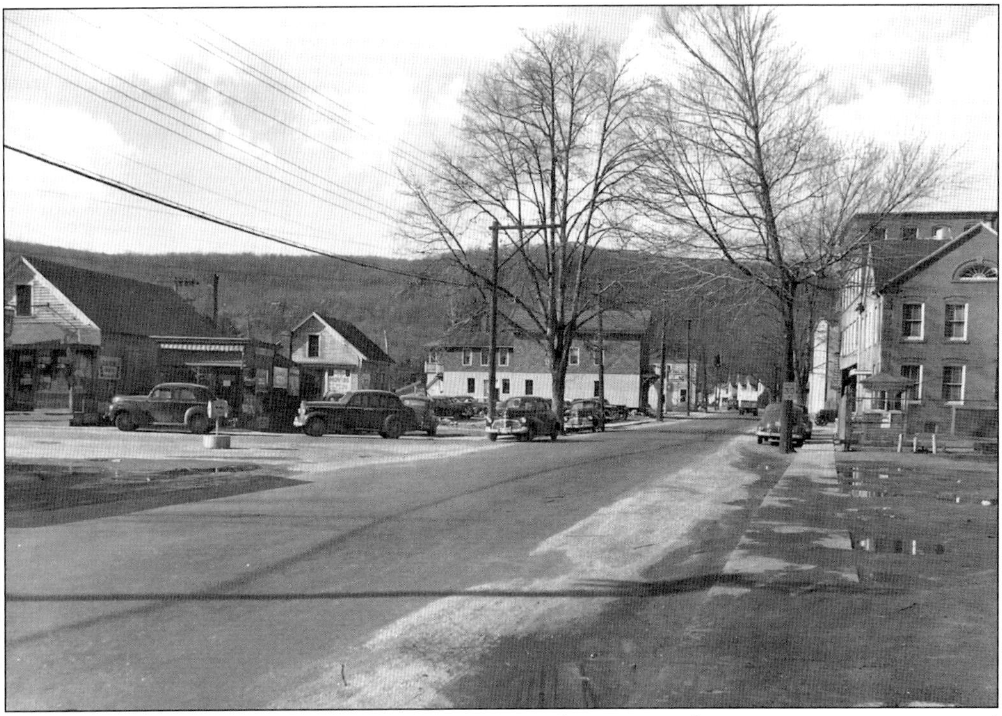

Looking north from the Rubber Shoe Company, the center of town is seen in its original configuration for the last time. When the road was widened, the drugstore on the far left was picked up, rotated, and moved a short distance up North Main Street. The building was deposited across from Burton Road essentially where the Top Notch Theater once stood.

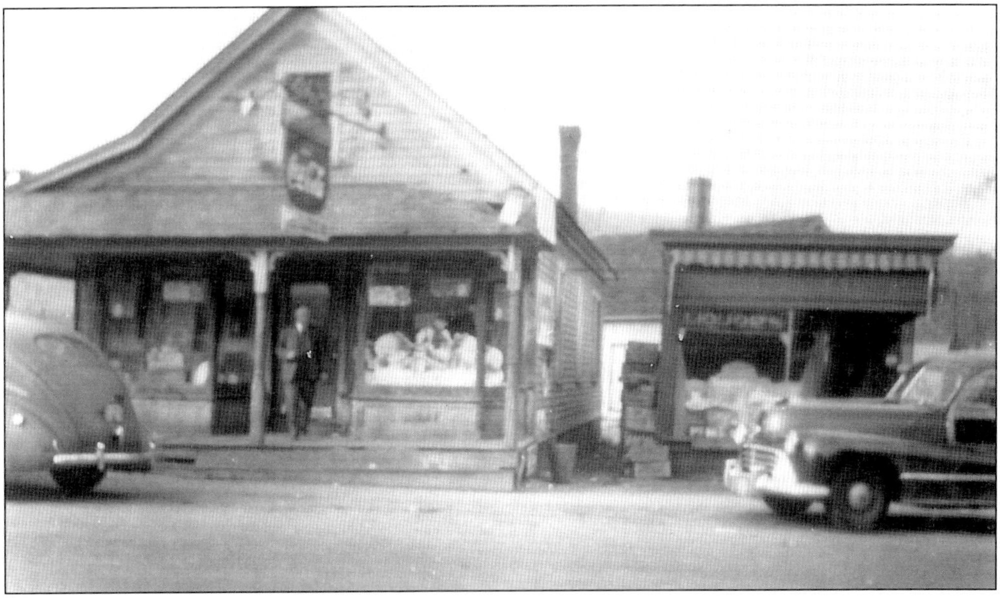

Here is a final look at the drugstore and the liquor store on Depot Street before the big move. Even after the move, the drugstore continued to operate for years as Wilcox's. Several other businesses have operated out of this building, more recently the Trolley Stop Creamery and Beacon Beer & Beverage.

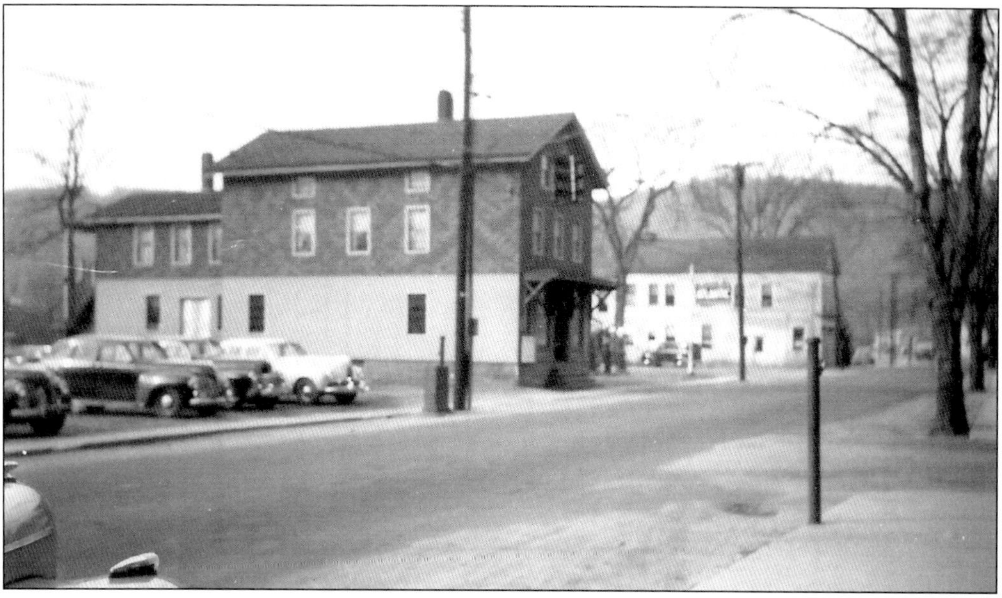

This northward view from the intersection at Burton Road shows Gruber's Store. By the 1930s, the days of the general store were numbered. As the automobile took more and more residents of Beacon Falls to other towns for employment, general stores such as these began to vanish. Gruber's would continue to operate until the death of owner Edward Gruber in 1951.

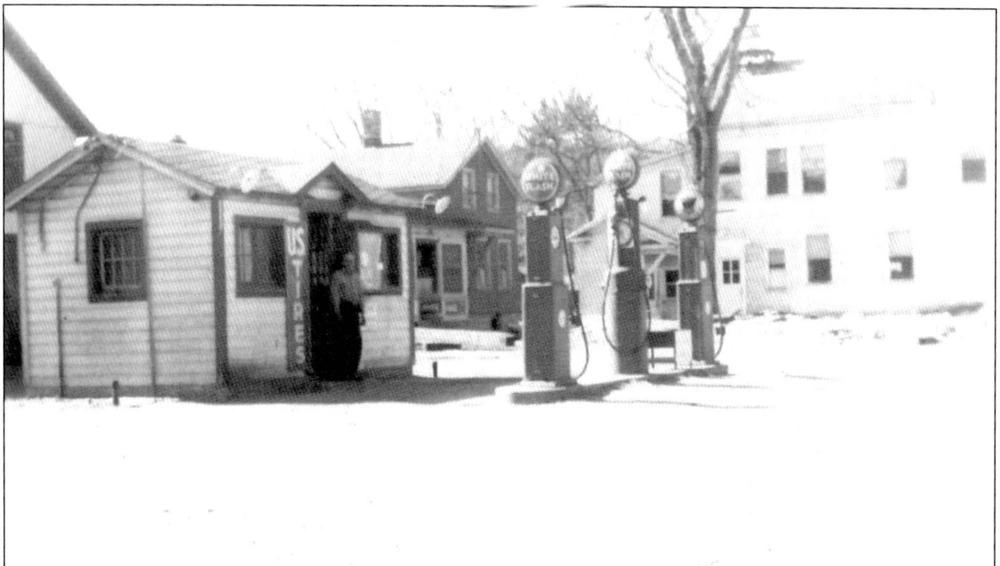

Christian Heiss operated the Atlantic Service Station next door to Gruber's Store. Chris Heiss can be seen in the doorway. The first and second gas pumps are labeled, "White Flash," and the third is labeled, "Atlantic Ethyl Gasoline." Ethyl gasoline was touted for its antiknock characteristics achieved though a tetraethyl lead additive.

At the time of this advertisement, Chris Heiss was also serving his first of two stints as first selectman of Beacon Falls; he was first selectman once in 1935 and again in 1937. Jones Garage was located in the building immediately behind the Atlantic Service Station.

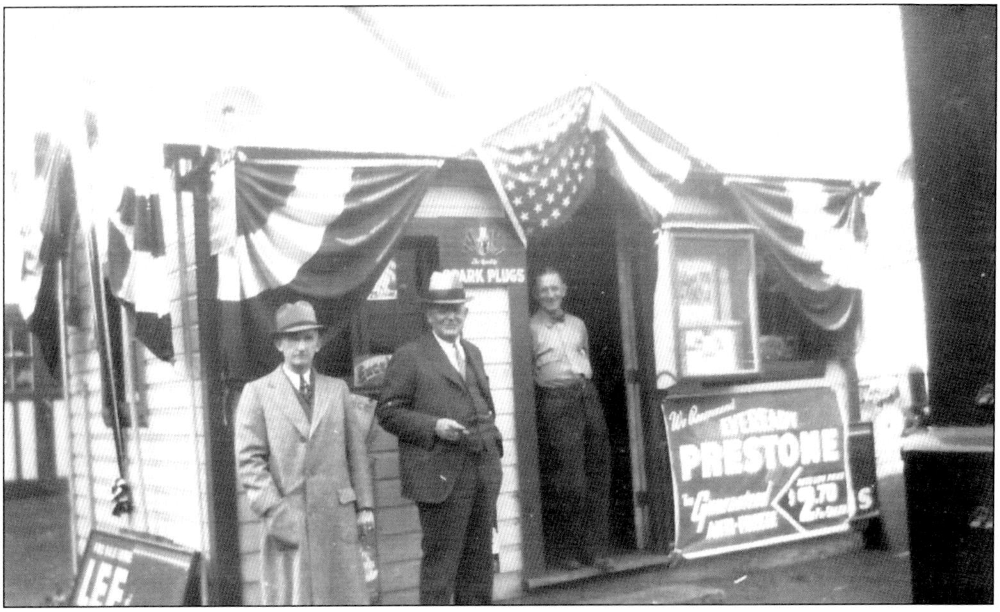

Chris Heiss stands in the doorway of the Atlantic Service Station. The two distinguished gentlemen and patriotic draping may be related to the dedication of the new bridge in 1935. The location of the service station next to Gruber's Store no doubt had something to do with the fact that Chris was married to Ed Gruber's only daughter, Charlotte. (MH.)

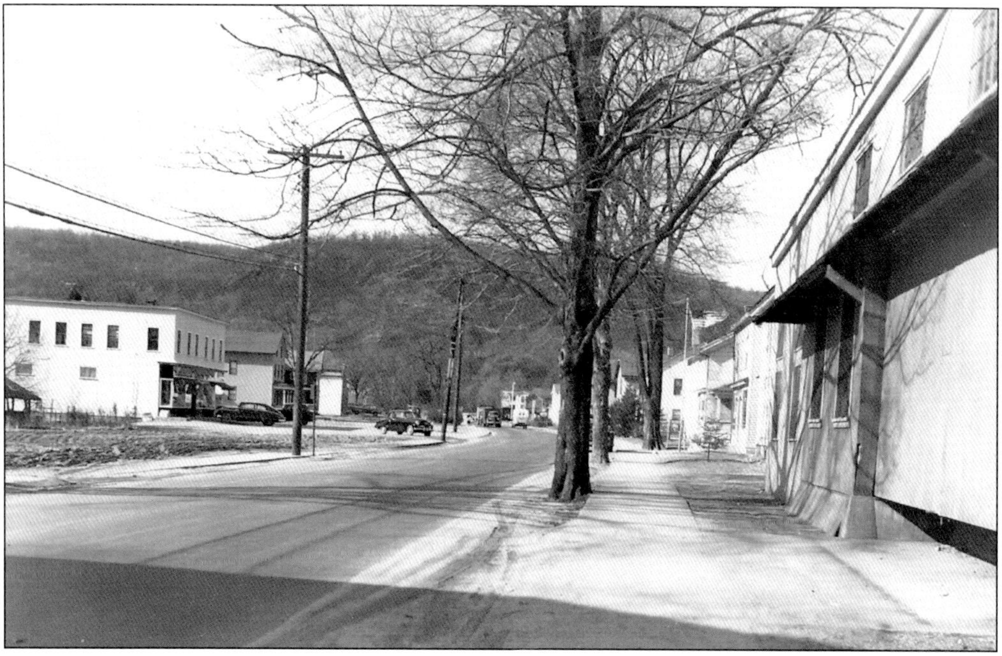

North of the bridge, there was little extra space to expand the width of Main Street. Rather than demolish the buildings on the left, the state decided to move them closer to the river. This view is just beyond Burton Road. The buildings on the left have already been moved back. The warehouse on the right was demolished in the 1980s. The land is now home to the Beacon Falls Pharmacy.

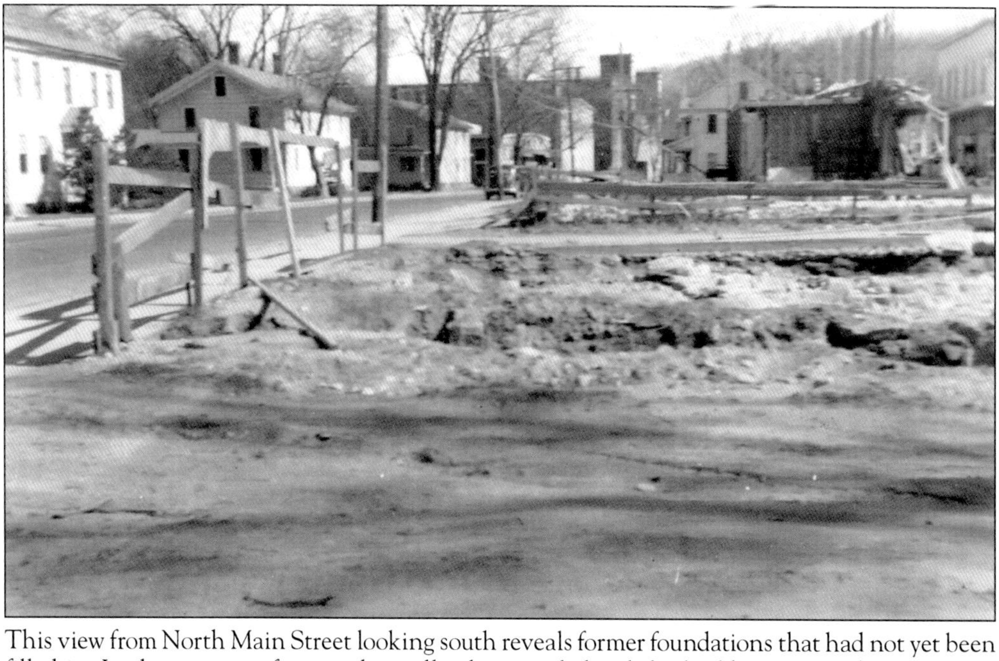

This view from North Main Street looking south reveals former foundations that had not yet been filled in. In this section of town, the trolley line ran behind the buildings west of Main Street next to the river. With the trolley line gone, its right-of-way was utilized when these buildings were pushed back closer to the river. The on-ramp to Route 8 North is near this spot today.

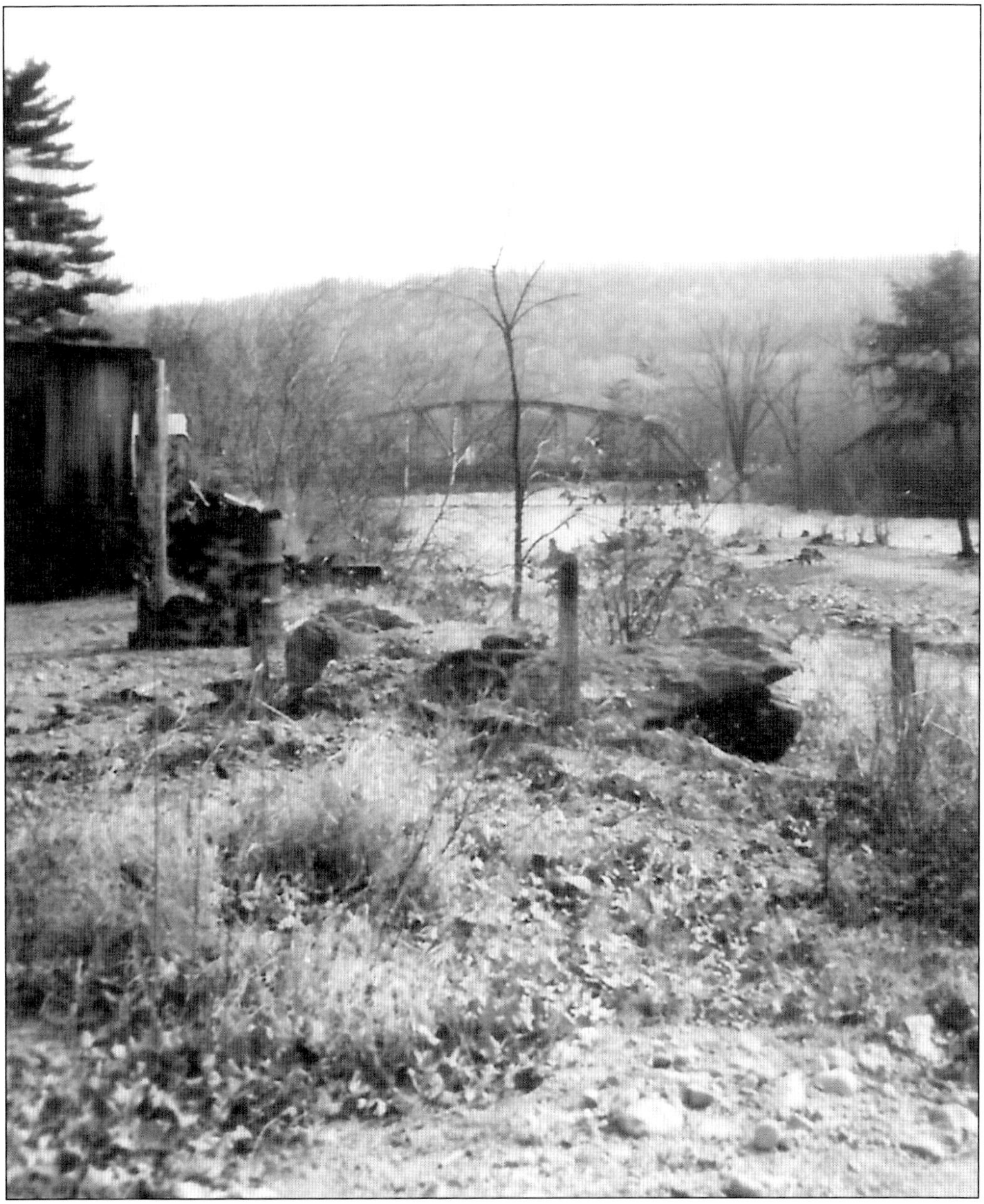

In this view of the Naugatuck River and the steel bridge from north of town, any evidence of the trolley line that once ran through this spot has been erased. In retrospect, moving the buildings along North Main Street closer to the river was both unnecessary and unfortunate. A flood would soon put these buildings in peril because of erosion of the riverbank, and a highway bypass west of here would later render the divided Main Street unnecessary. One would imagine that the Naugatuck River would be an ideal location for fishing, but alas, by the time this photograph was taken, the fish population in the Naugatuck River had been severely impacted by the major levels of industrial production north of here. Byproducts of chemical, rubber, and brass manufacture so severely polluted this river that fishing in it would have been considered foolhardy. Thankfully, river restoration and stocking projects in recent years have allowed the river to recover to a point that fly-fishing for Atlantic salmon is once again possible.

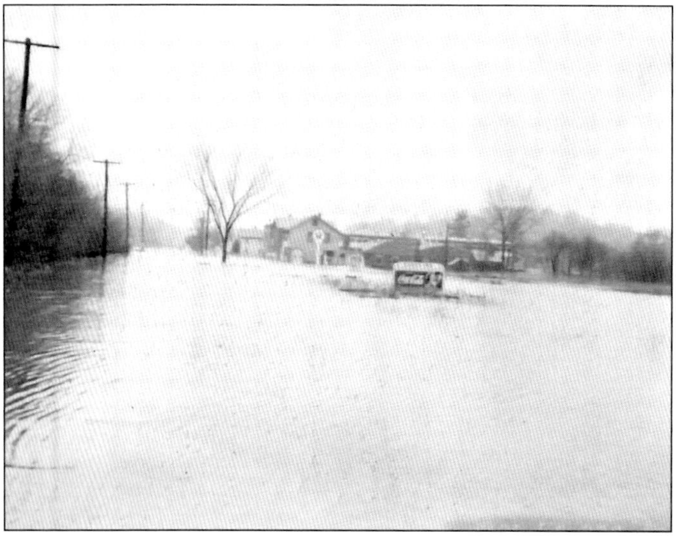

Living in close proximity to the Naugatuck River was not without its risks. In December 1948, the Naugatuck River overflowed its banks after as much as 13 inches of rain fell over the Hudson and Housatonic River basins in western Massachusetts. The effect of all this rain was felt in the Naugatuck Valley as well. This view looking south shows the flooding that occurred on Route 8 on the Beacon Falls–Seymour line.

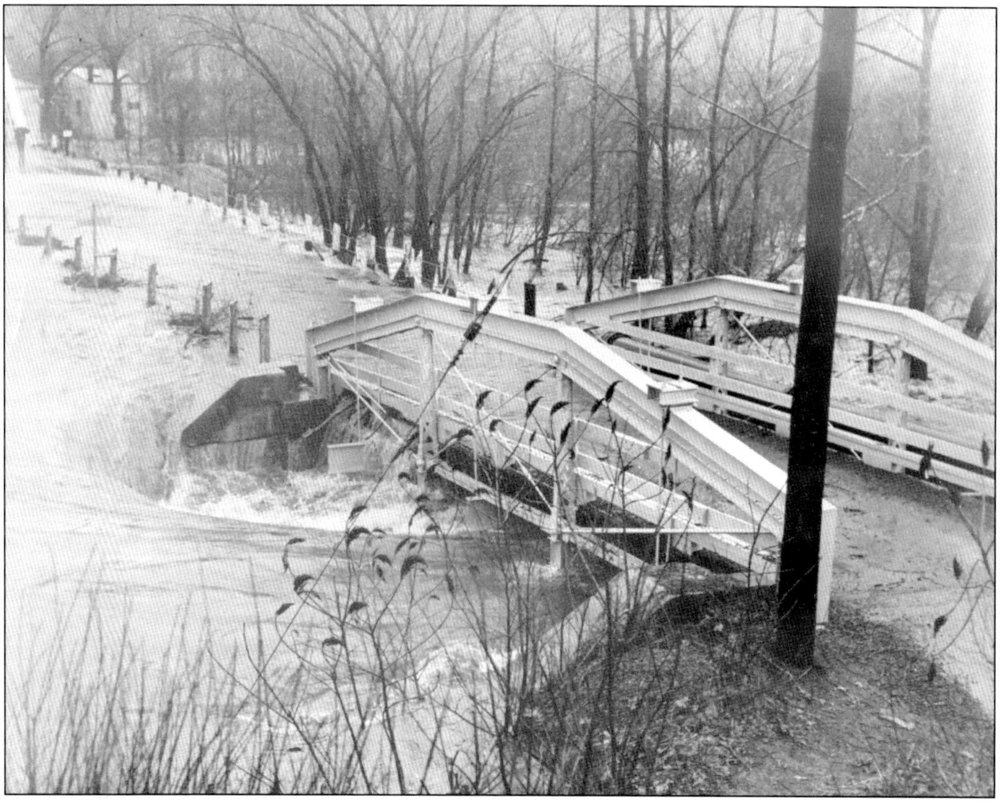

This photograph dated December 31, 1948, shows Pines Bridge viewed from the west shore during the flooding. Pines Bridge was always susceptible to high water on the Naugatuck River because of its modest clearance. Pines Bridge, one of the earliest river crossings in the area, utilized an island in the middle of the river to connect the overpass in the foreground to a steel girder span.

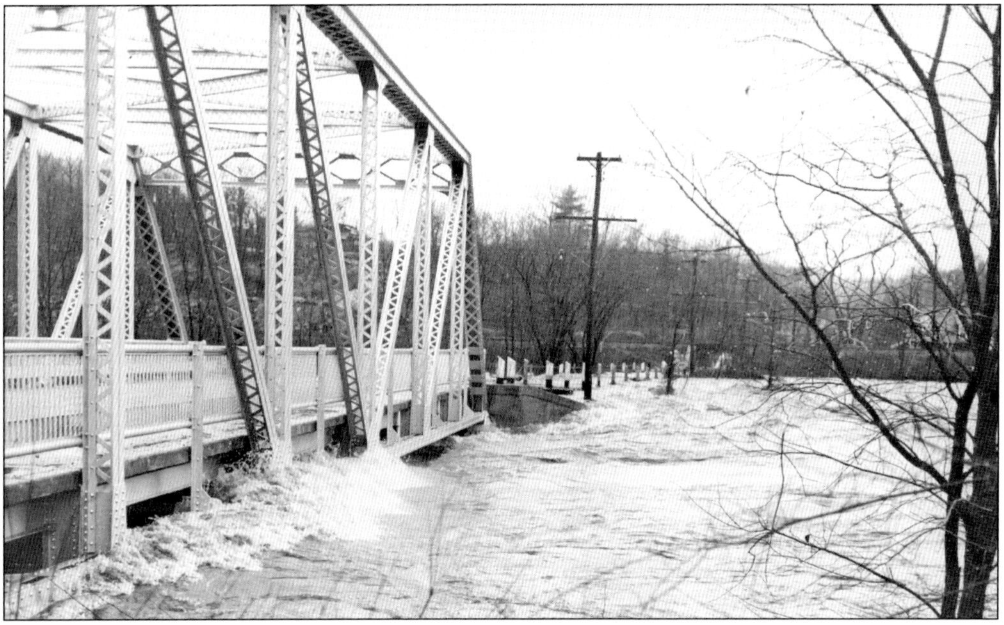

This view is of Pines Bridge from the east side of the Naugatuck River. The steel bridge in the foreground survived the 1948 flood, but the overpass in the distance did not. This storm was classified as a 100-year storm, meaning that a storm of this magnitude can be expected to occur only once in 100 years. This classification would soon prove to be greatly in error.

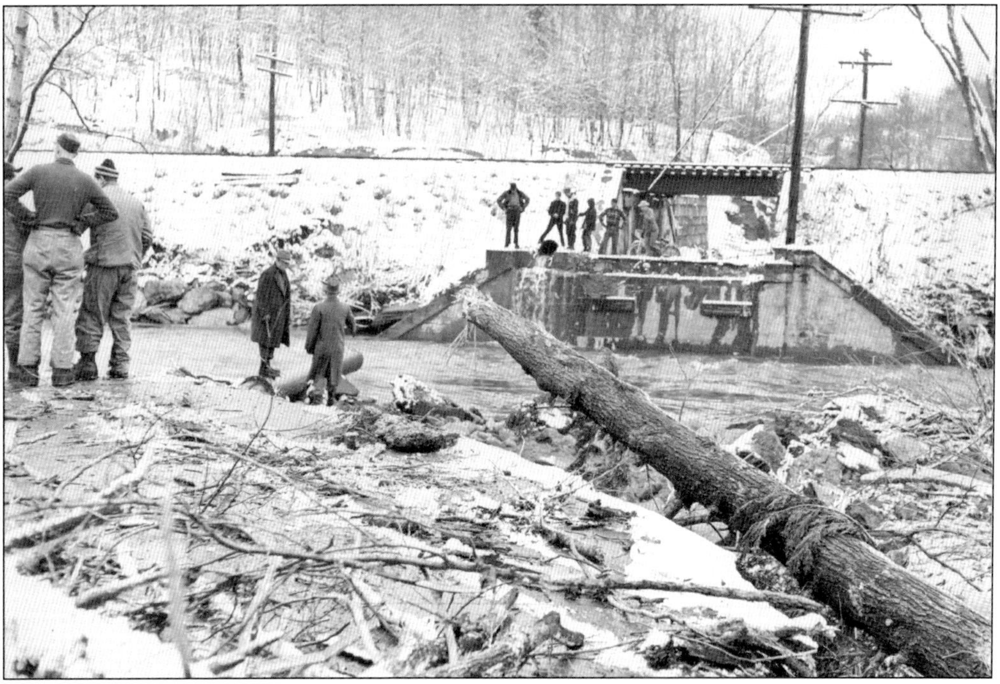

Not much remains of Pines Bridge in this view looking west after the December 1948 flood. It was unusual to experience flooding at this time of year. The Naugatuck River typically experiences its highest flows in the spring when snowmelt from the Litchfield Hills combines with heavy spring rains. Pines Bridge would be quickly returned to its original state, at least for the time being.

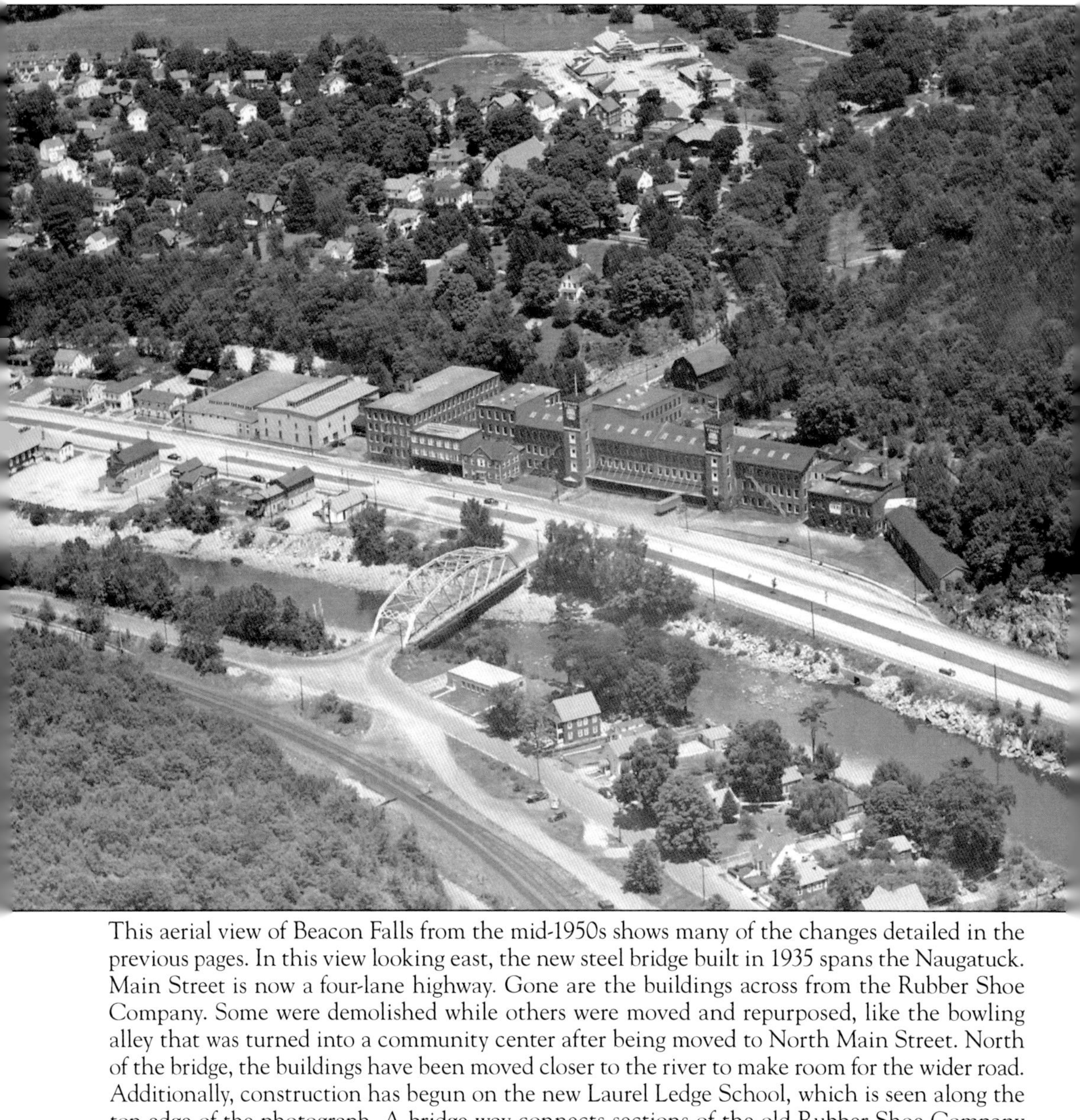

This aerial view of Beacon Falls from the mid-1950s shows many of the changes detailed in the previous pages. In this view looking east, the new steel bridge built in 1935 spans the Naugatuck. Main Street is now a four-lane highway. Gone are the buildings across from the Rubber Shoe Company. Some were demolished while others were moved and repurposed, like the bowling alley that was turned into a community center after being moved to North Main Street. North of the bridge, the buildings have been moved closer to the river to make room for the wider road. Additionally, construction has begun on the new Laurel Ledge School, which is seen along the top edge of the photograph. A bridge-way connects sections of the old Rubber Shoe Company building over Burton Road. Built in 1916, the bridges would last until the renovations of the factory building in 1986.

Seven

FLOOD

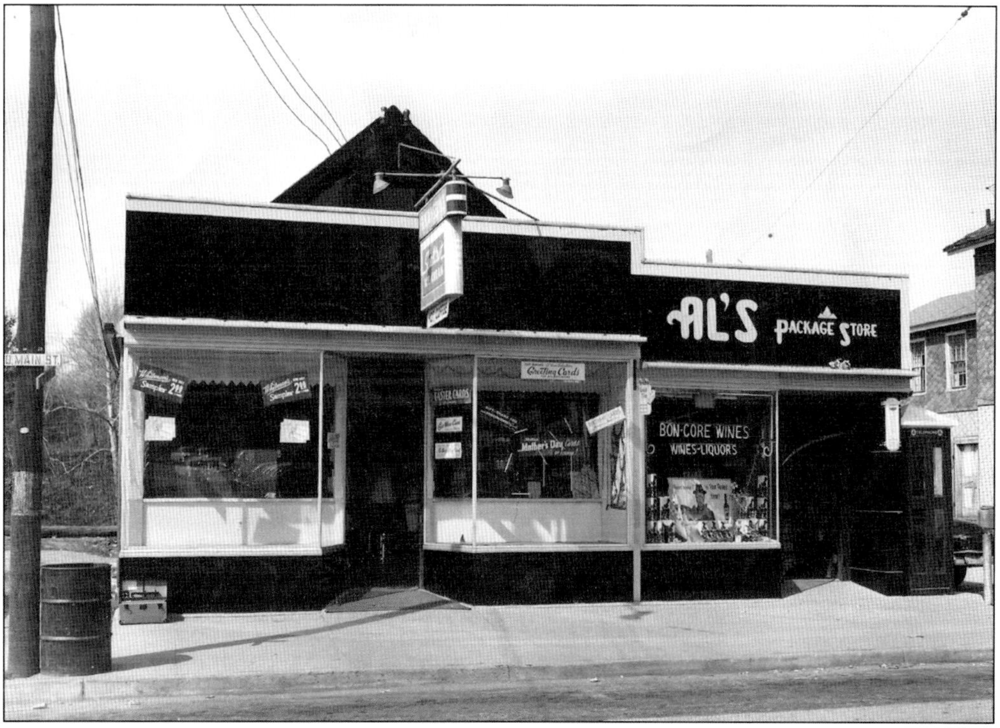

Numerous times in recorded history, the Naugatuck River pushed over its banks. But never has it done so with such destructive force as it did on August 19, 1955. The 1955 flood is still considered the greatest Connecticut disaster. This view of Wilcox's Drugstore was taken on May 4, 1955. The building, which was earlier moved, is now facing Main Street and sports a new Art Deco facade.

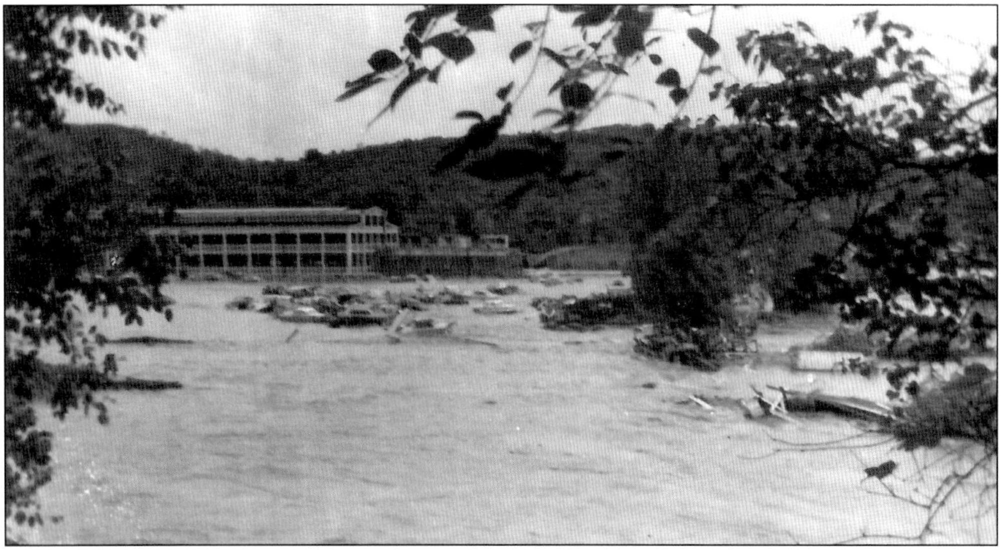

In August 1955, Connecticut was struck by two hurricanes: Connie on August 12 and Diane on August 19. Neither storm brought the damaging winds associated with hurricanes, but what they did bring was rain—and lots of it. The rivers of Connecticut could not hold the volume of water that funneled into them. In this view, the cars in the parking lot are being carried away by the swollen Naugatuck River. (BK.)

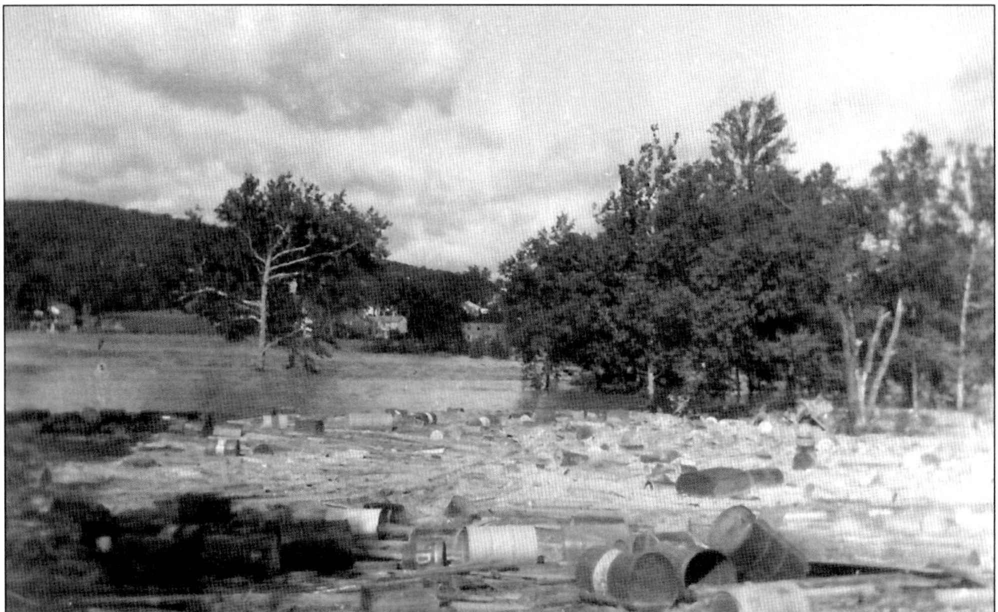

Hurricanes Connie and Diane delivered a one-two punch, dropping over 20 inches of rain on western Connecticut. After severely damaging the cities of Thomaston and Waterbury, the floodwaters struck Naugatuck, home of the Naugatuck Chemical plant. Naugatuck Chemical, whose origins trace back to the Goodyear rubber factories located nearby, sat right alongside the river. These 55-gallon drums are no doubt from the Naugatuck Chemical plant. Washed into the river by rising waters, these drums would become battering rams for the bridges and houses south of here. (BK.)

After leaving Naugatuck, the floodwaters passed through the High Rock area and entered Beacon Falls. The old dam that once provided turbine power to the woolen mill and the Beacon Falls Rubber Shoe Company was still here. In this southward view near Exit 25, Route 8 disappears into the water. Ultimately, the dam, which was no longer used, was destroyed by the rushing water, fragments of which remained visible to passing cars for decades. (BK.)

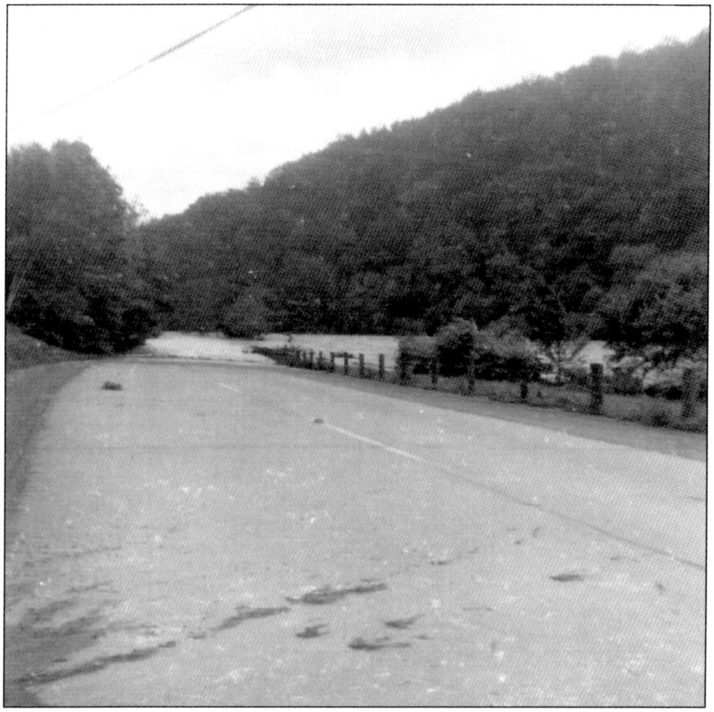

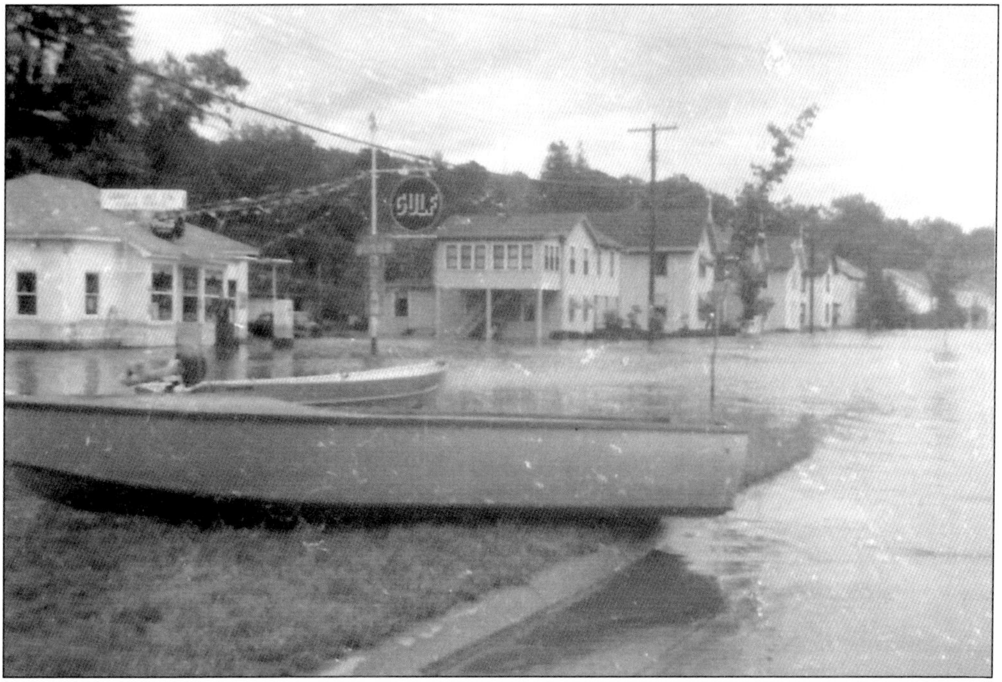

Here, the island on North Main Street between northbound and southbound lanes has its own marina. Many residents of the Naugatuck Valley had to take it upon themselves to rescue neighbors whose homes were surrounded by water. Helicopters from Sikorsky Aircraft in Stratford could be seen crisscrossing the sky, engaged in rescue operations. Over 500 people in the Waterbury and Naugatuck areas needed to be airlifted to safety. (BK.)

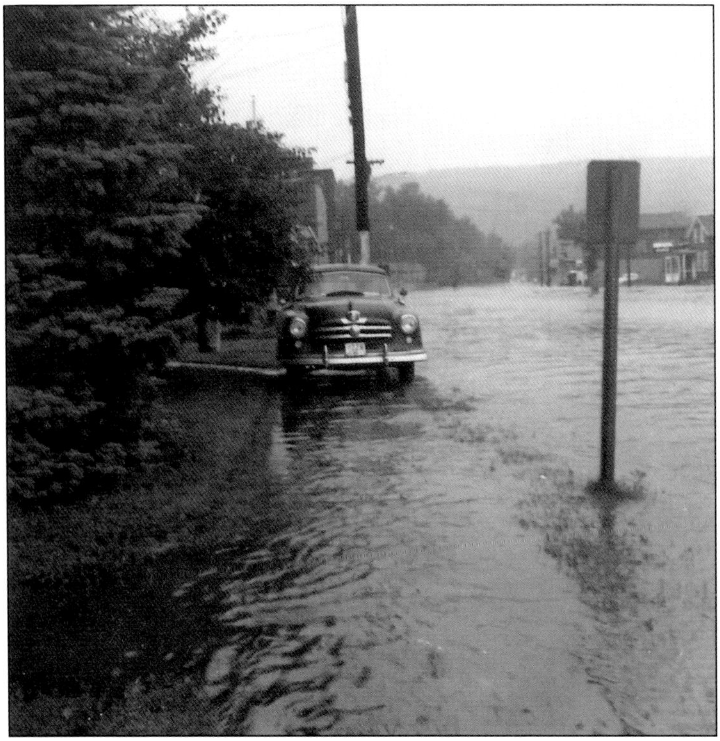

Here is another view from North Main Street looking south. The former Gruber's Store can be seen behind the street sign. A 1951 Nash Rambler appears to be stranded on the sidewalk. With Main Street flooded and floodwaters rising, this car may not have escaped. (BK.)

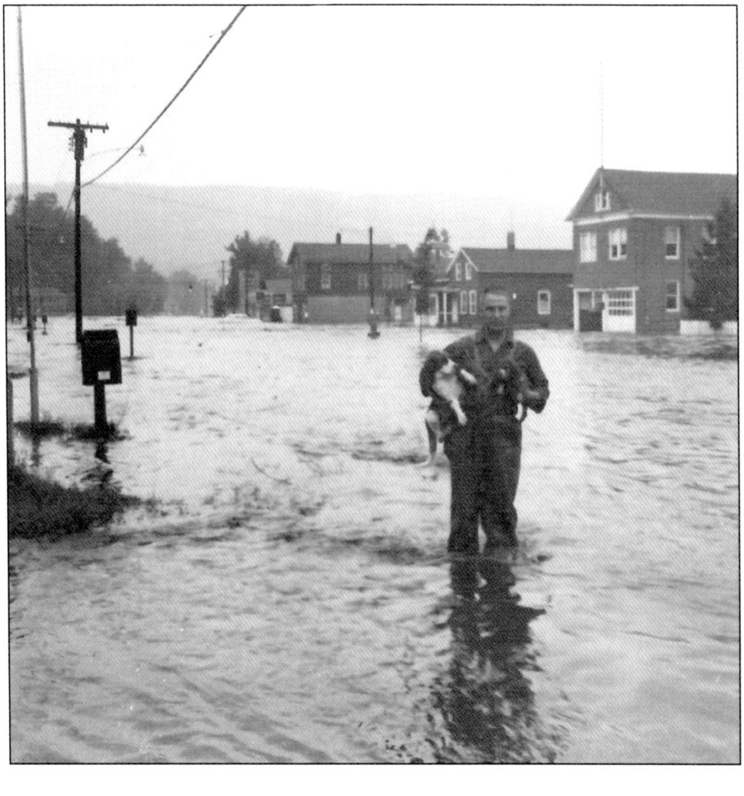

With Main Street now completely submerged, a Beacon Falls fireman holds a dog rescued from the water. Now emptied of vehicles, the firehouse can be seen in the distant right. It is interesting to observe how swiftly the knee-deep water is flowing in this area. Considerable damage was done to foundations along Main Street by this flow of water. (BK.)

The Beacon Hose Company is right in the middle of the action as the Naugatuck River spreads across Main Street. By this time, it must have been evident that the ladder and rescue vehicles inside the building were in imminent danger. (BK.)

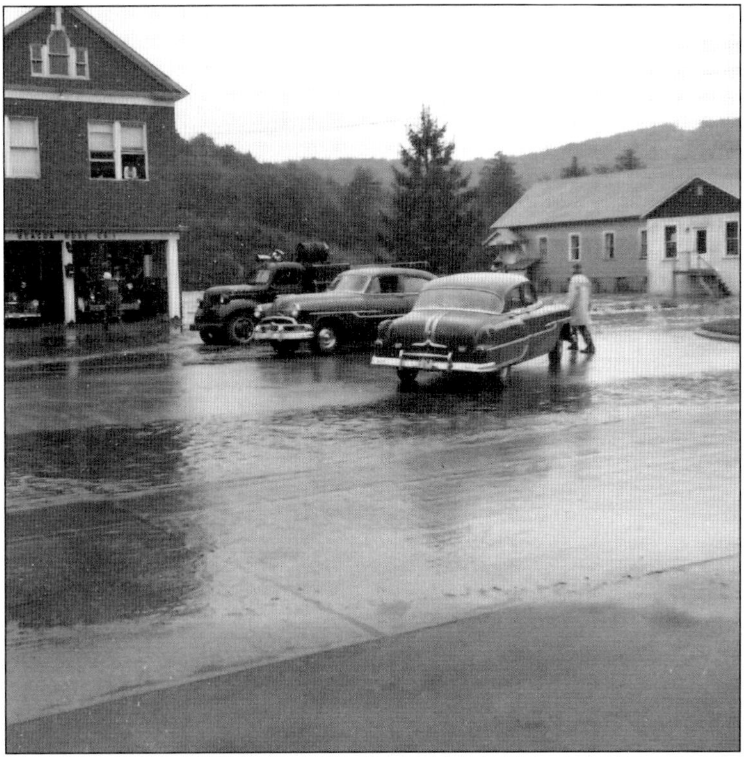

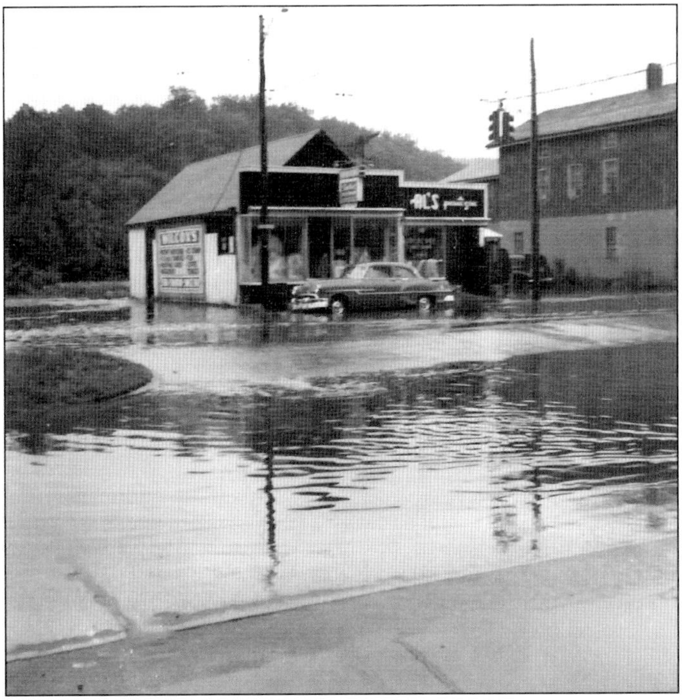

Closer to the bridge, Wilcox's Drugstore is also feeling the effects of the flood. The trunk is open on this 1953 Pontiac. No doubt people are trying to salvage whatever they can from these buildings. The escape route up Burton Road where this photograph was taken is still clear, as evidenced by the dry sidewalk in the foreground. (BK.)

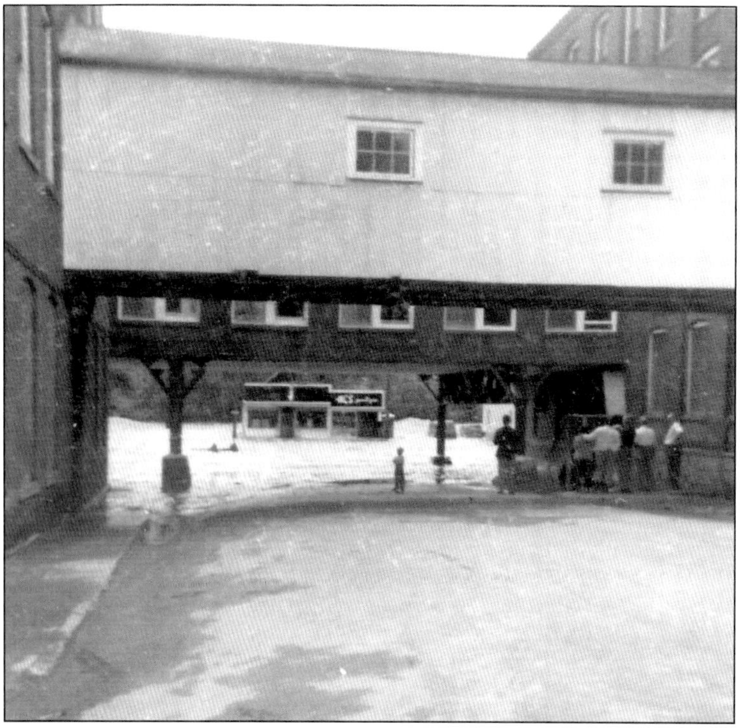

In what has to be the most photographed flood scene in Beacon Falls, Wilcox's Drugstore is seen framed by the buildings and bridges of the Rubber Shoe Company at the end of Burton Road. At nearly the height of the flood, sightseers gather to check out a natural disaster. The factory buildings were now used exclusively as warehouse space for US Rubber in Naugatuck. (BK.)

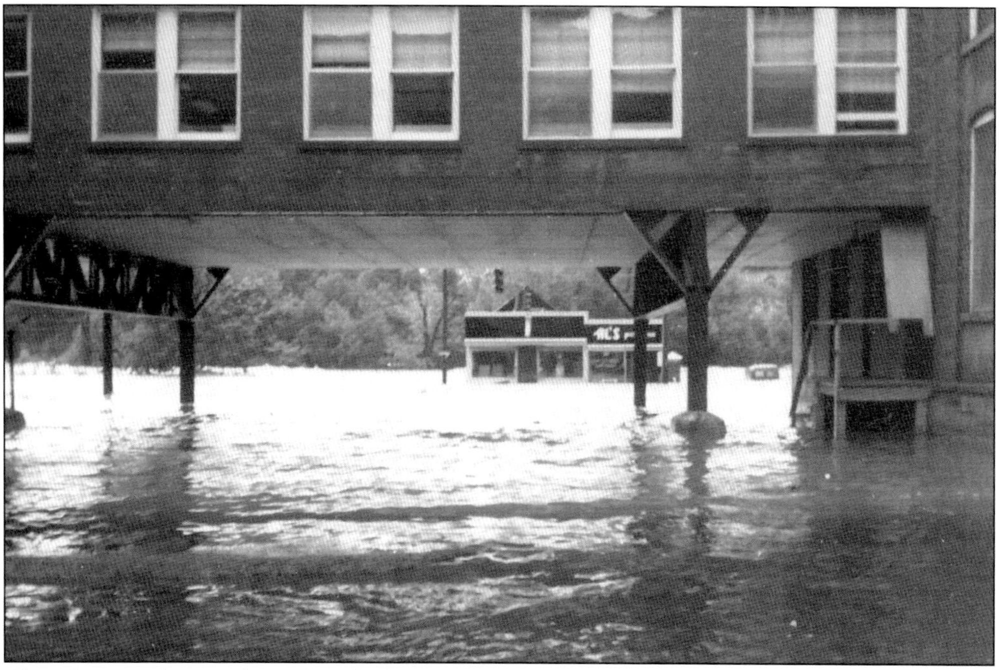

This photograph provides a closer look at the intersection of Main Street and Burton Road. The water level is approaching waist deep in the drugstore. The rear windows of a delivery van, nearly submerged, can be seen to the right of Al's Package Store. (BK.)

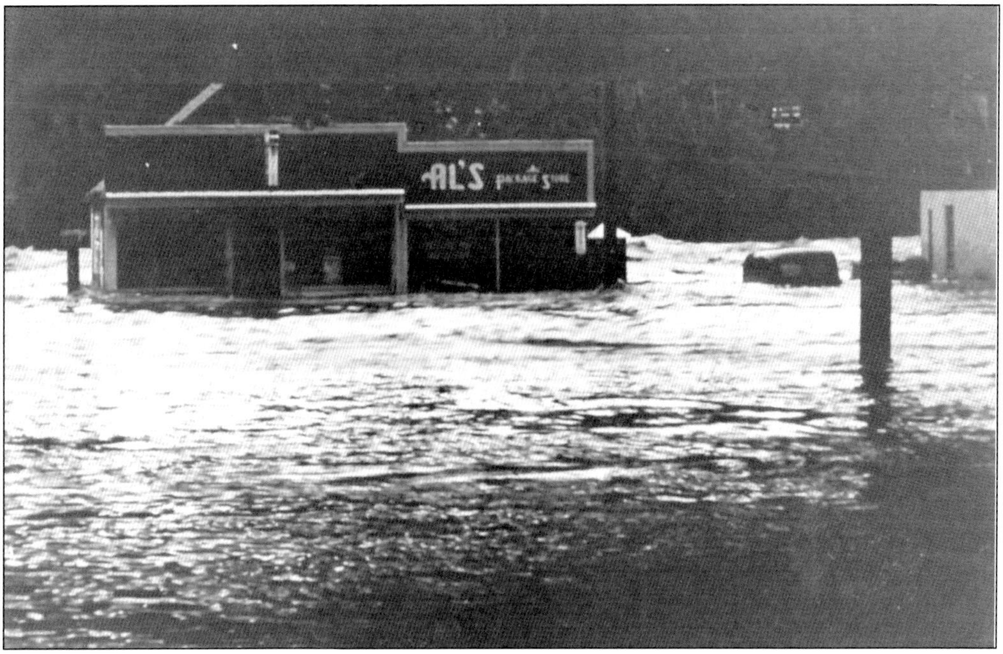

This view shows how turbulent the water was behind the drugstore. The churning was caused by the water not being able to flow freely under the steel bridge just to the left and out of view in this photograph. The water's action would do considerable damage to the riverbank behind Wilcox's Drugstore. (BK.)

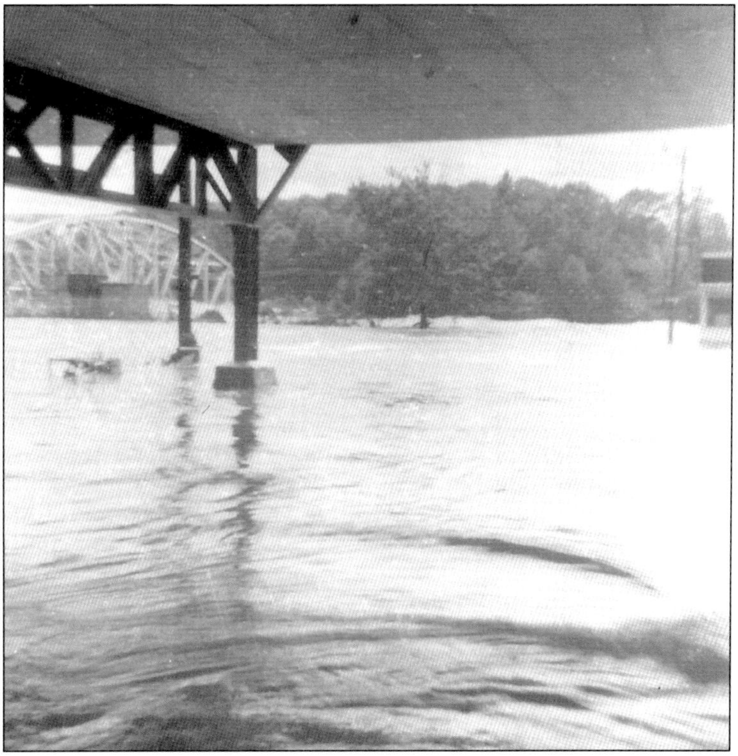

Despite the loss of many bridges throughout the valley, the steel bridge in Beacon Falls miraculously survived. This photograph shows the bridge holding on against the flow of water and debris. Many bridges were knocked down not just by the water, but also by floating remnants of upstream devastation moving downstream. The bridges trapped the debris, causing the water to build up. This created tremendous pressure on the bridges.

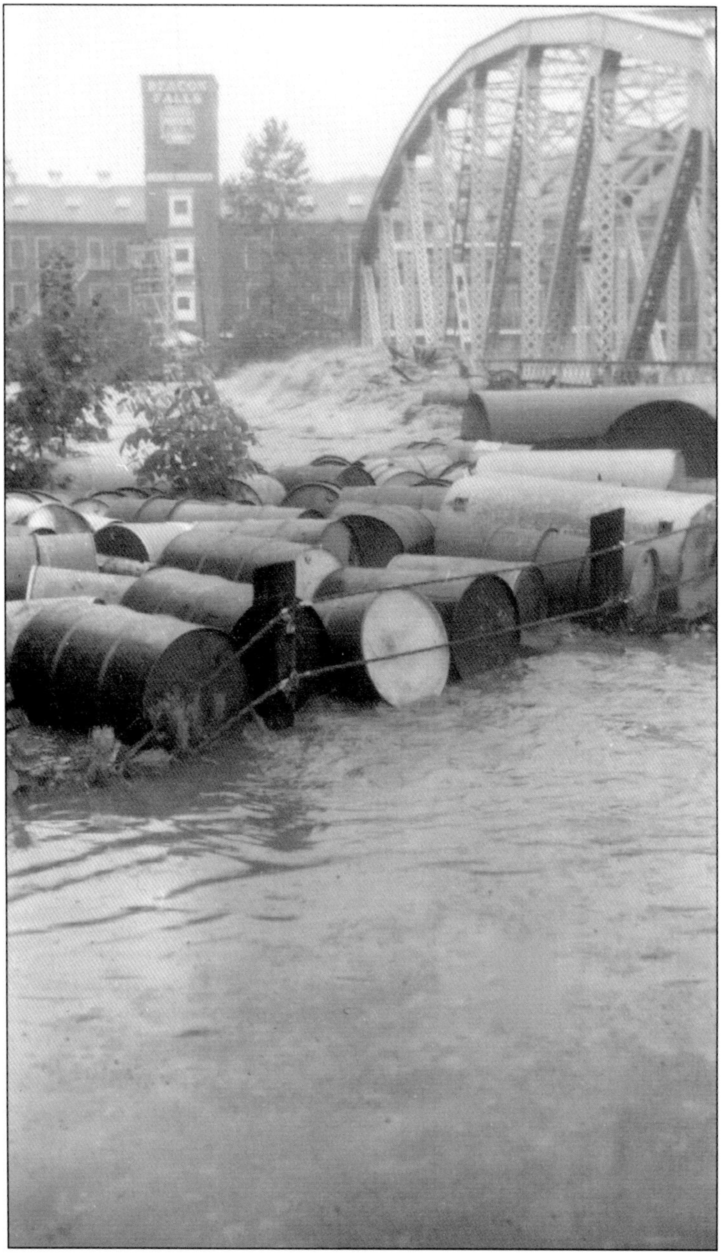

By 7:00 a.m. on August 19, the water from the Naugatuck River was already flowing over—not under—Pines Bridge, and the water was still rising. Here in the center of town, the steel bridge is dealing with a different problem, a build-up of pressure that threatens to take it down. As can clearly be seen in this view looking east from Railroad Avenue, a wall of water churning on the side of the bridge is pushing against trapped debris. Photographs of the bridge after the flood reveal damage to the railings in this area. One can speculate that water flowing around the bridge down Main Street and Railroad Avenue helped to reduce the pressure on the bridge somewhat and prevented its collapse. Of note are the scattered 55-gallon drums resting on the river's edge. Likely full of toxic chemicals, these almost certainly came from the Naugatuck Chemical plant three miles north of here.

At the foot of Feldspar Avenue, this view looks north back toward the steel bridge. The two men with rolled-up pant legs survey the vast floodwaters that fill the valley. The White Swan Grill on the right, whose foundation is most certainly flooded, is now the Full Harvest Bar and Grill. (BK.)

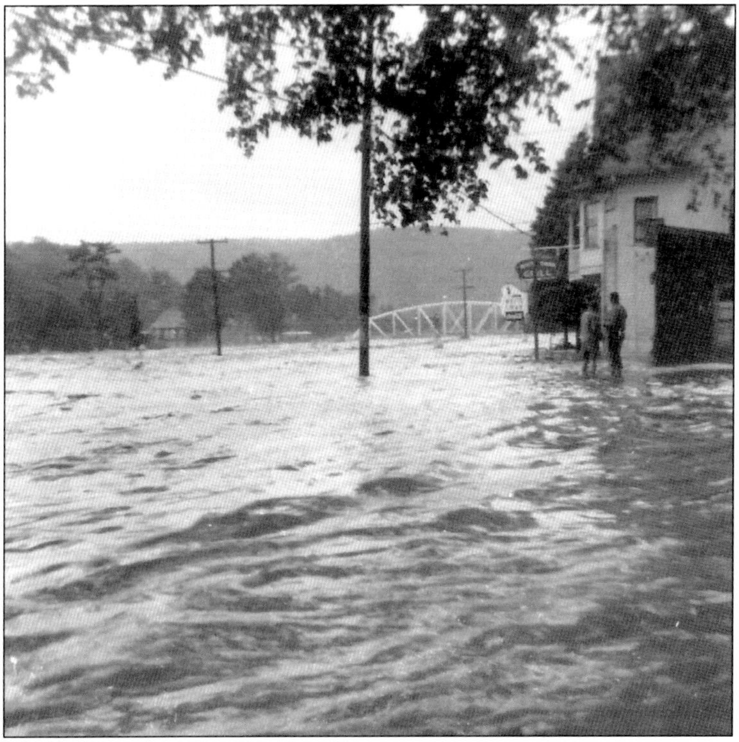

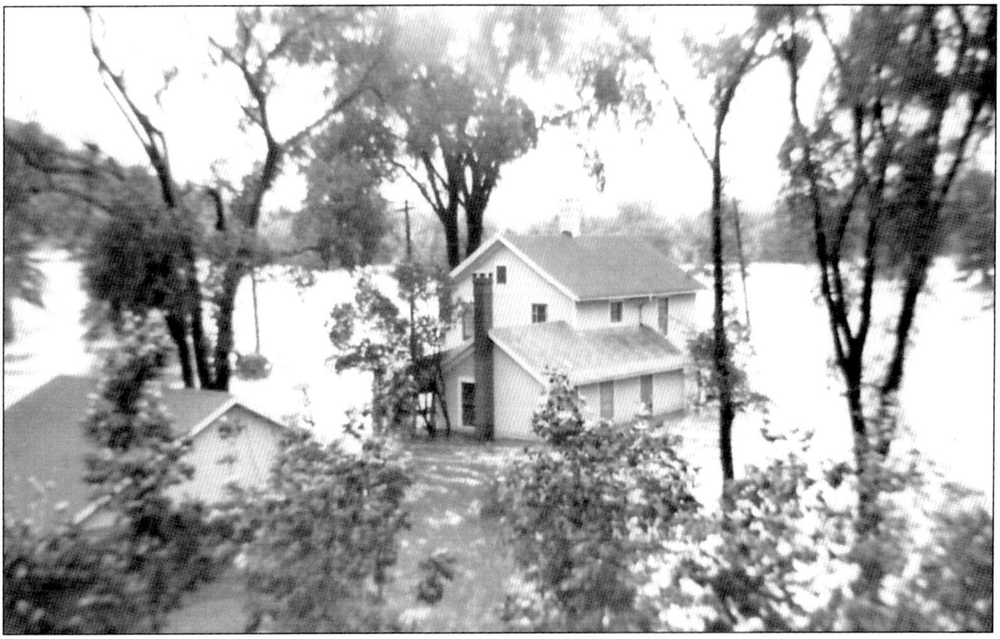

Another excellent vantage point for viewing the flood was at the base of Bethany Road. In this view looking north, a house is seen with the basement and first floor flooded. This house would survive the flood but was demolished to make way for the Naugatuck Valley Savings and Loan many years later. (BK.)

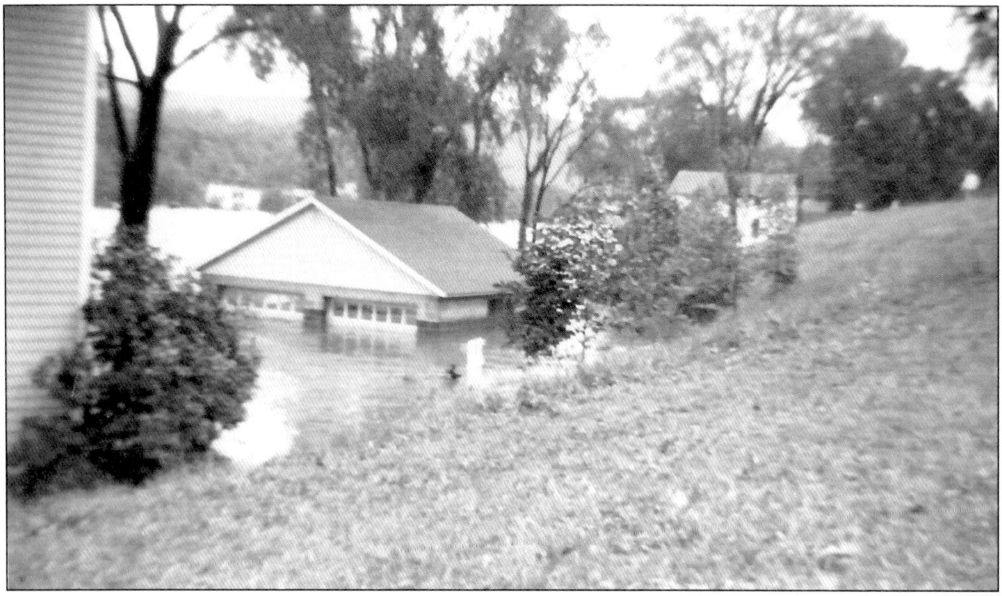

Like the house next door seen in the previous image, this house on the corner of Bethany Road and Main Street suffered similar damage. It was restored and remains occupied to this day. The vastness of the flooding is evident in this view to the north toward the center of town with nothing but water as far as the eye can see. (BK.)

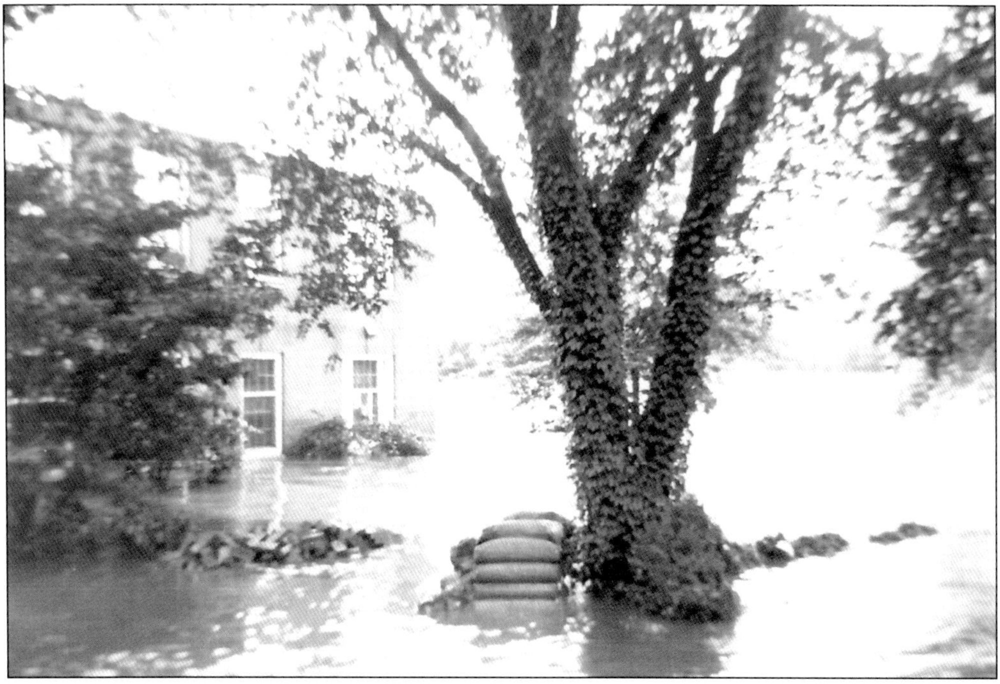

The Homer D. Bronson Company main office is shown in this view from Bethany Road. At the time of the flood, a second story was being added to the building. What appear to be sandbags are likely bags of mortar being used for the brickwork. Unlike the Rubber Shoe Company buildings north of here, the Bronson Company was an active factory. After the flood, a brass plaque was mounted inside the front door to record the high-water mark. (BK.)

Farther south is the Pines Bridge section of town. Located at a bend in the Naugatuck River, this section took a direct hit from the floodwaters, which resulted in some of the most serious damage in town occurring here. In the distance, only the second story of a home shows above the waterline. (BK.)

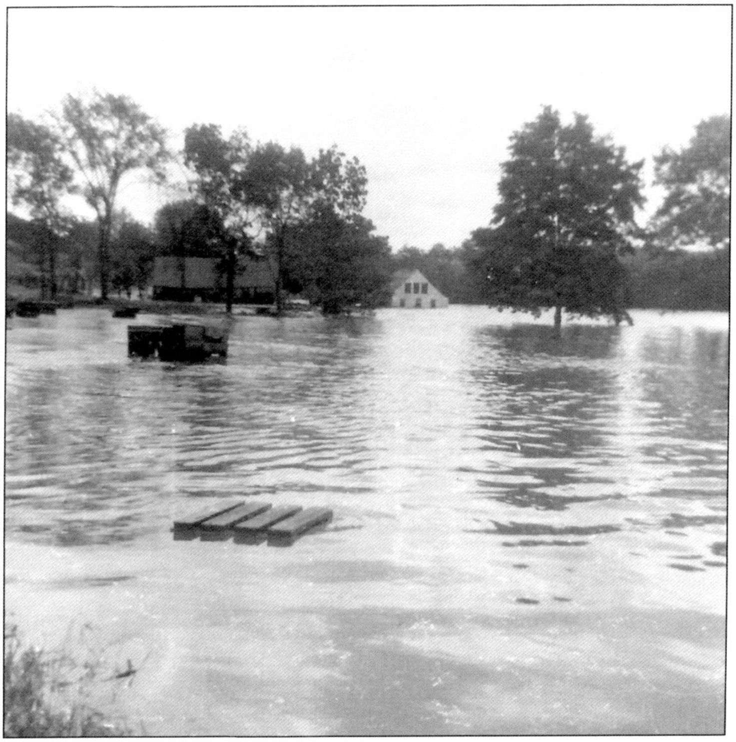

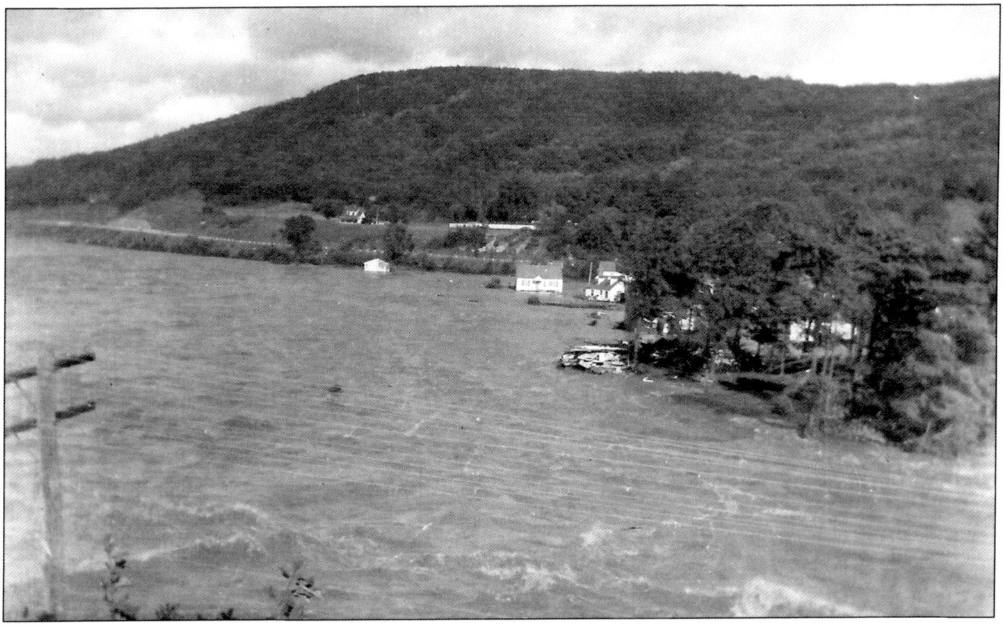

This view from the Naugatuck line railroad tracks on the west side of the river shows the Pines Bridge neighborhood fully under water. Today, this area sits adjacent to the southbound Route 8 on-ramp at Exit 23. Pines Bridge itself is slightly to the right of the view in this photograph. Only six years earlier, the bridge underwent significant renovation after the New Year's flood of 1948, only to be swamped again in 1955. (BK.)

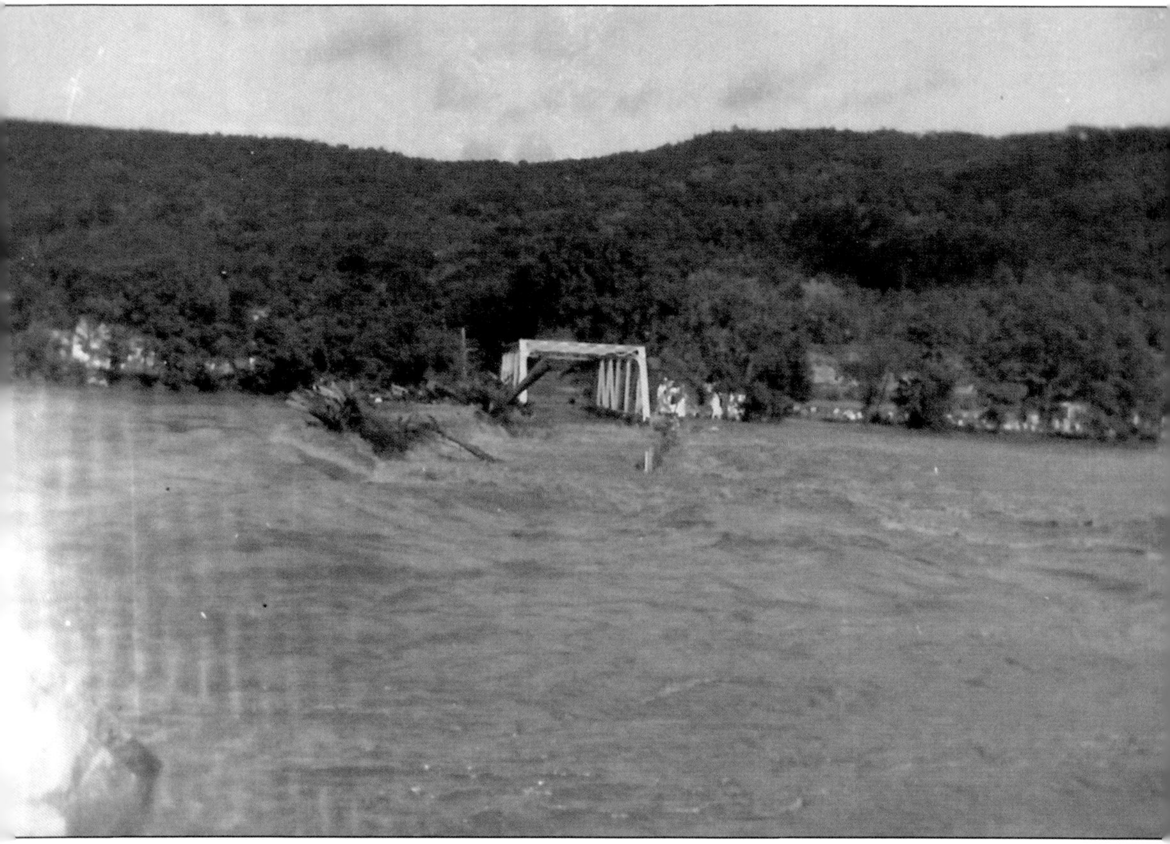

Pines Bridge was part steel girder and part concrete overpass. In this view east from the Oxford side of the river, the concrete portion of the bridge in the foreground is fully submerged while the girder bridge section is mostly above water. This photograph is taken from below the railroad underpass in what is now a nature preserve on Old Pines Bridge Road named in honor of the Indian slave Toby. So many bridges were lost throughout the Naugatuck River Valley during the 1955 flood that Bailey bridges were brought in to provide a quick solution in key locations. Bailey bridges, which were invented during World War II by British engineer Donald Bailey, are portable, prefabricated truss bridges typically used in wartime to replace bridges lost in battle. The use of Bailey bridges, which could be assembled by hand and erected without the need for a crane, were particularly appropriate in light of the fact the Naugatuck Valley was about to resemble a war zone.

Eight

AFTERMATH

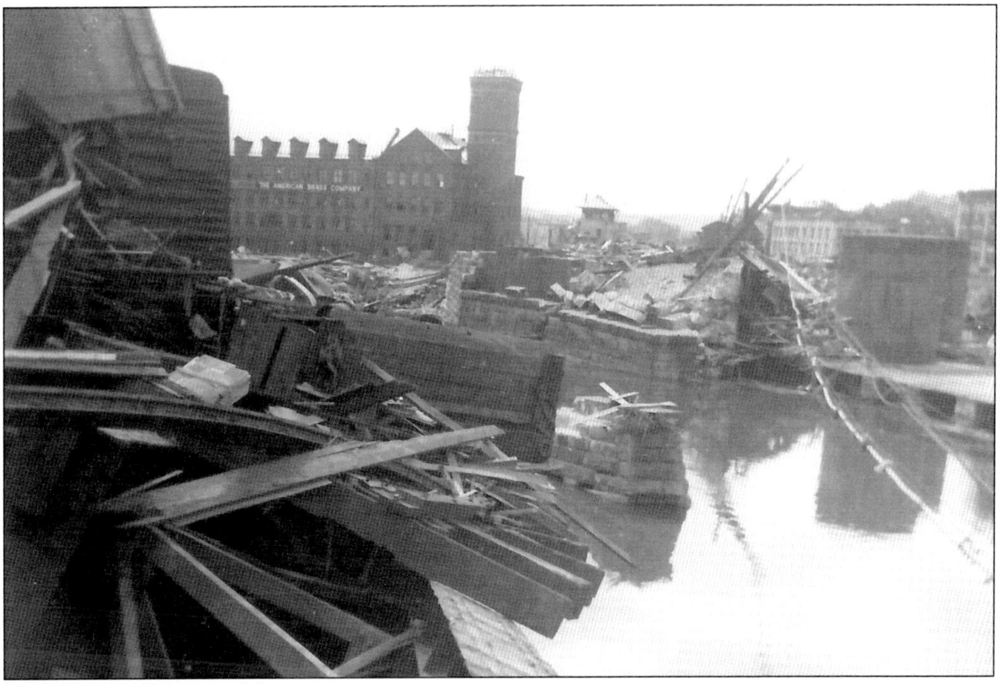

Within days of the flood, Pres. Dwight Eisenhower declared Connecticut a disaster area. A total of 67 towns in Connecticut were affected by the flood, and 91 people lost their lives with 12 people reported missing and presumed dead. One of the hardest hit was the city of Waterbury, especially the Brooklyn section of town shown here. This photograph taken near the intersection of Bank and West Liberty Streets looks south toward one of the American Brass factory buildings. (BK.)

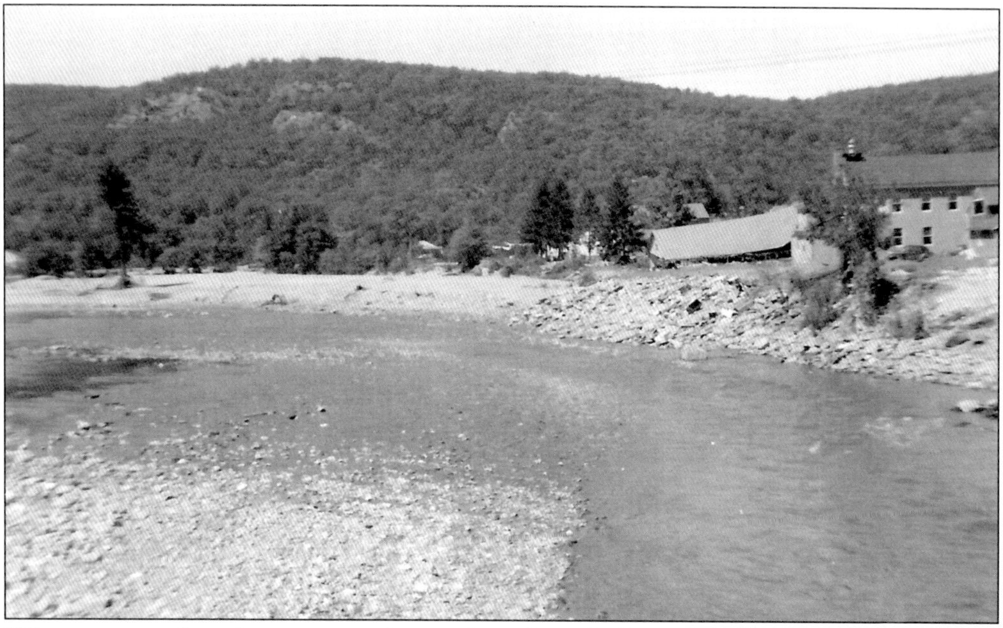

When compared to the towns to the north and south, Beacon Falls was lucky. The town suffered significant damage for sure, but it escaped the dramatic damage seen in Waterbury, Naugatuck, Seymour, and Derby. Of the more visible casualties of the flood was the collapse of the community center building on North Main Street, the roof of which is seen here next to the firehouse. (BK.)

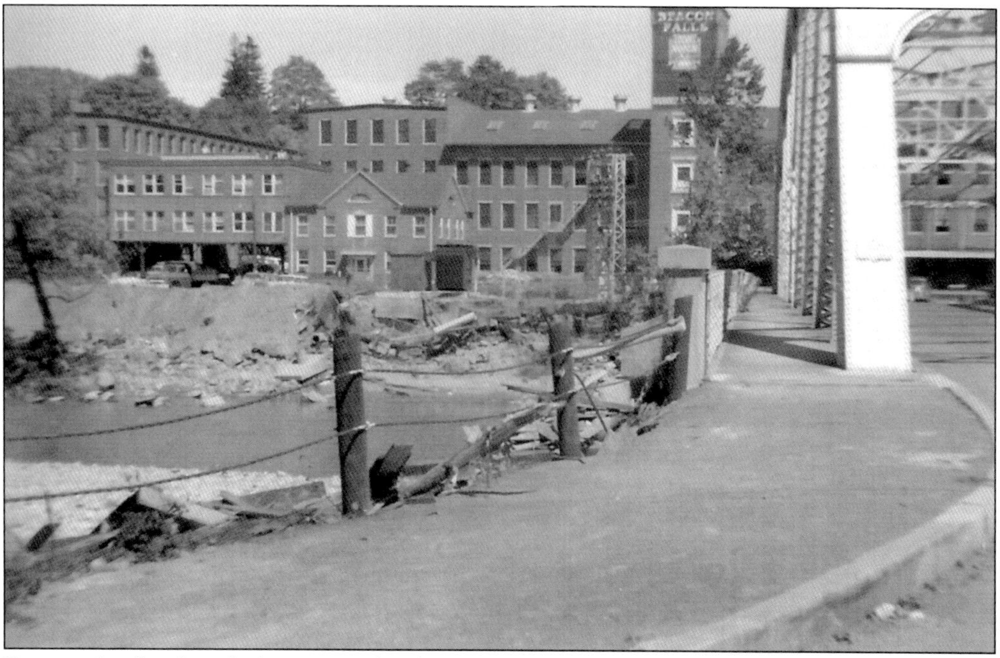

During the flood, turbulent water fought to get around debris trapped by the steel bridge. In this view from Railroad Avenue, erosion of the riverbank is evident on both sides of the bridge. Though the steel bridge seems no worse for wear, a sharp eye can spot damage done to the bridge railing during the flood. (BK.)

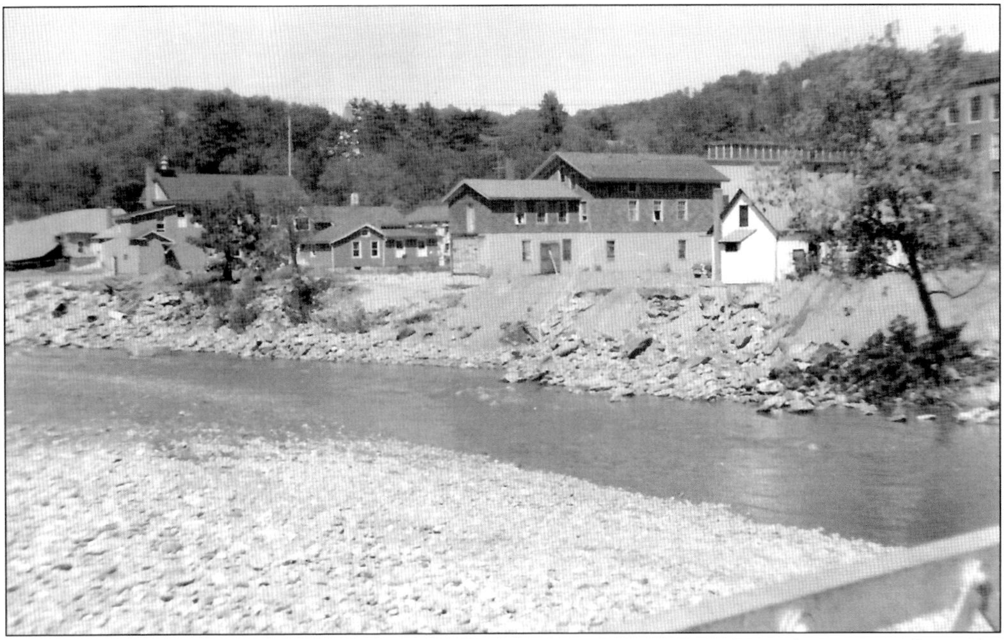

Some of the most serious damage to Beacon Falls was the erosion along the river's edge. The backup of water at the bridge dug away precious riverbank, virtually eliminating the backyards of the homes and business here. Only a few years earlier, these buildings were moved closer to the river; now, the flood made them closer still. (BK.)

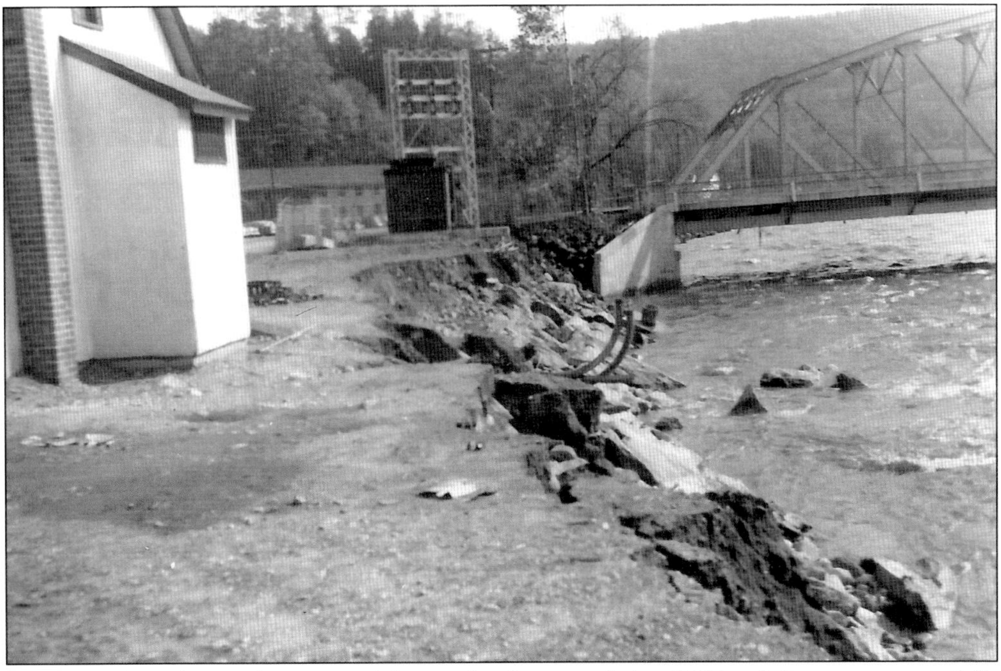

In this southward view, the extent of the riverbank erosion behind Wilcox's Drugstore is painfully clear. The bridge foundation also suffered significant erosion, but not enough to threaten the structural integrity of the bridge. The state restored just enough of the riverbank to protect the bridge foundation, but a lot of property was permanently lost. (BK.)

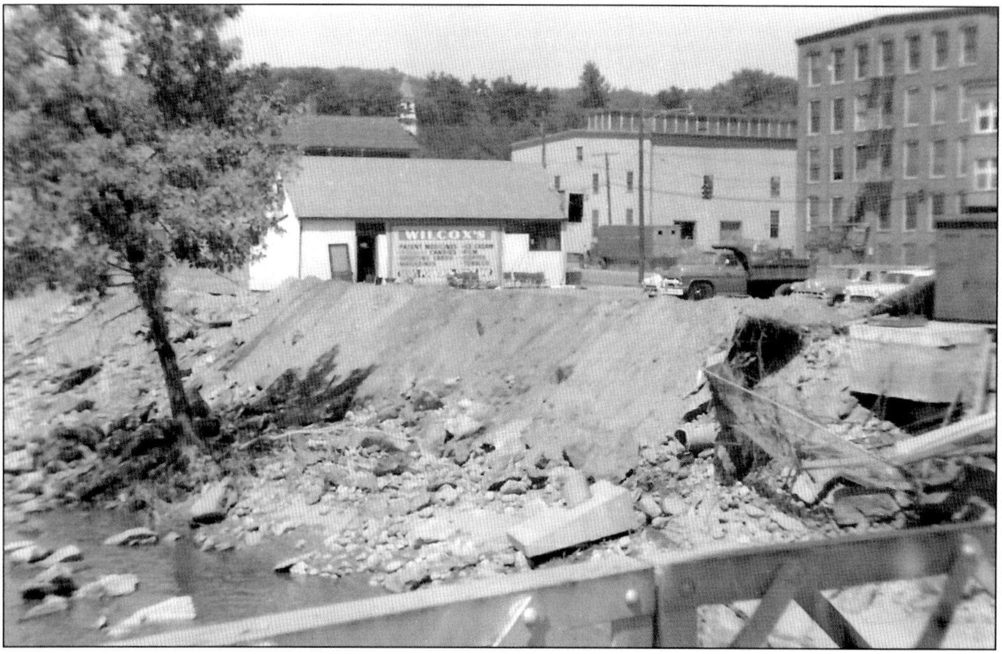

Here is a view of Wilcox's Drugstore taken from the bridge. The windows and doors are all open in an attempt to dry out the building. The remains of an electrical substation are seen to the right. Totally undercut by the flood, it seems in danger of toppling into the river. (BK.)

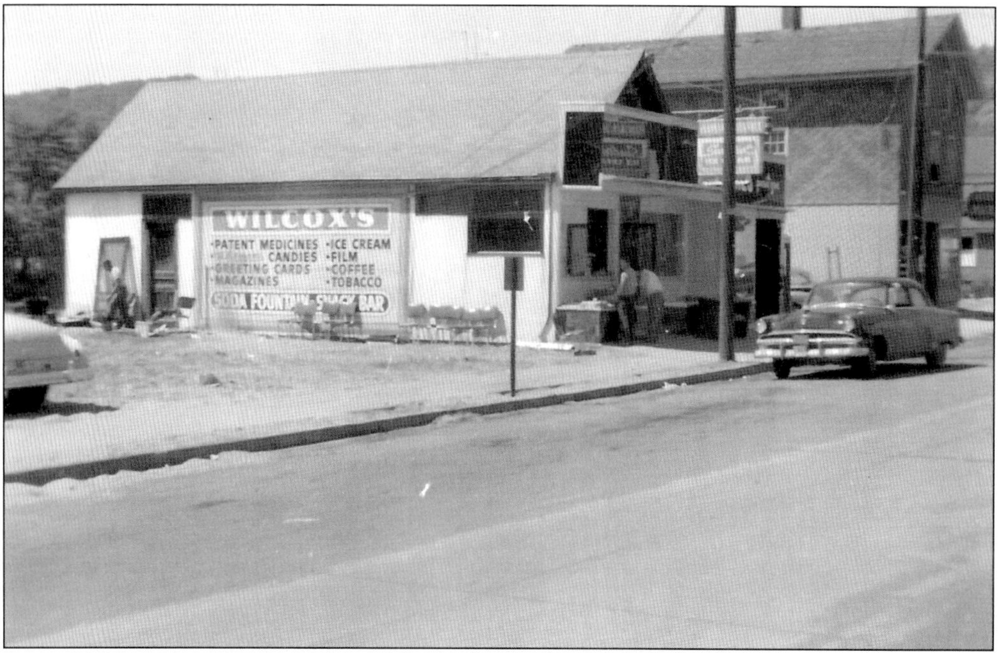

The renovations at Wilcox's Drugstore have already started. Because the water was chest high inside the store, all of the merchandise was destroyed. In this photograph, some items, such as the chairs along the side of the building, have been salvaged and placed in the sun to dry. The *Naugatuck Daily News* reported that in addition to Wilcox's Drugstore, two meat and grocery stores suffered damage in the business section of town. (BK.)

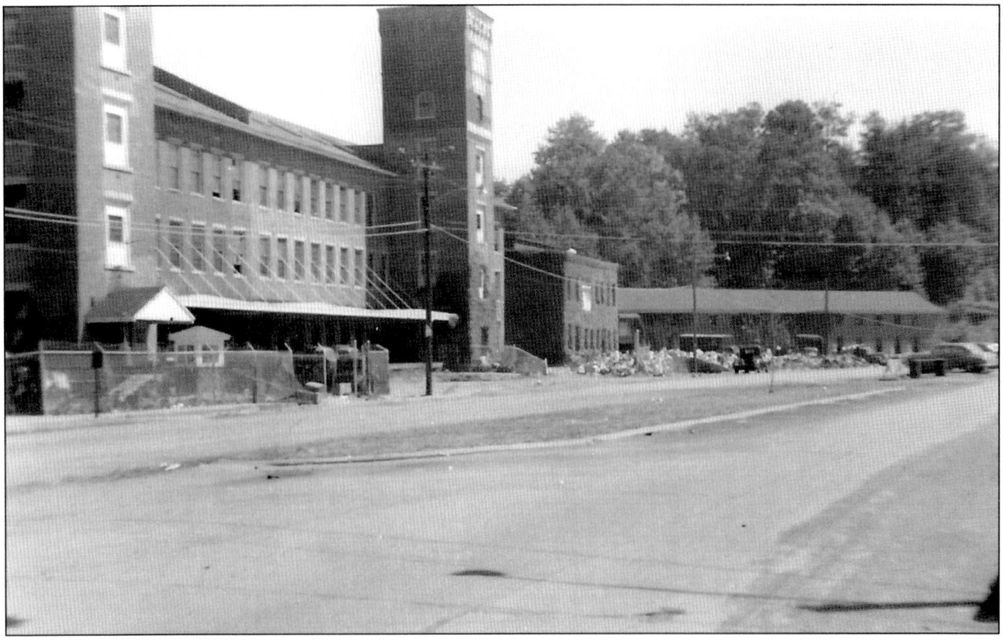

This photograph shows the view south of the intersection of Burton Road. People from the hill section opened their doors to help flooded-out neighbors, and Laurel Ledge School was opened as an emergency shelter. Electricity was out for a quarter of the town because a 5,000-foot section of cable was washed away. (BK.)

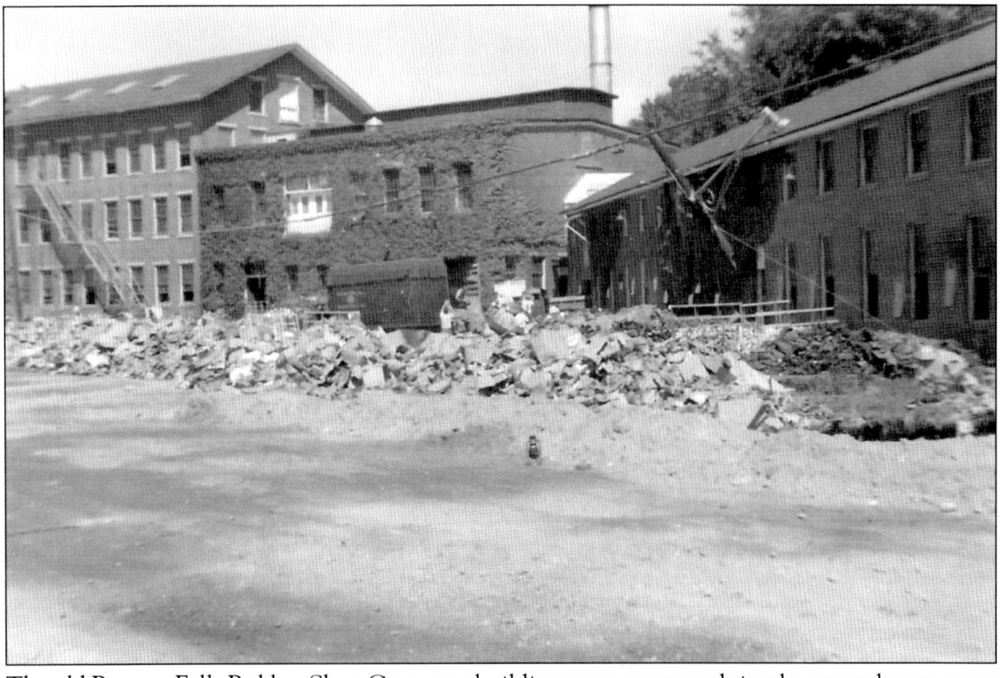

The old Beacon Falls Rubber Shoe Company buildings were now used simply as warehouse space for Uniroyal in Naugatuck. Damaged merchandise cleared out of the warehouse by truck shares the curb with dirt and rocks deposited on Main Street. A snapped-off telephone pole hanging haphazardly with the street light still attached is visible. (BK.)

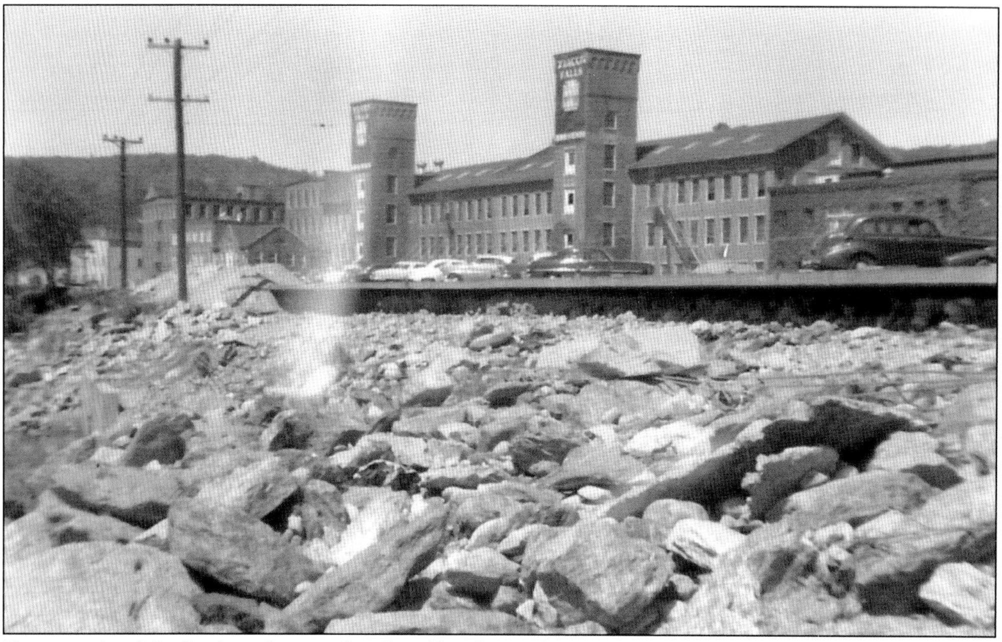

Even south of the bridge, the riverbank suffered significant washout. Here, the recently completed concrete base of Main Street, which was also Connecticut State Highway Route 8, has been undercut by the rushing water. The cars are parked on the island that normally would separate northbound and southbound traffic. (BK.)

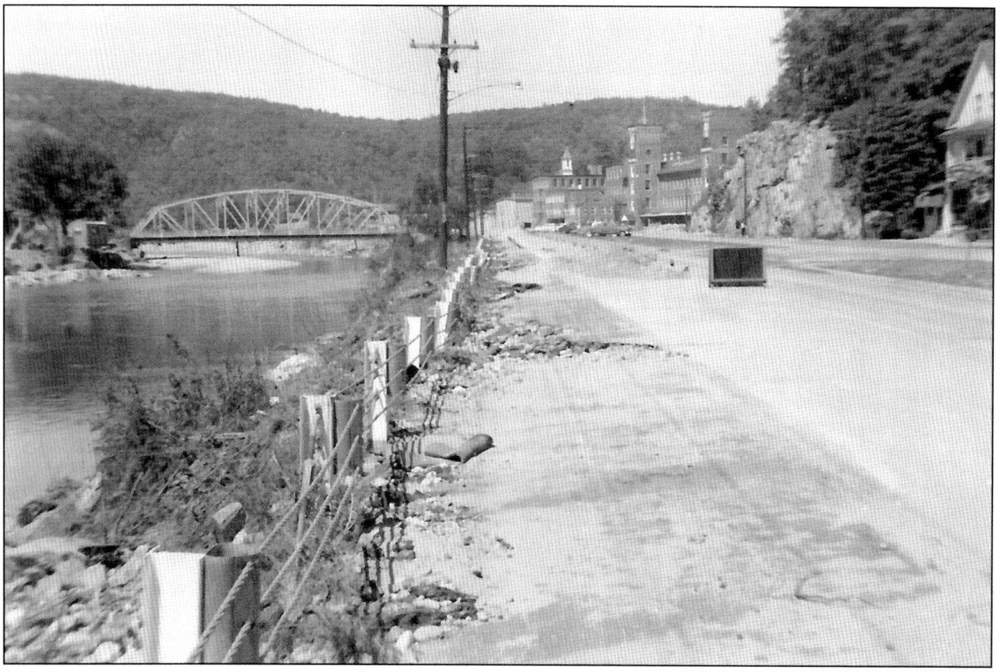

Moving farther south, the extent of the damage to Main Street can be seen. Here, the southbound lanes are blocked off until repairs to the roadbed are made. Today, the river's edge is protected by trees whose root structures help to maintain the riverbank. Unfortunately, they also block much of the river view here. (BK.)

Across the street from the river, homes along South Main Street show evidence of water damage. In this view, structural damage to the porch is evident in the house on the left. Soggy household items are piled along the street. Although nearly every house on Main Street had water in the first floor, most were restored. (BK.)

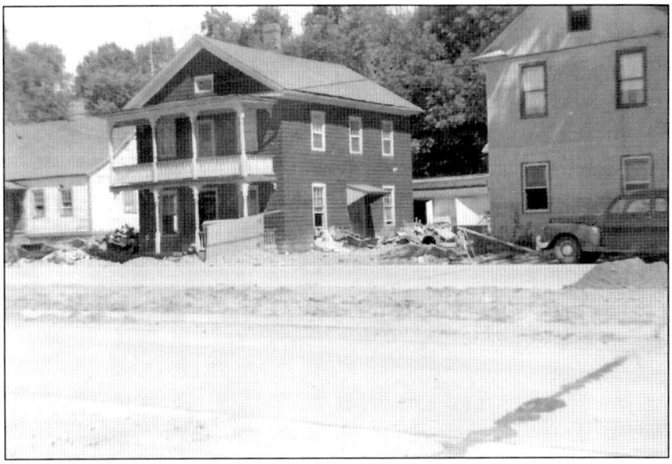

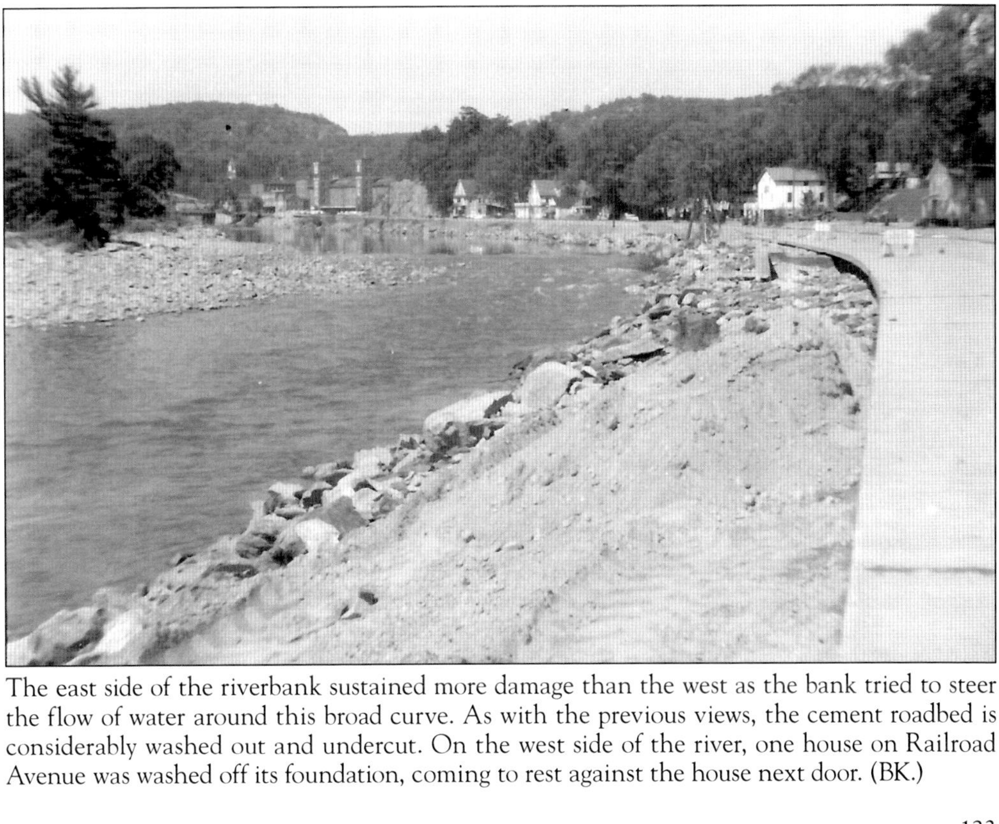

The east side of the riverbank sustained more damage than the west as the bank tried to steer the flow of water around this broad curve. As with the previous views, the cement roadbed is considerably washed out and undercut. On the west side of the river, one house on Railroad Avenue was washed off its foundation, coming to rest against the house next door. (BK.)

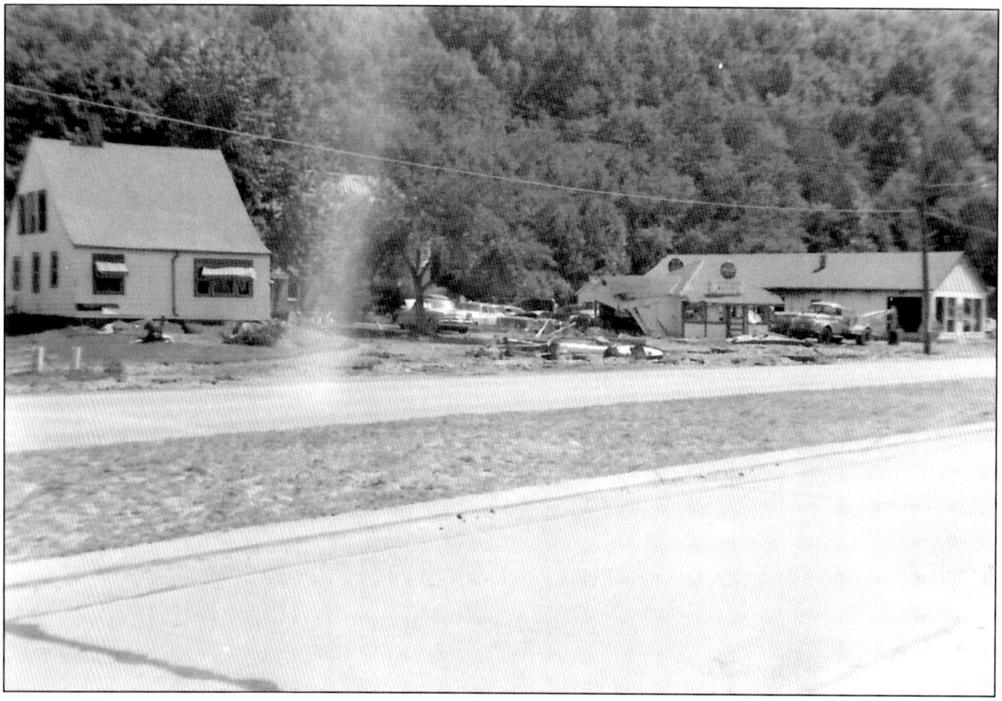

A veritable treasure trove of vintage automobiles sits behind Vardon's Beacon Motors just south of the Bronson Company. The building next door, whose sign reads "Outboard Motors," has partially collapsed. As a result of the flood, 86,000 people in Connecticut were left unemployed. (BK.)

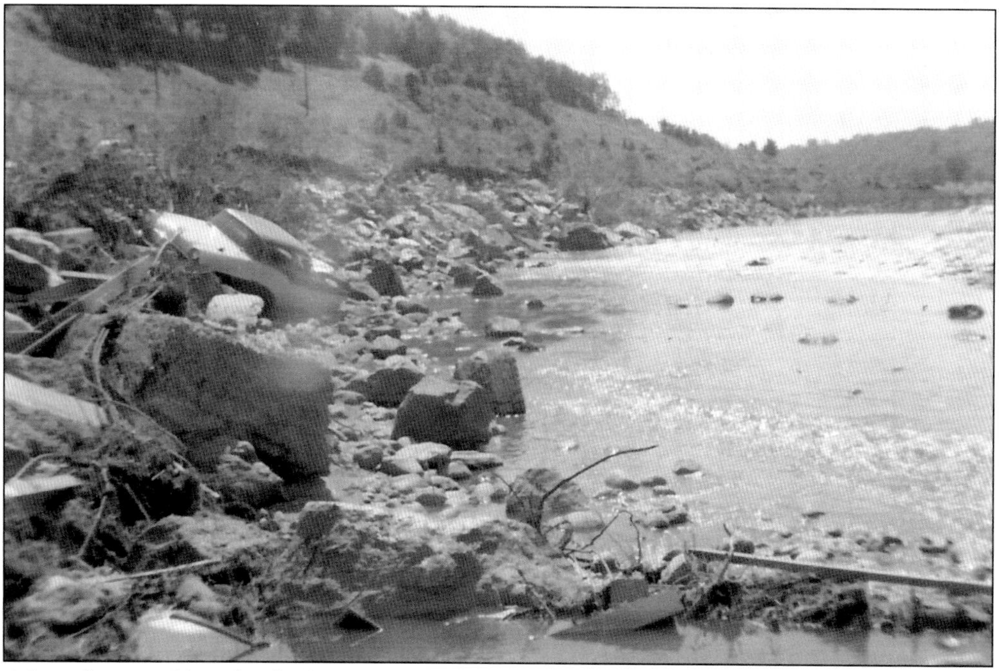

A brand-new 1955 Packard Clipper is seen stranded among the rocks and rubble after the water receded. The sweeping two-tone paint job was unique to this model and year. This view looks south toward Pines Bridge. South Main Street is barely visible on the left hillside. (BK.)

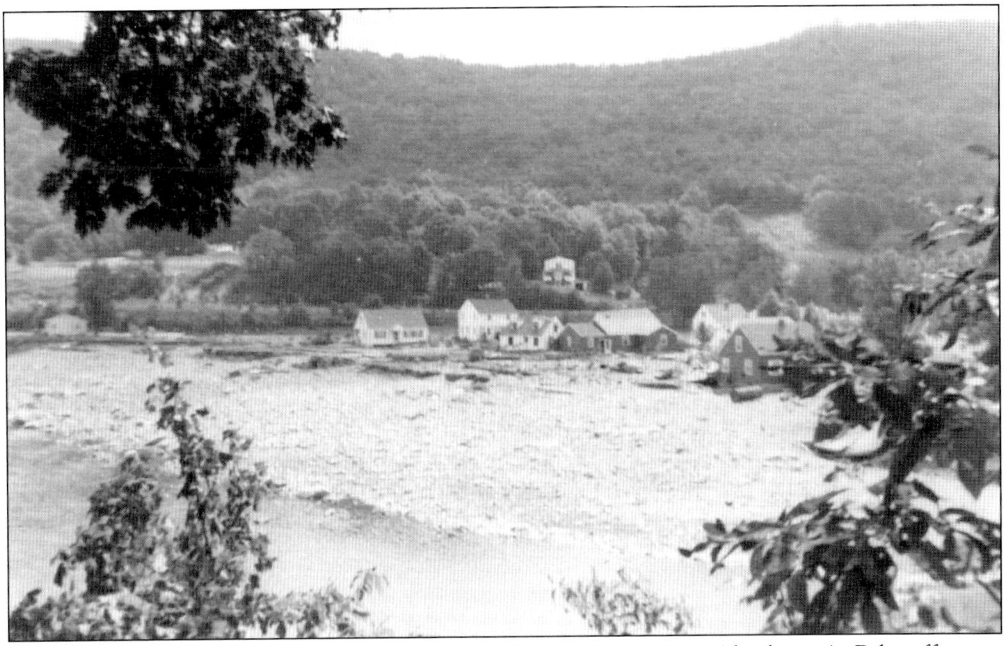

The statistics on the 1955 flood are staggering. According to Gov. Abraham A. Ribicoff, more than 1,100 families were left homeless, 2,300 families were temporarily without shelter, and 20,000 families suffered flood damage. The damage to individual property, business, industry, and state and municipal facilities was estimated at almost half a billion dollars. The Pines Bridge neighborhood is seen in this view. Some of the homes have been moved off their foundation. (BK.)

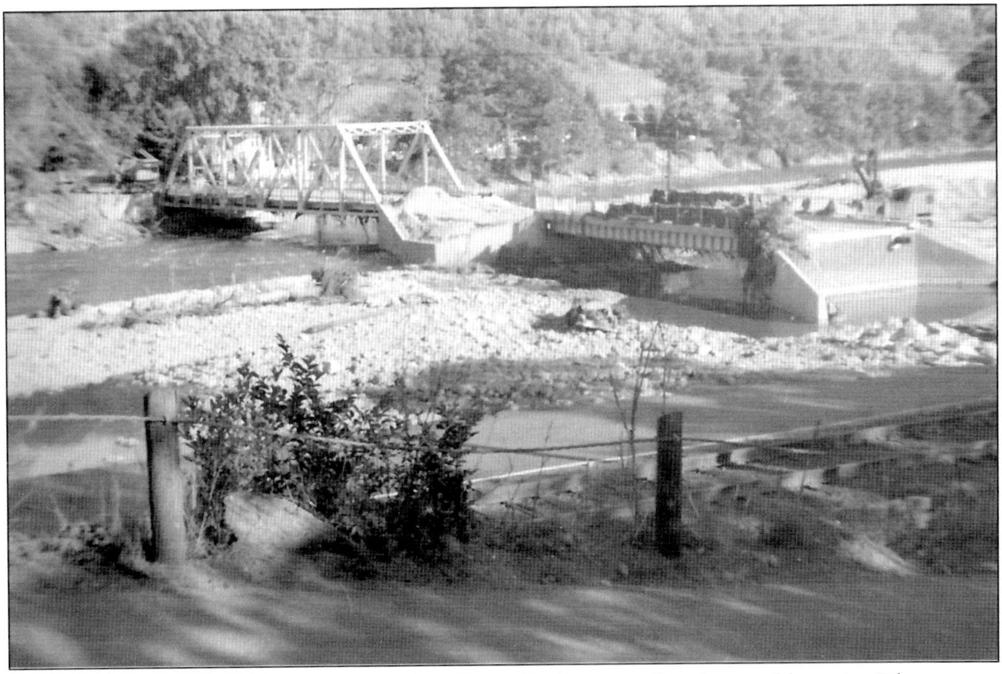

After being rebuilt only seven years earlier, Pines Bridge is rendered unusable again. The carcass of an old automobile can be seen resting on the rocks. In 1967, a new Pines Bridge would be built alongside this old one. The new bridge would tower above the river out of harm's way. (BK.)

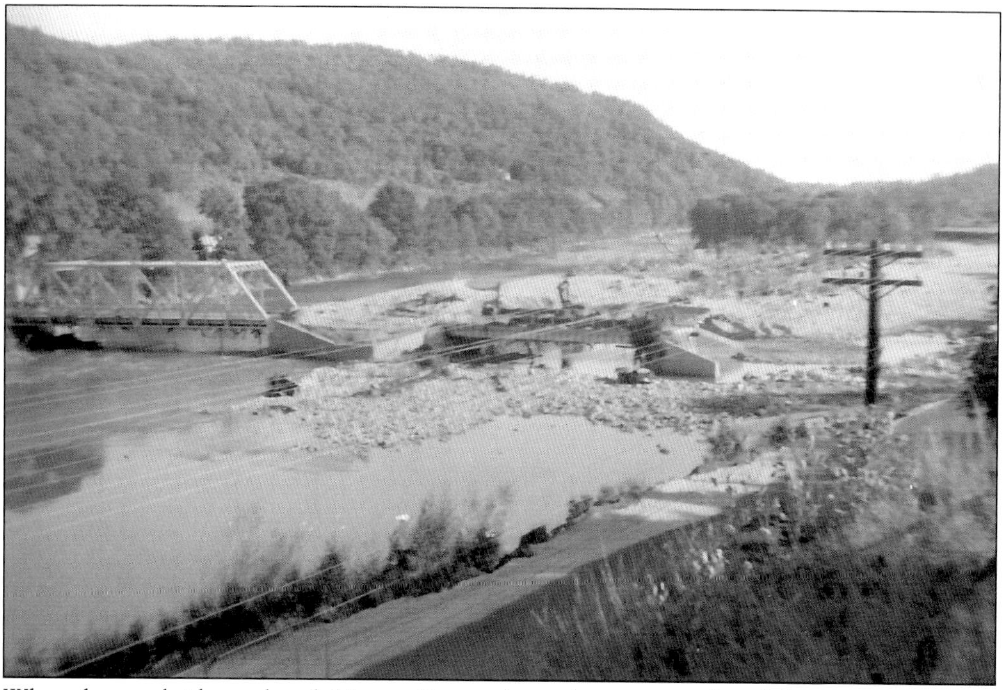

When the new bridge replaced this one 12 years later, the segment of road that accessed this old bridge was named Old Pines Bridge Road. The railroad underpass that one would have used to access the old bridge from the west remains today but is now the gateway to a nature preserve. (BK.)

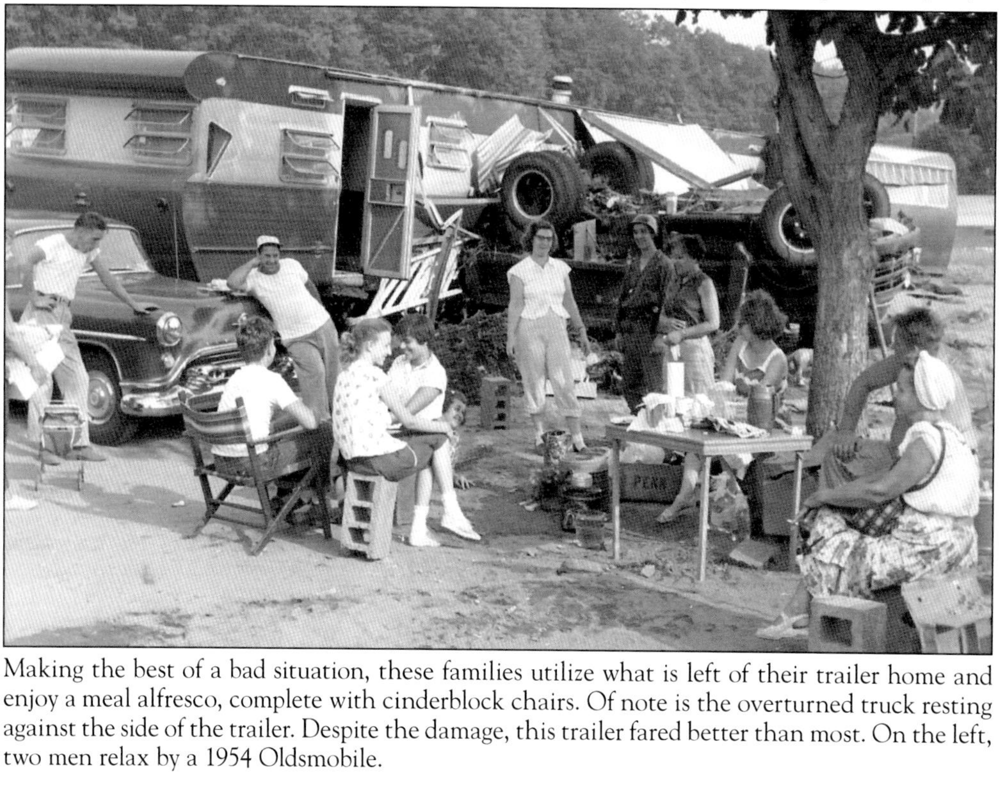

Making the best of a bad situation, these families utilize what is left of their trailer home and enjoy a meal alfresco, complete with cinderblock chairs. Of note is the overturned truck resting against the side of the trailer. Despite the damage, this trailer fared better than most. On the left, two men relax by a 1954 Oldsmobile.

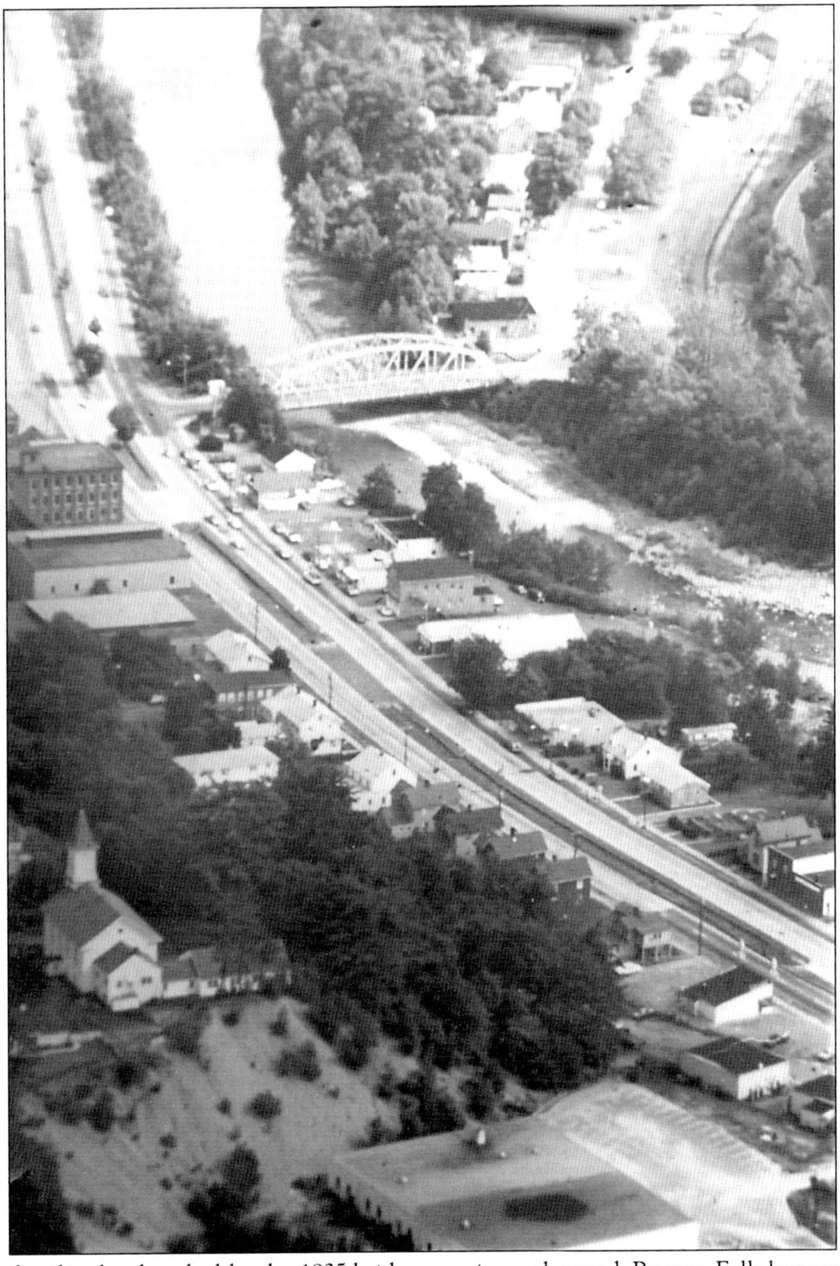

Though familiar landmarks like the 1935 bridge remain unchanged, Beacon Falls has continued to evolve over the years. By the time this photograph was taken in 1971, little evidence remains of the flood 16 years earlier. In the center of the photograph, the new fire station, built in 1969, sits alongside the old one. The year 1971 also marked the 100th anniversary of the incorporation of the town of Beacon Falls, and on June 30 of that year, the town kicked off a 10-day celebration. A year later, the town obtained 370 acres from Bernard Matthies to create Matthies Park. In the early 1980s, a new senior center opened on Main Street, the former Rubber Shoe Company buildings were converted into apartments, the Homer D. Bronson Company moved to Winsted, and a bypass opened that directed Route 8 traffic around downtown. In 2001, the new Woodland Regional High School opened its doors adjacent to the Matthies Park entrance.

Discover Thousands of Local History Books Featuring Millions of Vintage Images

Arcadia Publishing, the leading local history publisher in the United States, is committed to making history accessible and meaningful through publishing books that celebrate and preserve the heritage of America's people and places.

Find more books like this at
www.arcadiapublishing.com

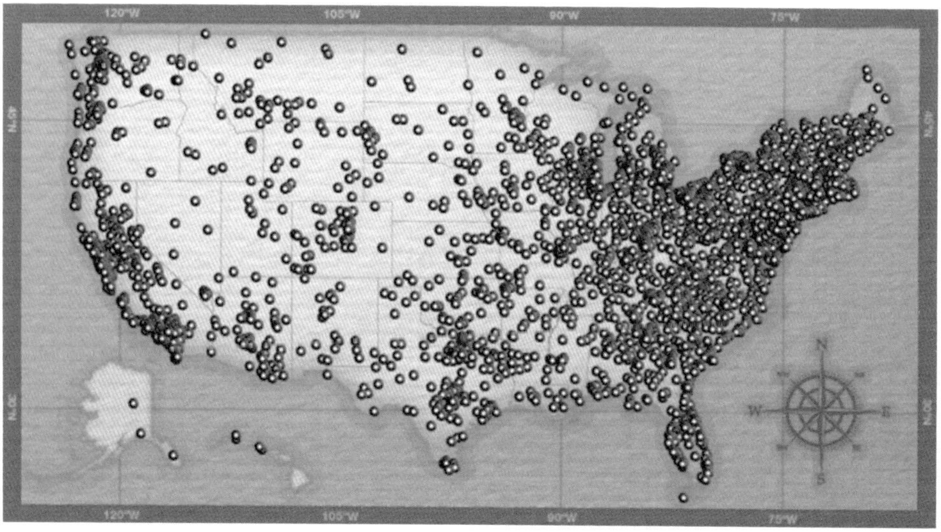

Search for your hometown history, your old stomping grounds, and even your favorite sports team.

Consistent with our mission to preserve history on a local level, this book was printed in South Carolina on American-made paper and manufactured entirely in the United States. Products carrying the accredited Forest Stewardship Council (FSC) label are printed on 100 percent FSC-certified paper.

MADE IN THE USA